images
of authority

Images of authority

WORKING WITHIN THE SHADOW OF THE CROWN

JOHN HIGGINS

Middlesex University
PRESS

First published in 2009 by Middlesex University Press

Copyright © John Higgins

ISBN 978 1 904750 63 5

All rights reserved. No part of this publication may be reproduced, stored in any retrieval system or transmitted in any form or by any means, electronic, mechanical, photocopying, recording or otherwise, without the prior written permission of the copyright holder for which application should be addressed in the first instance to the publishers. No liability shall be attached to the author, the copyright holder or the publishers for loss or damage of any nature suffered as a result of reliance on the reproduction of any of the contents of this publication or any errors or omissions in its contents.

A CIP catalogue record for this book is available from
The British Library

Design by Helen Taylor
Cover photograph by Anna Marlow
Chapter illustrations by Matthew Frame

Printed in the UK by Ashford Colour Press

Middlesex University Press
Fenella Building
The Burroughs
Hendon
London NW4 4BT

Tel: +44 (0)20 8411 4162
Fax: +44 (0)20 8411 4167

www.mupress.co.uk

Contents

Prologues

I – Dramatis personae vii
II – Dramatic contexts viii

Introduction

Chapter 1   – Who's this for (and why the title)? 3
Chapter 2   – A user's guide 9

Section 1   – **Revelling, thriving and surviving**

Chapter 3   – Stella: Authority as personal process 17
Chapter 4   – Martin: It's good to be the king! 29
Chapter 5   – Christina: Reflections on the nature of
                   thriving and authority 37
Chapter 6   – A short story about revelling, thriving and surviving ... 45

Section 2   – **Creativity, anxiety and metabolising shit**

Chapter 7   – Sam: Masked and unmasked authority 51
Chapter 8   – Luke: Creative authority 59
Chapter 9   – Thomas: Management writer, coach and refugee
                   from authority 67
Chapter 10 – A short story about creativity, anxiety and
                   metabolising shit 73

Section 3   – **Hanging tough**

Chapter 11 – Adrian: Combative authority 81
Chapter 12 – Michaela: Refugee from the malign 89
Chapter 13 – Giles: An ounce of ruthlessness 97
Chapter 14 – A short story about hanging tough 105

Section 4   – **Gods, elders and liberating mothers**

Chapter 15 – Lesley: Tough love 111
Chapter 16 – Bob: Burdened with responsibility 121
Chapter 17 – Marie: Working with authority from a
                   Freudian angle 131
Chapter 18 – A short story about gods, elders and
                   liberating mothers 141

Section 5 – Taking care of the self and others

Chapter 19 – Eve: Authority without a title 147
Chapter 20 – Lucy: Connected authority 155
Chapter 21 – Diana: Authority as authoring 163
Chapter 22 – A short story about taking care of the self
  and others 171

Section 6 – Cool passion

Chapter 23 – Roy: Authority from a Buddhist perspective 177
Chapter 24 – Bill: 'I have of late, and wherefore I know not,
  lost all my mirth.' 185
Chapter 25 – Mike: Tempered reason 193
Chapter 26 – A short story about cool passion 203

Endpiece

Chapter 27 – What the chorus saw 207
Chapter 28 – A singular conclusion 215
Chapter 29 – Further exploration 219

Appendices

A: An exploratory framework 222
B: Recommended reading 238

Prologue I – Dramatis personae

In the nature of things, much has had to be disguised in what follows. The experiences and positions of those who spoke to me about what authority had given and cost them through their lives include:

- A brace of the great and the good
- A fired-up theatre director whose troupe comes from those on the edge of society
- A CEO from the world of cement in the process of potentially doing himself out of a job
- A refugee from communist tyranny now enmeshed in the hierarchical trappings of a great British institute
- A renowned name from the world of construction now wrapped up in the delivery of the London 2012 Olympic infrastructure
- A world-famous medical researcher who got there without ambition
- A CEO of a small firm at the edge of being overwhelmed by family and entrepreneurial responsibility
- Two renowned filmmakers
- A fruit picker from the Ribena fields (who got there via Buenos Aires and Barcelona)
- A CEO of a nationally significant teenage counselling service
- A witness to the professional bitchery playing out at the highest levels of the health service
- A vice chairman of a global accounting firm
- A Freudian-informed psychoanalyst cum communications consultant
- The head of a business school's master's and doctoral programmes
- A school refusenik and consulting firm MD
- A trustee from a Buddhist meditation centre.

Prologue II – Dramatic contexts

Some of these people have had charmed lives, some have struggled and thrived and some have just struggled. Some dropped out of school, some were prefects and others were rescued by good teachers.

Some were drenched in malign authority, or Oedipal complexes, or switched off in the face of the indifference of others. Some loved authority, some were burdened by it, some can't get enough of it and some can't stop themselves being a magnet for it (even though their heads are barely above water).

Some dropped out and then dropped in. Some started feral and then went straight. Some looked after siblings; another counselled her parents from the age of eight. Some were eldest children, some were youngest and some were in-between. Some came from families riddled with the legacy of war and religious loathing.

Some talked about family history; some didn't. Some knew about psychology; some didn't.

Some had little or no ambition; others were comfortably ruthless or secure in their rightness to hold positions of power and influence. One had an evil primary school teacher who liked to bully the five-year-olds in her care (she was also the vicar's wife). No-one admitted to being a bully or a narcissist – although bullies and narcissists are to be seen in the worlds they inhabit.

Some talked of love, knew love and needed love in their lives. Some had had their comfortable certainties turned on their heads when uninvited love came to call. Some had an absence of love.

Some saw no difference between authority and power. Some saw no difference between authority and responsibility. Some took positions of authority because they wanted to stop others using authority badly. Some loved nurturing and bringing people on – others were impatient with the failings of others and their inability to learn or take responsibility.

Some stepped into authority, because 'Hey, why wouldn't they?' Some want to be liked and some like to be nice. Some see fairness at the heart of everything they do and know how terrible it can be. Some want those around them to take some bloody responsibility for themselves, their actions and their own bloody lives.

Some want and need the red blood of real conversation, of convictions and voices, crashing together to find the new. Some need calm. Some love reason and order.

Some are bossy and some are demanding. Some love their ability to find a way through the mess and take others with them. Some have been married, some have had children and some have been divorced.

Many have known untimely death and the travails of the care of the sick and the lame. One found enlightenment late at night on a tunnelling site… another in the eyes of her mugger.

Some have come close to or known depression and breakdowns.

Some (if not all) love their expertise, knowledge and experience.

Few like positions for their own sake.

★   ★   ★   ★   ★   ★   ★   ★   ★

There is order here, but what this tells me is authority is like an assaulted Gorgon – full of heads; as soon as you try and cut it down to size, new angles, insights and habits spring up.

introduction

Chapter 1
Who's this for (and why the title)?   3

Chapter 2
A user's guide   9

CHAPTER 1

Who's this for (and why the title)?

This has been researched and written for anybody who is in a position of authority, holds authority, hankers after authority, is being offered it – or simply wants to understand their relationship to authority better; be it their own or that of others.

For some it may be a matter of confirmation while for others it may raise unexpected questions or insights. It is not predicated on an assumption of inadequacy nor on the need to exhort people to adopt some idealised form – but it does assume that for many their relationship to authority is complicated by history, situation and the expectations of those around and inside them.

What it offers is an opportunity to explore the inner and outer experiences of authority as it plays out in the messy reality of others who have 'been there and done that'. This exploration may then result in further personal inquiry, for which material is available, into how authority works for the individual.

Images of authority – working within the shadow of the crown

Authority comes in many forms, each with its own particular brightness and shadow. Each of the stories I have written here has its distinctive character and provides food for thought – each has a particular relationship to the crown of authority. Some wore a crown to hide themselves, others stepped into the crown as if born to it – others had to be cajoled into wearing it or kept a tight hold of it in case it fell into the wrong hands.

The crown is a potent image that talks to us of power, the father, the anointed one, the self-anointed, even God. It evokes ideas and feelings that reach back into history and the deep roots of culture and family. How does authority bind us together? How does it set us apart? Does the crown unite people or divide them? Does the crown heal or haunt the king or queen?

Our culture encourages an aspiration for authority and yet rarely raises the issue of cost. When a person experiences themselves as having authority – and the definition slides and slips as it moves from person to person, situation to situation – it involves a shadow. This can be the shadow of personal fantasies held in check until authority set them free. It can be the shadow of the expectation of those around the wearer of the crown to save them, lead them, be the authority they've always needed in their lives. When you are in a position of authority people will behave differently towards you; it is nearly impossible for people not to at least in part play out their history of authority when engaging with you. You'll always be dealing with some previous good or bad boss, an absent parent, benevolent teacher or the idiotic evil of state police (as was the case with one of the stories).

You will also be easily caught out playing some historic or learned role of your own. In our culture two potent myths play out – the saviour and the man alone; myths which if combined can load up a person in authority with an all but unbearable burden, resulting in grim fatigue or an escape into an omnipotent sense of self-belief and destiny.

None of this is predetermined, but authority comes charged with meaning – some recognised and some unrecognised, some of people's own making and some an accident of the moment.

Some intentions

I wanted to talk to people 'off the record' about what holding a position of authority meant to them, what it gave to them and what it cost them. There is of course a paradox in play, given that the intention was always to publish what was said – so what I have here is what off-the-record material people are willing to put on the record. There is always the need to pay consideration to the confidences of others while at the same time finding ways of making available what is otherwise only ever talked about late at night in the company of trusted friends and family. As far as is possible I believe I have been able to shed some light on the back-story behind the experiences of those in authority.

I was curious about how much influence they found in their past, be it family, school, work, archetype or elsewhere. I wanted to see what sort of language they used to talk about authority: I wanted to break out of what I saw as a straitjacketed vocabulary of bland managerialism, can-do self-actualisation, victimhood made good, or other forms of limited prescription or simplistic psychology.

I didn't want to ascribe naïve causality; instead I wanted to see how people in authority saw themselves in the whole – not just the role. I also wanted to talk to more than the usual suspects, so I sought out a diversity of people from many walks of life. This included the arts and business, the public and private sectors, big and small organisations. I also wanted to find people who either had a natural disposition to self-awareness or personal disclosure or had reached a more reflective stage in life. I wanted to get behind the easy headlines, the publicly acceptable persona and look at the person in the position of authority rather than the position of authority in the person.

I also wanted to talk to academics and people who work with people in authority to hear their 'thinking' rather than their 'thoughts'. My interest was in finding out how people understood themselves and others once they went off-script and didn't follow the particular conventions of their discipline or industry – although knowing that they are drawing on a large body of documented theory and practice. These understandings are often messier and more paradoxical than the dictates of fashionable presentation demand, with their expectations of coherence, psychological arc and the triumph of the will. I set out to hear something more complicated, more believable and, I would go as far as to say, true.

Stories and themes

At the heart of this work are eighteen stories varying in tone and personal disclosure, reflecting how different individuals found themselves responding to my lightly guided questioning. In some I found myself wanting to pry and dig into loose threads or skated-over moments, but I restricted myself to polite prompting and if the person didn't want to go where I thought they should then I left it. I have learnt much more slowly than I care to admit that wilfully digging around in people's lives and sense of their publicly presented self is not something to be entered into carelessly.

The stories therefore reflect what people feel is safe and/or relevant to their authority rather than what Freud would tell them is the case. This is in itself interesting, for it speaks to me of how guarded we can become when talking of authority. In these stories I have not managed to remove the mist that surrounds our understanding in this area, but I hope that it has been lifted a bit. Authority is still seen through a glass darkly, but the darkness has a lighter tint.

Informed by the stories and my own philosophical practice, I have identified six perspectives with which the stories can be explored or that can be used to explore your own experience of authority. This exploratory framework (to be found in Appendix A) will also provide the basis for a more structured round of inquiry that will allow my work in this area to expand and live. The ambition for this explanatory framework is to be structured enough to allow for some comparison to be possible, while still being loose enough for the uniqueness of experience and understanding to be expressed.

Intimate inquiry

This work has been about trying to get the informal and the private sense of authority made available on a more formal and public stage. To achieve this I set out to approach people who knew me well and who knew to trust me with sensitive material; the complication was that I could not interview them – I knew too much about them and so would tell the story I already knew about them rather than the story that they wanted to tell. My resolution of this problem was to ask these trusting – and well-connected – compadres to introduce me to people who trusted them. I hoped that by being the trusted professional friend of a trusted professional friend, I would arrive at the interview with a borrowed quality of trust that would help people feel able to be comfortably open and would allow me to pay attention to what they told me, not what I thought I knew.

As always with my experience of inquiry processes, I broke my rules. There were people I knew well whose more general perspective I wanted to hear. There were also people who were the confidantes of others and I wanted to see what could be said from those perspectives without breaching trust.

The result has been that people have revealed a more intimate story of authority than is often written about and because of this it often uses a different language. In the first story presented in this book, Stella commented on the experience of being interviewed about her authority: 'Authority sounds such an external quality… [I'm] surprised how much it connected to my inner life.'

In terms of conclusions and identifying themes from the process I have also been walking a tightrope. I have grown up in the business school arena where the well-honed bullet point is highly valued. While appreciating the value of the concise opinion, I find that bullet point conclusions are often unhelpfully reductive – they boil out too much variety and often appear compelling right up until the moment when you apply them to the diversity of real life. I am increasingly drawn to the notion of leaving stories to speak for themselves, of letting sense and pattern emerge between reader and the read. In my conclusions therefore I have tried to leave a sense of the partial, of any conclusions being small pauses in an ongoing process of sense-making. My conclusions are not intended as full stops, nor as definitive statements of what there is to be known about authority in the lives of those I spoke to – the stories presented here are fragments not wholes.

Language and philosophy

Four principles inform this work. Firstly a belief that how people talk about things matters – words can never be neutral and their conscious or unconscious use is of note. To borrow from J.-P. Sartre, 'words are like loaded revolvers', they always carry a charge. This is why I have tried to use as many of my interviewees' words as possible, while doing what I can to turn spoken words into a coherent written form. It is also why I have not led this inquiry with the language of the multiple schools of theory that have examined authority or leadership or power or responsibility. I wanted to start with the lived reality, not the reality others have diagnosed as being significant.

My second informing principle concerns the stories that people tell themselves about their lives. I believe that we all live out the realities and fantasies that we tell ourselves fit with our sense of self, our story. To the best of our ability we make what happens to us fit within how we already see ourselves, or how we have been brought up to see ourselves. There are times when our plot changes and the voices inside us become more or less important, but momentum and continuity of story seem to be compelling features of our lives. In this research it has been this sense of inner story that has been of most interest to me, although of course this inner story both shapes and is shaped by a more objective external reality.

Thirdly I believe history matters – not to the exclusion of any sense of free will or personal agency, but I am convinced that our pasts are potent and that the challenge is to find a way of being informed rather than consumed by them. Within the managerial culture that I encountered in my time as an organisational consultant I experienced a fixation with the future – a desire to escape both from what has been and a historically mediated now, into some fantastical future that is free of all that has gone before. I believe such an orientation takes people away from the ability to work with what is possible in the now, and results in horrendous and unsustainable leaps into wished-for futures – where fantasies dominate rather than realities.

Lastly I have adopted an integrative approach. I wanted to seek out the connection between the individual and those around them, the family life as well as the professional one, the inner life and the outer expression, the head and the heart. As human beings we are all these things at the same time, we can shift what is figural at any one moment but everything is connected.

Ambition for this book

My desire to work on this came about as I watched my wife wrestling with the responsibilities and burdens that come from being a director of a company. There have been moments when the legal liabilities that come with that position seem quite shocking; there have been times when I have interpreted the behaviour of those who work for her as incredibly childish and I wondered how that mother–infant dynamic had kicked off and what could be done to shift it. At times it seems that people in positions of authority are simply there to act as punchbags for the frustrations of everyone else.

I want this book to be a small contribution to a more rounded and considered understanding of authority in our society. My fantasy is this can be brought about by starting with something akin to the reality of what it is really like to experience having, or being in, authority.

CHAPTER 2

A user's guide

People will of course read a book as they want. In its editing I approached a number of people with this book, some of whom read the end first, while others dipped in and out of particular stories that appealed to them. Some even read it the old-fashioned way, starting at page one and then working their way sequentially through to the end. My purpose in providing this user's guide is to make explicit my intentions and logic in structuring it the way I have. Those of you who don't use user guides can skip straight to the next chapter.

Why eighteen stories?

This is a subjective piece of work and makes no claims to objectivity (indeed I would hold strongly to the notion that there is very little in human society that is objective). Eighteen is not a magic number and when I set out on this project I had no real sense of how many stories were needed – or how many could be told. I knew more than a handful was required because of the need for contrast. By the time I had got to eighteen I felt that I was on the cusp of repetition and at the limit of what I could hold in my head. With a sense of emerging purpose I concluded that the eighteen stories provided enough food for thought and reflective companions for anyone wanting to explore their own unique experience of authority.

The value of having this large number of first-hand stories is, I hope, that it discourages people from trying to fit themselves into one particular synthesized category. If I had stayed with a smaller number the temptation may have been to try and see oneself as being of one category – what I hope the larger number offers is an invitation to explore how a blend of different stories touch on a particular person's take on authority.

Why the six sections?

There were not six themes that I wished to explore before starting off on this research. I divided the stories into six sections in order to provide some punctuation points for the book – although I do see the stories sitting well together in their various sections (which is not to deny that they could be repackaged into different groupings with equal validity).

In Section 1 (Revelling, thriving and surviving) Stella, Martin and Christina are brought together. These are people who, by and large, have found a way of being in authority that works for them. Their authority is grounded in a practical morality and is connected to a wider way of being in the world – integrity and respect for others are part of who they are and how they orientate themselves. Positional success is definitely an accidental by-product and they have ambitions to be well served by being in authority i.e. not to lose a sense of themselves or what matters to them for the sake of some collective or institutional good.

In Section 2 (Creativity, anxiety and metabolising shit) there are three edgier stories. These are people with a more suspicious attitude towards authority; yes they've found a way of making it more or less work for them, but there have been costs along the way and demons to be wrestled with (some of whom are still alive and scratching, biting and kicking). While Section 1 is imbued with a sense of optimism and/or aspiration, the shadow of authority is more strongly etched in this section. There is even a sense of unchosen fate undermining an individual's best intentions.

After the darkness of Section 2 comes the toughness of Section 3 (Hanging tough). Adrian, Michaela and Giles are tough hombres – they have something of the Spaghetti Western hero to them – the man or woman alone. They've all been able to exercise authority on their own terms, sometimes in the face of seemingly insuperable challenges. They make the world work for them but without surrendering to hubris, bullying or a sense of their own brilliance. They have all been tested in the fire and have emerged with strength and a sense of well-forged individual worth.

Section 4 (Gods, elders and liberating mothers) touches on the world of archetypes – those juju phantasms that some believe rise out of the ether and take over mortal man or woman. This section has people playing out unintended roles rather than wearing authority as an expression of themselves. It is very difficult not to repeat those early habits of authority everyone grows up in, be it as eldest brother, unwanted daughter or demanding mother. Sometimes the unintended roles are more demonic and can result in people wanting to surrender their lives to a great leader's authority. Of course it isn't as black and white as that, but in this section it is possible to have a sense of what it takes to live with almost hard-wired patterns.

Moving on from this brush with determinism comes Section 5 (Taking care of the self and others). These are the stories of three women who have all stepped from a less to a more visible form of authority, without surrendering their beliefs in enabling others or being consumed by ego. Their stories demonstrate the value of a well-developed sense of self-worth, which is also grounded in a care and attention for those around them. This is an exploration of authority as a mutual and reciprocal relationship – an expression of the benign feminine form of authority.

The last section, Section 6 (Cool passion), contains stories of understated steel. The three men who make it up are studiedly un-dramatic; they are men who seek to bring reason to bear in situations of high passion. They are a masterclass in how to keep your head while all around are losing theirs. But they don't do this by denying or burying strong emotions; their reason is one that acknowledges and works with the full gamut of human emotion – but does not seek to inflame. They are an expression of the benign masculine form of authority.

Why the images?

Authority and our relationship to it are as much to do with the gut or the unconscious as to do with our presentable conscious selves. In my professional life as a tutor, executive coach and consultant, I have worked with images and postcards when I want to escape from the habits of logic that tie me or my client to a particular way of understanding the world. In my work as an analysand (someone undergoing psychoanalysis), images have been important for getting me to go off-script, to see myself more fully than my words on their own let me.

The images presented at the start of each story are informed by a sense of each story and are meant as a provocation, a device for bypassing the conscious and an invitation to a less managed response in the viewer. The work is then to understand why we are moved by one image and not another; to pay attention to the feelings and thoughts that an image evokes in us and be curious about what it tells us about our relationship to authority.

These images are devices for personal reflection that complement the stories. Some may choose to work with these images without the help of others; I usually find it useful to talk through my reactions with a trusted friend or colleague.

Names, disguises and veracity

The majority of the names have been changed and where appropriate organisational identities played with. In certain stories I have mixed up experiences, shifting them around third parties, in order to avoid the game of 'is that so and so?' In certain situations I have had to write with a studied ambiguity or slide over events that are crying out to be explained in more detail.

Everything in the stories is 'true', in the sense that they represent my understanding of eighteen individuals' experiences – and they have all accepted what I have written about them.

Why research in this way?

This has been an inquiry into meaning-making, examining how people have created their meaning of authority and then the meaning that I have constructed in response to this.

It is in part an extension of the research philosophy I used for *Organisational Consulting – A Relational Perspective* (MU Press 2007) and is described in its Appendix 2, pp.190–4.

What is distinctive has been the framing of the inquiry in such a way as to blend the private and public self. For me this is consistent with the notions of Gregory Bateson and the concept of 'the pattern that connects' (Ibid. p.13) – in the inquiry I have been inviting people to explore the pattern that connects their present and historic selves. What people have then chosen to reveal or construct I have left up to them, although inevitably I did some prompting – whether verbal or non-verbal – which probably encouraged one line of inquiry over another.

This fits with the social constructionist notion of the participant–inquirer, or to paraphrase from p.190 of the *Organisational Consulting* book, 'authors of stories are not writing objective truths, they are writing stories that are heard through their own relationally and personally situated sense-making processes.' What was distinctive about my 'personally situated sense-making process' this time was that I was not writing directly in the service of, and to a great extent in the shadow of, an organisationally focused academic frame.

It's all about the stories

The structure for this book has been the normal collision of intention and happenstance – at its heart, however, are the eighteen stories, and this hasn't changed from the off. It is in these stories that authority lives and shows itself in its multi-coloured, potent, slightly stained, burdensome, haunting and sometimes wonderful totality.

section one

Revelling, thriving and surviving

Chapter 3
Stella: Authority as personal process   17

Chapter 4
Martin: It's good to be the king!   29

Chapter 5
Christina: Reflections on the nature of thriving
and authority   37

Chapter 6
A short story about revelling, thriving and surviving   45

CHAPTER 3

Stella: Authority as personal process

Stella puts her experience to work in the world. Three years ago she was viciously mugged, made eye contact with her assailant, saw that his fear mirrored hers and is now pushing hard for a film to be made for BIG TV based on her time spent with the kids and young men who inhabit her mugger's world.

Stella has been a filmmaker since her late thirties. Self-taught, she 'tends to write and research my own material' before reaching out to get the help of others. She is nearly 'always at the centre of what's going on'; what this centre is shifts as the film's life progresses. As with her work on the culture of youth violence, it frequently starts with Stella on her own. Then during the actual shooting she is in charge of a project involving several hundred people for two to three months. This falls away to a much smaller team during the backend work of editing and post-production. At each point Stella sees herself as 'being in charge' which means 'I have to be very clear about what it is I want others to do'. This experience of authority is something that she has 'increasingly learnt to enjoy'.

She described what it is like to be a filmmaker by referencing Truffaut's *Day for Night*, a film about filmmaking. In it, as in her work, 'the director is being asked endless questions' about what – for instance – colour the dress should be and on and on. 'All day long on shoot' she is bombarded with 'endless questions'. She has learnt that the director has 'to have an answer. The one thing I can't say is "I don't know." If I say that it sends a shiver of insecurity through the team.' This doesn't mean, however, that she is not willing to 'change her mind in a decisive way'.

She doesn't bark this decisiveness. She 'needs to make people feel confident and then give them the freedom to be themselves'. At the heart of this freedom and confidence is the vision of the project, which for Stella is nearly always wrapped up in her vision of the film. The vision is the touchstone that sets the boundaries and establishes the ambition of the piece; it gives Stella her decisiveness and so enables her to liberate her crew and cast.

Three types of director

After making her first film Stella taught one term at a film school. She felt slightly uncomfortable in her role as teacher given that she had not gone through the film school route. What struck her from this time was watching how the different groups of students performed as they worked on projects together. In each project one of the students would be the director and Stella observed what directorial styles were most popular with the other members of the team.

The most popular was Stella's personal favourite, those directors who were very clear about what they wanted but were also humane in the way they treated those around them. The second most popular was the style of the 'fascist bastard', who projected their own anxiety onto the group but were quite definitely in charge. The least happy groups, where the most moaning and complaining went on, were those led by 'woolly directors who didn't know what they wanted and faffed around'.

Learning to take charge and to stand out

One of Stella's earliest experiences of being in a position of authority was 'probably when I was 16. With another girl at school we decided to put on a review. We had to do it all; write it, organise it. I only recently remembered doing this and recall how surprisingly easy it was to do. I realised people would do what I wanted them to do and things could come off.' The 16-year-old Stella found nothing surprising about this at the time.

Prior to this experience of bringing others together around her own artistic vision, Stella had felt herself to be a bit of an outsider, 'slightly eccentric'. Up until this point she had grown up in the Anglo-Argentinian community, with its 'dated schools', where 'wanting to be an artist was something disgusting'. She knew that 'there were people like this' although not in her community, so when she was 15 she started 'wandering around Buenos Aires trying to find them'.

A sense of personal power

This forthrightness, this courage to seek out adventure may well have been furnished by her home setting where she felt herself to be 'quite a powerful force', although this was not 'maybe in a good way'. Her father had been 'very clever as a boy' but hampered by a 'terrible stammer. As a child and young man he had wanted to be a writer but didn't have the courage to pursue this. Instead he became an accountant and worked his whole life for the same multinational firm'. Stella was minded to quote Jung's observation that there is 'no more powerful influence on a child than the unlived life of the parent'.

There was also a fragility to her parents, as if 'both parents were missing layers of skin. Her mother had been orphaned at 15 and was not very intellectually able'. This was in contrast to the intellectual abilities of her father. To Stella it 'felt like a dead marriage that they plodded through'. By the age of eight both parents were confiding in Stella; she was the parent to the parents. In addition she was the intellectual stimulation and entertainment that 'my mother wasn't able to be'. Stella 'felt out of my depth but quite powerful'. This sense of personal power and drive was also shared by her younger brother, now a rich and powerful man in the commercial world.

Learning from not exercising authority

Stella enjoys being in charge and has learnt to feel comfortable with her authority. The toughness to her humanitarianism came about during her second film when she 'made every mistake you could... I was so excited that I felt I should give lots of others the chance to join in [in particular] I was picking women because they were women'. This resulted in her hiring a 'camerawoman who was having a breakdown' and 'didn't come to her senses until four p.m.' during a day's shoot. Rather than confront the situation Stella 'soldiered on', working with her camerawoman's incapacity. 'As a child I'd learnt to persevere.' Working on the film was a 'dreadful experience' with nothing being shot until late in the day. 'I was very anxious and therefore didn't give the actors the chance to be as good as they could be. I should have sacked her rather than persevere. By the end I hated her and she... probably returned the favour.'

It was not only the long-learned habit of perseverance that held Stella back, she was also steeped in guilt and a belief that she 'needed to look after people'. This was further reinforced by a political affiliation to radical Trotskyite socialism, which she had grown up in, and which meant 'only bastard capitalists sacked people'.

She operates differently now; 'if things aren't working' then Stella will sack people, something she had to do only a few weeks before our meeting. She sees the need to speak to people very early on if there are problems, 'I don't do it for fun or to make a point'. Usually her experience is that if it's not working for her then it's not working for the other person either. The very hard lesson is that in these situations 'things don't get better' and if they're not dealt with 'things only get worse'.

As she reflected on what this meant to her and how she'd changed in her life she repeated how at odds it was with her rescuer side and her sense of responsibility for others. She has within her that experience of being 'the small child responsible for other people'. She likes to run shoots where people are respected: 'some like a reign of terror. I don't; I like people working hard but enjoying themselves.' Stella is not passive in relation to her beliefs, 'It's never an accident what belief systems we have.' In her life this need to take care of others played out when 'I was a union representative in a hospital for a number of years. My job was to stop people being sacked (never mind if they were not doing a good job).'

Shit happens

At the end of this second film she realised that 'either I gave up making films or I addressed issues' such as those embodied in the camerawoman, and 'I embraced authority'. This embracing of authority 'took a while'. To begin with 'I blamed her', seeing that the 'shoot went wrong because she was useless'. With time and reflection came perspective and new insight, 'It was the point at which I was able to see my role [in the problems of the shoot]. I could see that there was something I could have done. I wasn't a victim of the situation.'

Stella appreciates that wishing problems away is not tenable, 'shit does happen. The question is how you deal with it.'

There will of course always be difficult people to work with; for Stella there is a very specific rule of thumb about how many difficult people can be incorporated. 'On big teams you can absorb one or two people who are very difficult. More than that and a negative whirlpool sets up with people complaining about them. With filming you have a short but intense period of time to work with and cannot afford to lose any of the energy. It must be focused on the film.'

The demands of filmmaking

'Filmmaking is brutal. You are working 12 hours a day on set, six days a week. Then there is the preparation time before going on set and on the seventh day you're preparing for the week ahead.'

Filmmaking also usually involves a lot of money. On bigger films there is 'film finance' and the 'bond', the insurance underpinning the financing. Every time a camera rolls over, the film finance people are automatically informed. They know from moment to moment, day to day, exactly how well the film is going in terms of delivering to schedule. The people who provide the bond have the right to intervene at any time to sack whoever they believe is slowing things down; they also have the right to sack the director.

Stella knows that she is hard to replace as a director because she is so personally bound up in the film, a fact that makes her unattractive to film finance people. Despite this 'I know that if I don't stay on schedule there is huge potential for interference'. Her authority as a director needs to be understood within the dynamics of her industry, where there is 'huge pressure to stay on time and on budget'. This explains her belief in the importance of giving fast and certain answers on set so 'when the armourer asks "what gun?" I have to answer if the prop is going to be delivered on time'.

Despite all these pressures to work to time and stick to the shooting schedule Stella believes she is able to be 'seen as an open and spontaneous director, where people can do as many takes as it takes... giving a sense that there is always time'.

Some roots of self-belief

I experienced Stella as having considerable self-belief and wanted to know where this confidence came from. To begin with, Stella spoke of the point in the filmmaking process when she loses her confidence. 'I lose confidence at the point where the film is shown. During the project I'm fired up. The film has to be done.' This sense of self-worth may be informed by her childhood. 'When I was little, one of the things my parents gave me was that they thought I was clever.'

She also seems to have acquired a capacity, a courage to engage with the unknown, the difficult and uncertain without being overwhelmed or frightened by it. This capacity to engage with rather than shy away from situations has been with her from childhood. 'I found the world quite a bewildering place when young… trying to make sense of things I don't understand is how I survive. How I breathe.' This desire to make sense of things using many types of creative forms is something she does. 'In November a horrible thing happened to me. I started writing a novel to make sense [of it].'

Filmmaking was not her initial creative expressive form and she explored many others before stumbling into it in her late thirties. Following on from her search for artists in Buenos Aires when she was 15 or so, she met someone, fell in love and 'ended up in Barcelona with a baby at 19'. She wrote stories at this time but didn't take them seriously. 'It was something I had to do.'

Wandering years

Before finding artistic endeavour as a job she worked in all sorts of ways to make ends meet – as a waitress, in a factory, picking blackcurrants in the Ribena fields and as a youth worker. She fell into this last and 'found I was good with delinquent teenagers because I'd been one… [I] wasn't afraid of them'. While working with these teenagers 'we put on a play, they got bored, so I said let's make a film'. They made a film, someone at Channel 4 saw it and so Stella's career as a filmmaker began.

'As soon as [I was] making the film it felt like falling in love. Everything I could do and was good at came together.' When it came to her subject matter she liked to explore things that were uncomfortable for her, as she said she 'always likes venturing outside of my comfort zone'. She knows that this was a turning point, 'a return to adolescence… adolescence being a time of potential with a life ahead. I'd had one kind of life and now had another.'

Authority from 15 to 35

When I asked her about her relationship to authority during these wandering years Stella's starting point was her role as a mum. 'I was a mum. I was skint. I had a very bohemian lifestyle, moved a lot. I was good with my son, very clear about boundaries.' In particular, being good with her son meant that he was able to leave home – a transition that is often problematic for boys growing up with single mothers. A psychoanalyst friend of Stella's suggested that this ability to be a father as well as a mother to her son came about 'because I identified with my dad more than my mum'. This paternal identification may also explain why Stella finds she is readily 'able to be in the world in a way many women find difficult'.

Stella was 'alright about my authority as a mother'. She had no trouble getting her son to do things like going to bed on time, not being rude, eating and so on. This ease with being in a position of authority also showed in her time as a union representative. At the same time as being in authority, she was also quite comfortable being an individual and seeing the world from her own point of view. This meant regular expulsions and suspensions from the local Trotskyite group that she belonged to. Stella does not respond well to the interference of others.

Her union responsibilities began when she was 26. There were 'only eight of us in the section [of the hospital]. Because I was more middle class and better educated than the managers... I developed a reputation at winning cases for people.' Originally she had meant the job to be undemanding, mindless even, leaving Stella free to paint – which was her artistic medium of the time. But her union work grew and grew as her reputation developed. What Stella took from this time was a belief that 'if you're confident, people will listen to you'. For Stella this belief was also anchored in a sense of what this confidence was in the service of. In the case of her hospital work, she was defending very poorly paid people and was energised by her 'strong sense of injustice'. She is aware that when she believes in something 'I'm very tenacious', which is 'one of the qualities of authority'. She is not mindlessly tenacious though – at the hospital she didn't 'go fighting cases that were stupid'. So when it comes to her current authority, 'You have to pick your battles, otherwise you become a pain in the arse. If I go into a battle, I go into it to win.'

The attractiveness of an iron will

Stella is currently fighting to get her film about her mugger's world made. 'Any sensible person would let go of this project' – she is having to fight hard in a TV world dominated by reality shows. 'But I know it's good and I know people need to know what's going on.'

In her attempts to get this project off the ground Stella has noticed something about those to whom she is appealing, those who at this time are in a position of authority with regard to her work. 'An iron will can be seductive when it comes to persuading people. They [the commissioners] don't want you to be vague, they want you to make them feel more confident.' From this Stella went on to make a general statement about people in authority. 'I have a sense that people in authority are not different from you or I. Part of your job [when engaging with people in positions of authority] is to make them feel comfortable. What you have to do is realise that this person needs you to be more powerful so that they can trust their own decision about whether or not to invest.'

Gender

Gender issues were touched on at various points as we talked. But Stella finished with a few words that struck me. 'I am hopeless with malign female authority… although I'm very good with benign [female authority]. I can deal with men whether they're malign or benign. I start to feel sorry for malign female authority figures – allowing them to behave very badly towards me. Gender is not insignificant.'

Reflections on a conversation with Stella

I was left with a series of explosive impressions, a firework display, when I ended my interview with Stella. My prurient side wanted to know so much more about points in her life that were alluded to or touched on briefly.

Significant parts of Stella's life would seem to be about inadequate boundaries, in particular her parents who expected the eight-year-old Stella to be a parent to them. Her bohemian lifestyle and seeking out of artistic adventure have a sense of boundarylessness to them – although I experience them as more of an escape from constrictions and constraints that prevented her from stepping into her authority. Now in the afternoon of her life she strikes me as having a very sophisticated, flexible and robust approach to boundaries. She sees boundaries between those in 'higher' and 'lower' positions of authority as a negotiation, where the 'lower' positioned person has a role in enabling the authority of the 'higher'. She is sensitive to the changing nature of what a good boundary is as the life of a film evolves. She understands that sometimes when a boundary is crossed the consequences need to be directly and robustly dealt with.

Boundaries exist in her life and her authority so that others can thrive. For people in positions of authority she has provoked in me some questions I find useful: 'What boundaries do I have to work with and what boundaries do I need to put in place? Are these the right boundaries for now? Do they serve the interests of the overall vision of the work? Do I need to let go of my boundaries so that I can encounter something new?'

Stella also has a courageous authority, something of the born-again delinquent – there is a boldness to it which I suspect gives her authority a thrilling edge. She has inhabited the counter-culture, the world outside of established norms and conventions – a world she is able to revisit. What this gives her authority is the potential for respect from those who would otherwise have little truck with people in her position. Shakespeare's *Henry IV* comes to my mind, with Prince Hal learning how to become king from those whose life is anything but kingly. These are insights and lessons that cannot be learned by visits or classroom lectures, these are lessons that are learnt through the actual experience of living differently. Maybe part of Stella's authority is the ability to draw on experiences where she has been – in some respects – without authority.

Stella believes in what she is doing and she understands that transmitting this belief to others is an essential part of her authority. Not to communicate this belief would be to fail in the exercise of her authority because it would derail others by bringing into question something that needs to be a given. She liberates others through her personal confidence. This characteristic makes me think of times when I haven't really believed in what I was doing or have witnessed others in authority around me failing to communicate this belief. It may be attractive to think that this believable expression of belief is something that can be grafted onto a person, but I suspect most people can smell this form of fake authority a mile off. She throws out a bald challenge to the world of leaders, directors, teachers, priests and parents – do you believe in what you're doing?

Stella's story embodies the marriage of masculine and feminine characteristics – or rather those characteristics we often talk about as being essentially 'masculine' or 'feminine'. There is a nurturing robustness to her, a desire to bring people on while at the same time not tolerating actions and behaviours that would undermine the work. Discussions about authority can often result in 'splitting', with the characteristics of authority such as forthrightness, decisiveness, boldness even ruthlessness, tending to be 'masculine'. The authority of the 'feminine' tends to be less witnessed, with characteristics such as care, nurture and sensitivity to relationships. Stella's story transcends this and provides a rich example of a human being living with an integrated (a holistic) approach to authority.

There can be a seductive pull to believe in a world where, if only everyone behaved as they should or could do, there would be no pain or difficult decisions. Stella's world is riddled with tensions and competing needs. Rather than looking to resolve the unresolvable, Stella holds the tension – say between the need for film finance to be kept happy and actors to feel free to explore and experiment. Then there is the sheer weight of events, of 'one bloody thing after another'. During her mugging Stella was not thinking about the filmic potential of the experience, she was too busy hanging onto her phone and being beaten up. It was only after the event that she could see the light in the darkness.

Authority is not about denying the difficult stuff or keeping everybody happy, it's about working with the messy reality of what is – and sometimes that'll be nice and sometimes that'll be nasty, but it'll never be simply sunshine and chocolates.

A follow-up meeting

Stella started our second conversation by referencing 'stereotypes of women in authority… the harpy and the ballbreaker. There aren't any calm pictures of women in authority.' She also said she'd 'felt very exposed' when reading her story and wanted to know my intentions. 'Are you investigating something you're quite hostile to?' When we'd last met I'd mentioned my father being in the army. We left that observation hanging and I asked if she'd recognised herself in what I'd written.

'Yes I did… which was a surprise. [It] felt really fair… you'd listened to what I'd said… [I'm] interested in what you picked out… [I was] relieved when I'd read it. I didn't feel judged… there was an acknowledgement that there were difficult jobs to be done. [I was] very struck by what I'd said about not being able to resolve problems with women… somehow I'd never learnt how to do that. My relationship with my mother never allowed for conflict and its resolution.' She noted 'how this is so common and so unacknowledged'.

Pain, learning and exposure

Stella is 'pleased that I'd learnt things. [I'd] started off not so good and learnt from bad/difficult experiences. Painful times are an opportunity as well as being painful… [although it would be] lovely if you didn't have to have the pain. [I'm] pleased that those difficult experiences have taught me how to do things better or alert me to [other] things. [I] protect myself better… [I've] stopped crippling myself by trying to rescue people, helping the halt and the lame.'

'I felt there was a lot of life [in my story]… it made me feel good. I felt I was alive. At the end [of our first interview] you said you were exhausted, "full up". That made me feel I'd exposed myself. Authority sounds such an external quality… [I'm] surprised how much it connected to my inner life.'

Other models of authority

Stella is experiencing a model of authority very different to her own at the moment – as she continues to try and get her latest project commissioned. A new young programmes director has come into post at one of the channels and 'rules with a will of iron'. Before he came, 'commissioning editors had freedom… now every single idea has to be personally approved by this man. People (commissioning editors) are becoming very afraid and won't fight for anything [for] fear of losing their job. The question is always, what will this director want?'

Women film directors and working with women in authority

There are very few women film directors. The ones there are 'either had children very young or don't have children at all… [it's] impossible to combine the two'. For Stella it is 'because of children' that there are so few women film directors – her assumption being 'why have children if you're not going to see them? When [you're] directing a film you disappear off the map… [you] can't do this with small children unless you're a very particular type of person.'

At this point Stella returned once more to the 'thing that struck me most when talking last time... the issue of working with women in authority'.

'When [I was] a child... if I argued with my mum she'd collapse and I'd feel guilty. She'd weep and talk about my dad. If I had difficulties... if I confronted her, she'd collapse. When some women in authority have been hostile to me... my fear is if I confront them I'll destroy them.' Stella stepped back and noted 'how strong these very early experiences are'.

'I could have it out with my dad... get very angry on occasion... I could shout at him and then it'd be alright. I wasn't damaging him by being angry.' Building on this Stella finds that when she's 'dealing with men in authority I'm not worried about being too destructive... I know they'll survive'.

Staying sane in the presence of others

'If a woman is not mad, then [it's fine]. If a man is mad [I] can deal with it. If a woman is mad [it's] impossible to stay sane.' A few years ago Stella was working with a mutual friend of ours – the producer on this film 'was vicious. Her anxiety meant she was very vicious to me.' She also had a condition that meant she was constantly bleeding. Stella was 'overwhelmed by how horrible she was to me' and she was also haunted by this 'image of her constantly bleeding. I couldn't say "no, you can't speak to me like that NOR could I say: she goes or I go."'

Things have got better over the years. In a 'recent experience of a woman in authority, she seemed to be setting out to humiliate me. I dealt better with it, kept a better sense of myself. She was very high up [in an organisation] so I had to work with her.' Stella 'was more able to realise what was going on and not get caught up in her stuff. Even though I didn't behave like a victim she must have smelt something in me. [I'm] still relatively undefended... but a bit better because I'm more aware.'

When dealing with the young male autocrat deciding the fate of her current project, '[I] don't feel crushed or humiliated [by him]... [I'm] able to accept it's just the way it is. [I] haven't turned it into an attack on myself.'

Noticing the presence of old bones

Stella describes having a 'sticky feeling when encountering something old [as if] amniotic fluid was attached to it... [it becomes] very hard not to obsess rather than deal with it'.

As our conversation wound down she returned again to the influence of father–daughter relationships. For Stella it is 'very telling [that] during the very passionate days of '70s feminism... how many of the women had better relationships with their father... [it was] easier to be in the world if you identified with your father.' Ironically, given Stella's political stance, she finished by referencing Margaret Thatcher and the way her 'mother is hardly mentioned'.

Given Stella's fear of destroying women, her final anxiety for this piece was not surprising. 'My one anxiety is that these women will recognise themselves and be damaged by what I say.'

CHAPTER 4

Martin: It's good to be the king!

Martin started our conversation by reflecting on the nature of success. He talked of 'interviewing youngsters' and 'asking them what position in life they were aiming for'. For Martin this was a trick question as the 'real answer is I haven't a clue'. Success is a random walk building on the skills achieved at each stage of life, maximising the opportunities that present themselves and then making a 'clear step forward'.

Authority and delegation

Martin was going to be 69 the day after we met and is 'trying to retire'. Although he does not carry as much authority as he used to he alluded to a strictly confidential role that he would be undertaking part time for the next few years – a job that will be firmly in the public eye and whose success (or lack of it) will be visible around the world. Subsequent to our conversation his role was announced – he'll be working for the Olympic Delivery Authority, chairing a panel 'set up to smooth London 2012 construction'.

In 1996 he gave up being a senior management consultant to take up the role of executive director of an association that exists to help its members to initiate and manage large-scale projects better. This association had members from over 80 organisations and institutions, covering all walks of life – from government to heavy engineering, from IT to the City. This was a demanding job firstly because 'the association had run down a bit before I took over' and secondly because 'all the people I was doing it for were senior executives who were accustomed to doing things well'.

He was able to turn this association around because 'I'm good at motivating people to do things. I've a pretty fertile mind... good at thinking of new ways of doing things. I'm a good communicator. Having been a project manager most of my career I'm good at identifying tasks and putting in place a plan to achieve [them]. I'm also very good at delegation, not because I'm idle but because more can get done. I can distribute.' Martin noted that delegation was 'the management skill that is never taught'.

'A lot of top managers are deficient at this. The classic is a manager who keeps all the decisions to himself and winds up with more decisions to make than he has time [for].' As a consequence of this the manager 'makes bad decisions and gets stressed'. In his view what gets in the way of delegation is the basic belief the more experienced or senior person holds that 'I can't let Young Snooks take that [decision] because he'll get it wrong. They forget they were once Young Snooks.' Martin gives 'full marks to the person who lets people learn from their mistakes' – which of course means giving people the opportunity to make them in the first place.

Motivating others and himself

'The main thing [is to] create an environment where you give people a lot of responsibility but also a degree of comfort that you're not going to let them foul up. You make a point of praising people who've done something good.' As a person in a position of authority you need to keep a flow of both praise and criticism going. Without becoming too mechanistic about it you 'shouldn't criticise someone unless the last comment was praise'.

Motivating others is also about 'taking time... talking about their work... making suggestions, giving confidence about things they're nervous about'. People like to be well paid, but motivation 'really isn't about money'.

His own motivator is 'achieving things. Setting new tasks and achieving them. I hate doing the same thing more than once', and if he does have to do the same task he'll 'always do it differently'. He also likes 'the approval of other people... people I respect'. If they're not people he respects then he 'couldn't care'.

Martin's first sense of personal authority – having to cope

Martin qualified as a civil engineer and went to work for a big contractor where he spent time in the design office. After a year he 'went up to Teesdale on a dam building project' where he was soon 'put in charge of the night shift' carrying out the tunnelling work. This was in 1962 when Martin was 23 years old. 'I had charge of about 30 men and lots of machines.' He was 'clearly the youngest person there' and was in charge of the whole site at night. The men were 'tough Irish navvies going from one big tunnel to another. They used to enjoy making life difficult for me... to get them to do things was tough. It was a very formative period.'

'One night [after] it had been snowing hard all day I went up to the site. [There was] no-one there. I drove back down to the village and found them in the pubs. I got them out of the pub and got them back to work.'

Martin relived his 'sensations as he drove to find them'. Part of him was saying, 'Why don't I just slope off home?' Another voice said, 'Let's give it a go. See if I can get them back to work. I'd set myself a challenge and I wanted to meet it.'

Other formative experiences also occurred at that time. There was an accident in the tunnel and someone had been injured. 'The men were thrown and didn't know what to do. I had to make the tunnel safe and get the man to hospital. I expected a foreman with experience to step forward, but they turned to me. I was thrown into a situation and had to cope. A lot of people never get this. In an office environment you never have lessons in exerting authority like you get on a big construction site.' It gave Martin 'practice in dealing with and leading others', which was 'something I was interested in'. There was a class dimension to this; Martin had grown up in a middle-class, grammar school world and in his words 'didn't know working people'. He certainly did by the end of his time in Teesdale.

Sources of courage

I found this tunnelling story compelling. Martin exhibited a courage that I would never have had if faced with similar circumstances – so I wanted to know where his courage came from.

'I used to like being in the school play and standing up on my hind legs and debating; situations where you put yourself in front of people and have to perform – both literally and metaphorically.' There was more to the school influence than providing him with a stage to perform. 'The school was very good, with a very strong ethic for developing boys as people.' Although it was one of the country's top academic grammar schools, it was in the other activities that were offered that Martin thrived, be it in the CCF, music or societies. Martin 'indulged in these to excess and failed my A levels'.

This behaviour at school demonstrates a distinctive pattern to Martin's life. 'I'm not a very disciplined person... I tend to do the things I want to do and not those I should. I'm not lazy', it's just that 'I've got to decide it's a good thing to do'. The things that he puts his energy into are those that he finds personally rewarding, so at school the piece for the school magazine on Birmingham's railways took precedence over homework.

'I'm generally blessed with high intelligence... I don't see it as an achievement.' Getting into this school was one of 'the most important events in my life [but] it was not an achievement to have got in'. Martin had been given brains and so to be intellectually capable was not an achievement, but a gift. 'I was lucky to get in and then I made full use of the school in everything but academics.'

Addressing failure

As has been said, Martin's love of extra-curricular activities resulted in him doing badly in his A levels. He was sure his parents were disappointed with this but they never showed it; his family was one where '[I] never talked seriously to parents about personal things'. Martin was disappointed though, especially after his father said 'I'm sure there are professions you can enter without going to university', such as architecture or quantity surveying. Martin 'decided I didn't want to do that, so I set myself a challenge and went for it'.

He did his A levels a third time, part time and in the evenings. During his last two years at school his A level Maths mark had declined from 35 per cent to 25 per cent. 'I then spent a year not at school', living with fewer distractions, and scored 98 per cent.

Other experiences of stepping into authority

When Martin was about 25 he went to work for a very badly managed contracting/building company in the Midlands. This was an excellent experience as his previous company had been very well run and he'd assumed this was normal. He was involved in building an extension to a factory in Manchester that was going badly – badly enough for top people from the factory owners in the US to fly over to the UK and demand a meeting with the MD of Martin's company. Since Martin had been helping with running the job, the MD asked Martin to join him at the meeting with the irate American clients.

On the morning of the meeting Martin's MD phoned him, saying he was unwell and would be unable to make it. Rather than cancel he told Martin to go on his own. When Martin went into the meeting the Americans were very angry that 'the boss had not turned up'. Once things got underway Martin said 'I can tell you what the problems are and what we need to do to sort them out' and by the end of the meeting 'this really tough American said "[This is] the first time one of your guys has spoken sense."'

The kicker to this story is that 'the MD wasn't ill… he'd flunked it'.

Being taken seriously

I was very intrigued about what enabled Martin to be taken seriously by these angry clients who had wanted to talk to the head man and instead had been palmed off with a relative youngster.

'I'm very good at seeing ways through difficult things. My main career was in management consulting [which is] about helping others manage things better. I've got a particular type of intelligence [that is] good at seeing ways ahead.' With regard to the Manchester experience 'I didn't go waltzing in all confident… I didn't achieve what I achieved through dominating… I said what I thought.' This is one of Martin's general characteristics – 'I find it very easy to say what I think.'

He also seems to engender a sense of enjoyable purposefulness, a view confirmed by four captains of industry who emailed him with these sentiments following a meeting he chaired recently. He even talked about finding fun in his work and seeking to promote fun when working with others.

What is fun?

'Life can't be fun all the time… fun is a relative thing. Fun is not just a laugh a minute. A component of fun is a group of people interacting well together and achieving things together.' Fun and achievement go together – and Martin is 'very much achievement orientated'.

Martin describes his career after the Manchester experience in a very focused way; while there was no grand plan he made the best of what every opportunity presented. As a result he worked in Canada, moved into the university world to research into the management of civil engineering and by the time he had finished his PhD he had access 'to everyone in the civil engineering world', with his particular specialty being financial control. He became the leading light in establishing new standards in this area and 'made my name in the civil engineering industry'. He became well known in the industry and he enjoyed the approval that came his way. 'I like people to like what I've done.'

He does not experience a fear of failure – seeing nothing in his life that would count as a crisis brought on by significant failure. He does 'not have a lot of self-doubt'. This doesn't mean he is nerveless; simply that fear doesn't get in his way. His wife Diana believes that 'he's built on experience... started small and built on this'. Martin believes that you are 'only frightened if you think you can't do' something.

This informs how he has managed people in his life, making sure that he delegates to people but provides the right level of support so that they feel able to do something. For Martin 'his monument is the ranks of people he has brought on'. Bringing people on 'is a hugely important part of the job'. Bringing people on is about helping 'people take steps and building up confidence'.

Important people and what makes for satisfaction

When I asked Martin who'd been the most important in bringing him on, he replied without hesitation 'my wife Diana'. With 'all the successes you have in your career and all the times in the day you do something you're proud of... [there is] no point in doing it if it's not noticed by someone you love. Wanting to be successful and achieve things is important... having Diana appreciate me is very important.'

Martin sees the satisfaction of his life very much in terms of how he is experienced by others, even if Diana is a *primus inter pares*. 'I do like to be appreciated... I get as much of a thrill when I know people warm to me' as he does from what has been achieved together. After a pause, he put this even more strongly: being warmed to 'is more important than what we have achieved'. This led him onto a wider point about how he sees business. There is 'no point in making business wealthier if this is done at the expense of people you work with'.

When he considers all the big projects that he has worked on, 'the thrill is not just [about] the date you completed, the amount it cost or what it does'. The thrill comes from being a leader and a part of a group of people. 'Hell is when you can't get people to work together. It is very unpleasant when relationships don't work. Not rewarding' at all.

Reflecting on Martin's story

For a while I played with the idea of putting two quotes at the front of this book. The first would look to tap into the more angst-ridden aspects of authority and make use of Shakespeare's observation that 'Uneasy lies the head that wears a crown'. The second quote would look to draw out the pleasure of authority, which is how I experience Martin – and although he seems a bit more serious than Mel Brooks, the line 'It's good to be the king!' speaks to me when I think of him. He really enjoys leadership, not in and of itself, but because of what it enables him to get done in the company of others.

Martin has had the experience of being in situations where boundaries were not taken care of – in particular the abject failure of his MD at the time of the Manchester problem to step into his authority. I wonder how much his concern with giving people sufficient responsibility to extend themselves, even fail – but within the context where they are not going to hang themselves – is informed by that and other experiences. Martin's concern for bringing on people speaks to me of the 'good father', one who is both able to nurture and also to step back so that those around him do not stay in his shadow. His self-confidence is a gift to others because he does not have a need to 'keep people in their place' but instead seeks to enable them to do the best they can in the service of the shared endeavour. The authority he embodies emboldens others around him, by being in their service (not his) and also owning the fact that there will be times when he needs to take charge and use the position he holds.

This was the first time in many years of conducting these sorts of interviews that someone has talked of love, in this case Martin's love for his wife Diana. It was only mentioned briefly but its presence when I met with the two of them was tangible. His authority has a moral, even spiritual, anchor that is based around his relationship with Diana. It is her opinion above all others that he values. The implications of this are that his authority will always have a yardstick outside of the job itself or the immediate priorities of the work – which should mean he has a healthy inoculation against being swept away in the mania of any particular moment or cutting corners that should not be cut, especially in the arena of human relationships. The love for and of a good woman provides more support for Martin than would a legion of coaches or consultants.

Martin does not seek out positions of authority, they arrive on the coat-tails of achievement. He certainly enjoys being at the heart of things, but that's because he enjoys getting things done. Authority in Martin's life is an inevitable by-product of his personality and how he wants to be in the world; the key word though is 'by-product'. Much of his authority may come from how others experience him – they do not see him as someone interested in grandstanding or self-aggrandising behaviour, but as someone whose attention is grounded in the here and now of what needs to be done so that things can be kept going and progressing. This may sound an obvious and simple feature of 'good' authority, but history and organisational studies are littered with kings and chief executives who started off with good intentions and then became obsessed with the trappings of authority rather than its purpose.

Milan Kundera wrote *The Unbearable Lightness of Being*, which explores the overwhelming intensity of life. Martin's lightness is of an earthier kind, more to do with 'the enjoyable lightness of authority'. He invites people to enjoy what can be enjoyed while getting on with a shared endeavour. He does not want people to be crushed or overwhelmed by the seriousness of what they're doing, to experience the shared task as a joyless burden. His authority is there to leaven and lighten the moment, not make it heavier. This doesn't mean trivialising what is serious, knotty or important, it simply means giving a process some space to breathe, some humanity. Martin enjoys having authority, both personal and positional, and seeks to share that enjoyment and what it makes possible with those around him.

There is a strong sense of personal agency in Martin – he is not passive in his relationship to events or his ability to influence and shape them. However, he has never fallen into the trap of mistaking personal agency for an ability to control the world; his life is built around the notion of making the best of what opportunities present themselves and then seeing what this makes possible. His agency is grounded in a thorough appreciation of the present – he works with what is, rather than what he hopes or wishes the world to be. He seems to live the tension between free will and accident with considerable ease, probably because that is the nature of reality as he has experienced it; to find this tension difficult would be most illogical when reality is constantly infused by both.

CHAPTER 5

Christina: Reflections on the nature of thriving and authority

Long pause.

'It so depends on the person and what people want to get from a position of authority.'

'I could give you lists of opposites.'

'If I'm someone who wants to be in control or seen to be in control I want compliance and I'll thrive with compliance.'

Christina thrives in conversation and I was trying something different with her, asking her to do her thinking on her own rather than as a collaborative effort. Prior to sitting down in a café in Waterlow Park, we'd talked about the context for this interview, about what enables people to thrive or not thrive in positions of authority. I wanted to hear Christina's point of view on authority because of her experience of working with so many people in positions of authority, her own professional responsibilities – and her academic credentials. She's also a friend.

For Christina people don't thrive when they are 'disconnected from their awareness, their feelings, their thinking… thriving has to mean they [and I] get connected… and compliance to autocratic behaviour, however good it may feel, is not thriving'.

'Thriving comes from connection', and this presented Christina with a difficulty with being interviewed. She didn't feel adequately connected having me just listening and taking notes.

Stepping into a position of authority

Christina is in the process of taking over leadership of an academic programme. 'I've been discovering how I like to lead. It's no use just trying to perpetuate the previous leader's approach. I've realised that I'm not someone who wants to lead from the front. I really enjoyed a recent faculty conference because we were "thinking together". I noticed how I was influenced to change my mind by what colleagues were contributing to the conversation. I was thriving in my new position of authority by contributing to this experience where people flourished… our brains were aching because we'd thought so hard together.' What a contrast with the previous and following meetings, which were business oriented, with a long list of tasks to work through. And yet that work has to be done too. 'I'm currently wondering about how to make business meetings more fun whilst staying efficient and on course. Not a straightforward proposition!'

'One of the things I've noticed is that I discover who I am as a leader in response to others' behaviour. I am learning how people's personal agendas influence the way they engage with me, more so than in the past before I took on this role. It's quite natural of course, but I notice how some of that behaviour can be quite disturbing.' Christina is wary of people who are in a position of authority and need to be overly in control and equally wary of people who invite authoritative behaviour from her, especially when it serves their agenda.

When it comes to thriving in a position of authority, 'a very important issue is your context', how you interact with those around you. To thrive in authority you 'need a context that invites you to operate with integrity [which is] a big ask in our current corporate environment'.

Integrity as a lived essence not a thing

In her native language people talk of an 'integral' person, that is a person 'who is imbued with integrity'. Christina notices that the English equivalent 'doesn't quite feel the same. In English you talk of integrity as something people have, rather than it being an intrinsic quality of their character.' Being an 'integral' person means 'I can speak my truth without fear of losing my job or getting my head chopped off'. This quality exists within the context of particular relationships and situations. Thus Christina may on occasions feel that she cannot 'speak her mind' to a senior colleague because it will upset them, it's not the right moment to speak truthfully and/or because the colleague is likely to respond in a counterproductive way. 'This is how organisations go down the pan either morally or economically… [when] it is not safe for people to say what they're seeing or experiencing… [and] that's true upwards, downwards or sideways. Having to censor oneself becomes a pattern… some things can't be spoken of… for instance we may know some senior person is not up to the job but no-one dares talk of it and so it becomes impossible to do something about it.' Christina is currently reading Harlow Cohen's *The Dinosaur in the Living Room*, which describes this point, of 'everyone knowing something is wrong but no-one talking about it because people are untouchable'.

'I need to have some difficult conversations with my colleagues in the team… thriving is about not avoiding them.' To have these difficult conversations Christina gets the courage she needs when she realises that 'by not having this conversation with A, I am short changing B'. This doesn't make it any easier 'when you know the impact is going to be heart breaking'; for instance, 'How do you sack someone and do it with integrity?'

'For me thriving in my position of authority means I lead with integrity and that my team members are thriving too.'

Being in the right job

'A necessary condition' for thriving in authority 'is to be in the right job, not being put in a position where you are out of your depth in terms of skills, knowledge or any of the attributes required to do a job well'. And at the same time as having the necessary knowledge, skills etc., 'in my view humility is a requirement for thriving. I've seen people go under because they lost their awareness of the extent to which they really are dependent on others to deliver their agenda, [a leader] "whose ego gets inflated and in the way" – as we would say on our master's programme.'

Having come up with this definition of thriving she added: 'I find it very hard to think of someone who is thriving.'

Thriving at great personal cost

On reflection Christina identified 'Andrea' – who could be said to be really thriving, although 'at great personal cost'. She works for a well-known health organisation and has a 'clear view of the contribution the organisation could make to patient care'.

'Over the last few years she has really, really held people to account – including herself. It seems like a tornado has hit the organisation.' She has 'developed new initiatives and contributions, in line with the purpose of the organisation, whilst stopping people going off to do their own thing, and misusing or on occasions abusing organisational resources, and she's held the line in the face of enormous adversity'.

'I've seen her very close to crumbling… [but] now even sceptical or downright hostile people are coming round… I've seen the dark days and months, when she came close to giving up, and now I can see how she's flourishing as she sees the fruition of her hard work.'

'Thriving is associated with staying true to yourself. I'm not talking about how I maximise profits (my own or my organisation's) at the expense of everything else. Thriving is an expression of deep ecology.' This is a phrase that I, John, interpret as being about how the health of the whole is informed by and plays out within individuals.

Part of this ecological thriving is to do with 'doing no harm to yourself, or others or the environment you're part of'. To thrive ecologically requires a person in authority to do 'no harm even if what you are going to do will cause distress.' This plays out in the practice of 'tough love in organisations'. S, a coaching client of Christina's, is 'beginning to see that not speaking a painful truth is a collusion that could result in damage'.

'To really thrive [requires a] fantastic awareness of self, others, motivation and awareness of one's dark sides.'

Thriving as a human being

'Thriving can be a not very exciting and potentially bland word. If thriving is the same as a big bonus or a big corporate profile I'm not interested.' Christina is interested if it's about thriving as a human being.

'To thrive as a human being you need to get reconnected to yourself and others… [to] the web of life. To thrive in a position of authority you need to find ways to give of the best of you in a way that's true to you.'

'If I'm an introvert in a position of authority that requires me to make public statements with confidence... I need to be allowed to do my public speaking in a way that works for me.' But there is more to it than simply working with a particular preference such as introversion. A strength certainly needs to be built on and worked with but people also need to 'become more even handed', by building up those preferences that are less developed in them. 'Some people start off even handed and become one handed. [It's] tempting to just revert to strengths.'

Redemption and healing

'Thriving has something to do with redemption and healing', this is 'partly related to developing two-handedness'. Christina comes from a family environment in which she was not encouraged to put herself forward. 'If I think of the number of times I've been infused with the message: "You mustn't draw attention to yourself. You mustn't take centre stage." The idea I'd ever take up a position of authority' was laughable at that time. Her family can still be less than supportive when they hear of Christina 'stepping into a position of authority'. During the time between the three conversations that went into this story Christina's father died; at our last meeting she said: 'I'll be interested to see how strongly this "injunction to be modest" continues to play out for me.'

Taking on authority 'appears to be a very different experience for me compared to friends who were encouraged to be the leader of the pack'. She reflected on a client who had always expected to be a leader in the familiar public school fashion. 'For him taking up a position of authority was more right-handedness... what he needed was people who were willing to challenge his autocratic behaviour.'

In this definition of thriving, Christina is 'associating thriving with maturity' as presented in the work of Gilligan with its notion of 'balancing agency and communion'. For her public school client there was a need to learn about communion, whereas 'for me [it is] more to do with learning about agency'.

Thriving in the service of self and thriving in the service of an organisation

'I'm not sure any of the standard leadership literature is really interested in leaders thriving... it appears to be more about how you can shine, sparkle; NOT how you can thrive. Shining is about being seen to be successful... [this] could just be a person simply developing single-handedness. I've seen people lose themselves in very successful jobs.'

'I was concerned about this when I first took up a leadership role. Would I notice if I was becoming Teflon coated... becoming inappropriately defended against feedback', no longer being 'open to see the good or bad impact I'm having'?

She returned again to the theme of connection. 'We seem to have disconnected ourselves from ourselves, from our context and from our web of life. Thriving has become defined by the bottom line. I've seen people become inhuman… only when the edifice collapses does it become evident what a monster they were turning into.' She recalled the heyday of Robert Maxwell who at the time was 'getting accolades about being a thriving businessman, whilst most of his staff suffered under the brutality of his leadership'.

Taking a sideways look

After another long pause, Christina came at the issue of thriving in authority from another direction. 'I'm thinking about parents… when are parents thriving?' For Christina 'good parenting always has a sense of the parents healing their own wounds rather than passing them on'. This insight from parenting then translates into authority and leadership. Good authority is 'about not acting out the unhealed wound but acting in a way that is consciously informed by what went before'.

'Many successful leaders are acting out their distress', and are not experiencing this redemptive quality. Their wound is 'the worm in the apple'. For instance 'having been abandoned early on in life' they develop the habit of 'not trusting anyone – of being exceedingly self-reliant. Sometimes this is appropriate for their situation but it doesn't mean they're thriving… [it's] not doing [them] any good. It's like abused parents, abusing children to instil discipline.'

This charged reflection led Christina to make a series of strong statements about the importance of reflection. She started with the well-known saying that 'the unexamined life is not worth living', concluding that 'thriving is about consciousness and self-awareness'.

She then challenged herself, recalling a particular chief executive she knows. 'Malcolm doesn't do self-awareness, yet he's having a good time in his job. Is he thriving?' She left the answer uncertain. 'I notice I'm making a big moral judgement there… I'm sure he'd say he's enjoying himself. Tricky one isn't it?'

This uncertainty seemed to be centred around the question of 'thriving from whose perspective?' Christina considered another senior executive, this time in the field of research. 'He's very successful, does good work and gets lots of grants. I wouldn't say he's thriving at the moment because he's not willing to grow up around [certain issues]. He's very good at research, seen as very bright – but he's not a very good manager. In my view he's not thriving but others, and he, may see [it differently].'

Taking power and position into consideration

'I know I'm rather judgemental in my view of what constitutes thriving. My definition is rather narrow. Thriving is to do with growing up... becoming a more mature, balanced, connected person.' But Christina could see that 'I've been ignoring position and power'.

Position and power can provide a wonderful opportunity to pursue a particular course of action as 'Andrea' did at the Health organisation. It also brings with it the risks of hubris, of believing oneself to be both irreplaceable and superior to all.

Mature authority, which may then enable thriving, is one where it is possible to have an honest acceptance of both potency and limits. Christina quoted from the well-known prayer to summarise this – 'Give me the wisdom to know what I can change... and the courage to leave well alone what I can't.'

As well as this mature appreciation of one's own boundaries, a similar appreciation is needed of what is going on with people who are around a person of authority. Firstly authority makes a difference to relationships, 'When you are in a position of authority people will behave differently to you than they did before... you have to accept this, not criticise or deny it.' Secondly, 'People in positions of power can enable, but also disable, others.'

Authority within the context of circuits of mind

As we approached the end of our meeting Christina returned to Gregory Bateson's notion of circuits of mind and the concept of an indissoluble web of connection within the world, between thought and action and their consequences as they ripple out through the wider sea of interconnectedness – human and non-human, material and immaterial.

'If I'm willing to sacrifice myself to make my organisation successful, I establish a toxic circuit of mind – by damaging myself, I damage the web of life. It is the counterpoint of the insight that indigenous people have always understood: "If I damage the web of life I damage myself."' This has been a theme in Christina's life for the last six months, paying attention to the 'connections between different ways of knowing, sustainability, indigenous peoples and phenomenology'.

Final words on thriving in authority

'Thriving means seriously examining your levels of narcissism and finding a healthy level. Our current organisational culture encourages narcissism. People become more and more defended and more and more narcissistic, so that they can't hear any basic truth about themselves.'

For Christina as she becomes embedded in more and more positions of authority her inoculation against this is a question to her husband: 'I keep asking John, am I getting attached to my position? Is there a risk that my integrity is being eroded? Am I becoming seduced by the accoutrements of positional power?'

A short story about revelling, thriving and surviving

These three stories have a generosity of spirit to them. They appeal to my own philosophical and psychological bias, a bias that allows for personal ambition but not at the expense of others. They are also stories of people who have not followed simple linear paths; these are lives with bumps in, where privilege is not taken for granted. My reflections on authority informed by this triptych fall into four areas:

- Don't lose yourself
- The wellbeing of others matters
- Don't simply repeat what you've been through
- Practical integrity.

Don't lose yourself

Stella, Martin and Christina have ways of staying grounded. Martin has his Diana, whose love and respect he desires above all else. Christina has her John who she can check in with to see that she's not getting overly attached to position. Stella has the brute reality of film finance, a wealth of life experience and a well-honed habit of self-reflection to keep her real (a psychoanalytically informed friend helps as well).

They all exist in situations and relationships that mean they are able to hear basic truths about themselves – even better than the voice behind the triumphant Caesar reminding him that he is mortal, they have voices reminding them that they are people who need to be lived with – and if they expect to get away with bringing that chariot into the house they've got another thing coming.

None of them seem overly impressed by the trappings of authority and are still curious enough about themselves to have someone, such as myself, rummage around their lives. They are all self-assured but haven't fallen into arrogance; they are well voiced and don't let what matters to them get drowned out. They have all known success, but it doesn't define them nor has it gone to their heads.

My sense is that people in authority can easily lose themselves; to begin with they are probably competent, or lucky, but as time passes and success accretes to them so they can begin to believe themselves more able than they are – and others around them can fuel this self-referencing myth. Without people who can tell them basic truths and with a diminishing capacity to hear anything that doesn't fit with their increasingly unchallengeable fantasy, so the human being gets lost and the authority figure steps into the world – as god, monster or mother/father to us all.

The other form of losing yourself is when the self disappears, becoming invisible rather than grandiose. The self becomes the role, the cipher performing what others need the role to do, the one 'who does not count the cost' – a truly awful and inhuman image of selflessness. I have seen too many workaholics, and bitter wives referring to these role-defined husbands as 'sperm donors', to see such consuming self-sacrifice as healthy.

The wellbeing of others matters

All three are concerned with the wellbeing of others around them – sometimes to their personal detriment. They are people who enjoy seeing others doing their best; Martin's observation speaks for them all when he says 'Hell is when you can't get people to work together.' Being in a position of authority in the company of others brings with it great responsibility because, as Christina says, '[they] have a huge potential for enabling and disabling others'. Even if the burdens of authority can make it difficult to thrive in authority, not paying attention to the thriving of those around you is a dereliction of duty. The wellbeing of others matters.

It is important though to pay close attention to what wellbeing can mean; it is not some simply defined term that can be applied willy-nilly to all people in all situations. Thriving is not only about supporting and bringing people on, it is also about challenging people who are playing games or engaging in behaviours and actions that are damaging to others. Thriving has both a personal and a collective dimension; a person in authority needs to look at the needs of the individual as well as how the needs of the collective are knitting together – a need that includes a frank acknowledgement of what a person in authority can or can't cope with given their own history, ability and character.

Thriving is also not to do with supporting others in whatever it is they wish to do. This is a bounded thriving, where the ambitions and intentions of the work set the limits. Thriving is in the service of the task in hand, it is not about helping people address psychological problems or become free children. Thriving may require a strong recommendation to seek support or help outside of working on the collective task, but it is not the job of the authority to support all forms of personal or professional development. Authority is not all things to all people, although people who wear it will have all manner of matter thrown at them.

Don't simply repeat what you've been through

All three, professionally and/or personally, have experienced people in authority not holding boundaries – abdicating their responsibilities. Their response has not been to repeat this and do what was done to them, but to do something different. In psychological terms they have been able to work from a position of healing or reconciliation, rather than directly from the original wound. They set out to support those around them by owning their responsibility combined with an attention to how they have constructed its meaning and the associated action.

They have been tempered by the experience of what happens when either they or those around them have failed in some duty of authority – they are also informed by experiences that have shown them to be resourceful and authoritative in the past. They have an embodied, as compared to a purely intellectual, understanding of their own capabilities as people in and with authority.

This may be one of the critical features of good authority that I have been seeking; an applied practice of authority that draws upon personal history and preference wisely. This is not about a knee-jerk acceptance or rejection of one's experience of authority and its practice; it is a considered use of personal insight – the wise application of experience rather than an arrogant (and unreflected on) belief that what worked for me in the past (or at least didn't kill me) will work for others in the present or future.

Practical integrity

I experienced them as being principled without being priggish – they have an integrity in terms of their orientation to the world and what they see as important. This provides them with a way of living from which they try and work. This doesn't mean they seek to impose their way of being onto others, nor does it mean that things always work out as they wish or that they don't sometimes get derailed by the storms and disturbances of others.

But by holding to a way of being in the world, that I would describe as an example of applied ethics, they provide people around them with a practical consistency that can be grounded in the day-to-day – which does not blow around according to whatever happens to be fashionable, expedient or the flavour of the month.

The shadow of the ethical person can be rigidity or moral absolutism; what prevents this is the ability to put yourself into the shoes of those around you – Stella's connection with her mugger being an extreme example of this. Authority that can't understand the world from the point of view of others is doomed to being perceived as self serving, self referencing and insensitive. Being able to see through the eyes of others does not mean surrendering yourself to that point of view, but it is at the heart of the old managerial cliché of using 'different strokes for different folks'.

section two

Creativity, anxiety and metabolising shit

Chapter 7
Sam: Masked and unmasked authority   51

Chapter 8
Luke: Creative authority   59

Chapter 9
Thomas: Management writer, coach and refugee from authority   67

Chapter 10
A short story about creativity, anxiety and metabolising shit   73

CHAPTER 7

Sam: Masked and unmasked authority

Sam is both chief executive of Teenspeak and also a qualified psychoanalyst. When I spoke with him on the phone prior to our meeting he wanted to know whether I wanted to talk to him as a CEO or as a psychoanalyst. I asked him to see his CEO role as figural, but to use his analytical training as a reflective frame for our conversation.

He joined Teenspeak, a counselling service for teenagers, in 1997. He started off as a counsellor, before becoming an assistant director and finally chief executive. He has a background in teaching and has been a deputy head; experiences at that time convinced him that children underachieve because they're unhappy so in 1994 he started a school counselling service and became trained as a psychodynamic counsellor. He then moved out of schools and worked in a Primary Care Trust, with no intention of going back to working with kids. An invitation to join Teenspeak changed that.

Personal responsibility and the need to achieve

'I was five years old and going to school for the first time and was not going to be like the other kids.' He was contemptuous of 'kids who were upset at being parted from mum'. For Sam it was his responsibility, on his own, to deal with this move from home to school.

After a few weeks or months at school he realised that while he couldn't read there were others who could. He remembers sitting in the bath at home, really trying to make sense of the words HOT and COLD written on the taps and then finally being able to make sense of how the letters combined to make words.

'From an early stage I had some very complex Oedipal patterns. Mother was a very strong personality; bossy, demanding and very loving.' She was the oldest sister and was also bound up with her brother, Sam's Uncle Robert, who died from muscular dystrophy when Sam was five or six. He remembers his mother's physical and emotional absence at that time and his personal sense of 'having to get on with it' on his own. The family was very poor and his father worked long hours as a printer. The parental dynamic at that time was of an uncommunicative father and an absent, fiery mum.

Once the trauma of Uncle Robert's illness and death had played out, Sam increasingly experienced his mum as being 'guiltily intrusive'. Sam and his brother were surrogates for a disappointing marriage. His dad would observe, 'She was only ever interested in her two bright boys.'

After his slow academic start Sam now felt he 'needed to be big and grand enough for my mum'. His parents however thought that he was getting too full of himself, teased him about having a head too big to come through the door and engineered games that he would lose. A difficult mixed message played out for Sam about 'needing to achieve, but it not being okay to achieve'.

Authority and the false self

Sam went to grammar school and stepped into authority roles without really enjoying them. He feels that by then he was already playing out a false self and was not able to feel comfortable in his own skin. He was leader of the sports team and head of house; he was voted form captain five years in a row as well as being a patrol leader in the Scouts. 'I turned myself into Mr Nice Guy. I'm energetic; I listen. That's why people voted for me.' All the time though Sam experienced a sense of inadequacy and inner emptiness. He knew that somehow this was not him – even as he went on doing it.

Sources of self-mistrust

One of Sam's fears was that he was being grandiose in taking on these leadership positions; somehow he was being too big for his boots. The other source of doubt concerned his mother's dislike of the masculine. 'My mother distrusted men. Her father had been an alcoholic and there was sexual abuse on Granny's side.' Then there was muscular dystrophy, which is transmitted from women to men. Sam's mum desperately wanted girls not boys. 'I was supposed to be Samantha', even the clothes for the baby Samantha had been bought.

Calculating how to succeed

It was no accident that Sam took on the roles he did at grammar school: 'I have a neurotic need not to be caught out.' Right from the start he understood that school was a very competitive place and to succeed he would need to do well at classes and at sport. So 'I turned myself into a damn good rugby player' all the way through school.

Because he felt so intensely under threat at all times, Sam developed a really good social and environmental radar, becoming adept at 'tuning into what was going on'. This capacity was immensely useful not only at school but also as a teacher where he had a 'very good understanding of where kids were coming from'. As a deputy head and now as a chief executive this sensitivity to what is going on supports his ability to develop a strategic vision, a sense of the whole and how to work with it. 'I'm good at strategic vision', an ability which has helped him to launch an umbrella organisation with county and even national reach that sits alongside Teenspeak. 'But the neurotic energy that fuels it is exhausting.'

Not only does his calculated success cost him a lot of his energy, it also – historically – has given him very little satisfaction. Pride and satisfaction in achievement is fleeting and he is 'very good at rubbishing anything I can do'; his mother's disappointment and anxiety with him being the wrong type of child worms away at him. He has 'difficulty in valuing who I am, so I do it through achievement but that is never enough'.

I shared with him my reflections that this might well make him a godsend for an organisation — a leader who would never become complacent or too in love with his self-image, although at a potentially disastrous personal cost.

Healthy and unhealthy positions of authority

When I asked him how he was making Teenspeak work for him, he began by talking of a situation that hadn't worked. He recalled taking on a deputy headship at a failing school that he successfully turned around prior to the arrival of a new head. He remembers being the target for everyone and being the one who had to take a lot of tough decisions. He was squeezed on all sides and filled with a huge sense of personal doubt. I would categorise this as the ongoing pattern of external success disconnected from any sustaining sense of personal value and achievement.

Teenspeak is run on collegial lines. 'People want me to be more visible and I'm [getting] better at this. I can take pleasure [in success] without feeling my head's getting too big.' For Sam a critical aspect of what he needs at work then became apparent: 'working with other counsellors I can be more real emotionally'. He recalled how last year there had been a life and death moment for the organisation as they waited for a crucial decision to be made by a funding agency; when it came through 'I cried.'

Sam can wear his authority more comfortably when he is in an environment where his emotional reality can be expressed. Prior to Teenspeak he had had to keep his emotional reality, and the emotional reality of the organisations he belonged to, under wraps — or rather, denied. He is also 'less afraid of leading from the front' these days; in his deputy head days he felt himself to be 'leading from behind'. The shift has become possible thanks to a lot of 'good therapy, more ego strength, more self-esteem', although he still remains fearful of 'sounding too grand'.

For Sam it is 'wonderful to be in an environment where I can be more present, a boss who cries when the funding comes through. There's less that needs to be covered up… I can bring more of myself with less risk into this scenario.'

Crippled by his lack of self-esteem, authority was a burden for Sam, especially when he felt unable to bring his vulnerability to work. Authority has become something pleasurable now that he is in an emotionally real environment, both in terms of the organisation's work and also because of the emotional competence of his colleagues — and himself.

The demonisation of authority figures

'People in authority… teachers, police, prime ministers get so much transference… [they] get demonised.' As a deputy head Sam 'took so many projections' from people. He recalled one incident where 'parents stormed into my office and gave me ten to fifteen minutes of abuse and hate'. Sam defused the situation, acknowledged the perceived hurt and turned it into a potentially positive opportunity. But 'I needed supervision. It was very hard to talk to my colleagues. In their view this sort of encounter goes with the territory.'

Another time a psychotic came into the school with a knife and Sam had to put himself physically between the intruder and a child. Again the common room adopted an ironic 'glad it wasn't me' attitude. For Sam authority 'is not just big balls… it's about intelligence and space. Not being all things to all people and having the opportunity to be imperfect.'

I sense that in the past being in authority was about having to cope with whatever came up on his own; it was about putting a strong mask on for the world and not showing how he had been touched. He talked often about a sense of false self – I now see it as a mask he felt he had to wear; authority as a mask of capability in a world where others are less capable.

Authority now

In his role at Teenspeak Sam feels 'understood and valued' by his colleagues. There are lots of mechanisms in place 'for paying attention to and containing adolescent splitting.' There is 'space to metabolise powerful pieces of shit. I get very few bits of shit from inside the organisation… [and] this releases me to fight battles outside.'

In terms of crude archetypes Sam feels much more of a 'hunter–gatherer' going out into the world, 'much more masculine. I have [always had] well-developed nurturing parts; [now] I've got the balls to occupy the full masculine.' Sam's authority is now informed by a more integrated and valued mix of the feminine and the masculine; historically owning his masculine authority had been a problem. Now healthy authority is about 'bringing the masculine and feminine into balance'.

This healthy balanced authority is in stark contrast to the very negative and authoritarian masculine authority he grew up with through the Church, which he experienced as anti-human, and the grammar school, where only a very negative and belittling authority existed.

In his work he is also meeting an unmet need of his adolescence, the provision of an empathetic masculine presence – an authority figure who can be talked to by the young. When he was 14 he became convinced that he was being struck down with muscular dystrophy, but found himself unable to talk to anybody about this. He knows about the intensity of adolescence and 'I open up space for them… they can talk to me.'

His current practice of authority is about putting his experience to good use, providing adolescents with an experience of generative masculine authority.

First experience of benign authority

Sam's sense of authority in much of his life has either been negative or solitary, i.e. something that he has to take on by himself. His first experience of benign authority came when he was a deputy head and a counsellor advised him to seek out a genetic counsellor. So it was he discovered that with the birth of his own two daughters, his Uncle Robert's particular strain of muscular dystrophy was dead. He also learnt that he and his brother had had only a 50 per cent chance of both being healthy – no wonder home was an anxious place and he held within him such a sense of being under threat.

The fond dad

'I am a very fond dad. It was so easy to look after and enjoy my daughters.' Sam has brought this into his work and 'found I do enjoy colleagues. I enjoy being an "in authority" figure, to nurture and bring people on. Authority and nurturing have come together – the masculine and the feminine.'

Sam's views on what represents a good practice of authority

Sam gave me six points that spoke to him of good authority, all of which come back to emotional intelligence.

1. *Emotional intelligence* – 'the best leaders are those who understand themselves and how they construct relationships with others.'

2. *Awareness of the need to resolve inner conflict* – 'if inner conflict is not addressed then it will become external conflict.' A good practice of authority seeks out a healthy integration of the masculine and the feminine, the hunter and the healer.

3. *Having a good radar* – this shows itself in an attuned awareness to the needs of others and an ability to really hear what people say, stripped of inner paranoia and disturbances.

4. *Respect for others* – including their 'grittiness and survivability'. Sam is aware that if he is 'not careful I can be so keen to support I can be patronising'. A key feature of this respect for others is a respect for what currently works for them, what useful roles their defences serve and their overall ability to cope.

5. *Space to grow* – this is about giving people the opportunity to be noticed, the time to lie fallow and 'bollocks to 9 to 5'. Allow people to be creative, encourage them in valuing themselves and valuing the task they're engaged with. With this in place an evidence-based culture isn't needed.

6. *Sharing the goodies around* – 'share in a sense of achievement… not in a neurotic sense but driven by people's sense of purpose and self-esteem.'
   'If you put all this together, you try stopping people.'

Reflections on Sam's story

My conversation with Sam was a charged experience. His reflections and commentary on his experience of authority were strong meat and I felt nervous on occasions at the transparency with which he weaved together the personal and the professional. To begin with I wanted to avoid writing my own reactions to his story, preferring to leave it with his own conclusions about a good practice of authority. I am aware that I am anxious about how to treat what he has said with sensitivity, kid gloves even – but then I remembered to respect him and his own grittiness and survivability.

Throughout much of Sam's life he has been aware of somehow being out of step with himself and for much of his life he just kept on with his established ways of being, despite his disquiet. Anxiety and disquiet are useful sources of data to people in general and especially people in or seeking authority; they are feelings worth paying attention to. By taking his inner-emptiness seriously he was able to begin the work required to find a form of authority that didn't fuel or distract from this gnawing lack.

He has found a framework for his authority that is based around intense emotional honesty and reflection, both personal and collective. He is in an organisation that acknowledges the active presence of strong emotions, both conscious and unconscious, and this works for him. He knows what it is like to try and exercise authority in a way that does not allow him to fit his own skin and knows that the personal cost is too high.

In other stories people talk of the significant effects of positive and benign authority at early points of their life; Sam's life had an absence of benign authority until very late on. I sense that this has made his struggle to find an authority that works for him a tougher piece of work than it may have been for others. The benefit is that he carries within him a burning desire to practice benign authority, that healthy integration of the masculine and the feminine.

Sam's transition in his practice of authority has been in part a shift from a standalone authority to a supported authority. Sam talks about his authority at Teenspeak within the context of a complex web of collegial relationships, based on a shifting mix of hierarchy, professional support and personal attention. Authority is understood in terms of relationship rather than absence of relationship.

All organisations involve strong emotions. Teenspeak has the added complexity of clients who bring the particular charge of troubled adolescence, but all work places have people experiencing and dealing with all that human beings can feel and go through. Strong emotions cannot be ignored nor dealt with by a tick in the box, they take time to be engaged with. People in positions of authority can be lightening rods for shit and space must be provided for it to be metabolised.

CHAPTER 8

Luke: Creative authority

Luke is a renowned documentary filmmaker and a man whose life has been touched by the upheavals of the Second World War and the institutionalised insensitivity of the British boarding-school system.

He is a committed liberal with an instinctive desire to side with craft workers and unions when faced with the deadening hand of authority being used for its own sake. He knows that he can be very negative about the whole notion of authority, even though he works easily with his own particular definition of it. Luke is a practitioner of creative authority.

Authority for a purpose

Luke had told me to look out for a white-haired man when I'd agreed to meet him outside WHSmith. When I saw him he struck me as a poised and self-contained individual; there was a certain stillness to him. As we walked to the pub for lunch he soon warmed to his antagonism towards much of what passes for authority.

'Authority must exist for a purpose,' he said, a sentiment he repeated when we returned to the self-same spot two hours later. For much of his working life he made his films within the institutional context of a big TV company – a company that over the years he feels has moved away from management as an enabler of creative talent to management as a career path for managers. When he spoke of the negative aspects of authority he tended to use the word manager; when he talked about his own directorial role (I wouldn't dare to use a word like 'leadership' to describe what he does – far too managerial) he described it in terms of the creative process of bringing a group of talented people together to achieve a vision – and as the director, that meant his vision.

Diffidence and steel

There is a strangely elusive quality to Luke that coexists with a directness and frankness. He is not naturally someone who puts himself forward – a characteristic that is core to his sense of what makes for a good documentary. He can enjoy those films where the filmmaker is centre stage, but he wants his documentaries to be about his subjects not himself.

He is dismissive of those who put themselves forward too forcefully as 'loudmouths' and remembers initially missing out on a director's training opportunity because of his diffidence. Yet he is absolutely certain of his self-worth, seeing his work as a high-water mark of quality and good managers as those who seek him out because his work is of quality. 'When they [managers] are supporting me, they are supporting quality.'

Written as starkly as this he may come across as arrogant, but in person I experienced it not as arrogance but as a sincerely held sense of his ability – he may not shout about what he can do, but he does not deny it. This aspect is well described by an executive producer he once worked with who wrote of

Luke, 'beneath a diffident exterior he has a steely desire to succeed'.

Respecting ability and ambition

Luke respects not only his own ability but also the ability of others. During his school days he recalls being 'dissed' by many of his teachers, because he was a late developer. At its worst this 'dissing' included a sadistic maths teacher taking a twelve-inch ruler to the thirteen-year-old Luke and rapping his knuckles for his bad homework; given that maths was not (and never would be) Luke's thing, he was the subject of frequent punishment.

In his early working life he also came across the experience of being grossly disrespected. Seduced by the idea of making much more money than he had ever done to date, he got a job as an assistant editor on a feature film – even though it was not what he really wanted to do. He worked on this for nine months, seven days a week, giving 'my whole life' to the film. Throughout this time, outside of the immediate camaraderie of the cutting room, he was made to feel completely menial and underused. 'I was just someone who stood in a room servicing a more senior assistant.' But his real venom from this experience is focused on the director, a well-known feature filmmaker of the time.

'The director was a very unpleasant guy. He treated us like shit... [it was] probably my first completely negative experience.' The director expected the young Luke to be starry-eyed at the experience of working for him and saw no need to acknowledge any of the people working for him; they were simply pairs of hands to him.

He fitted into a particular and very negative view of what people in authority can be like. He was overbearing, assumed that no-one around him was worth very much and made no attempt to communicate what he was trying to achieve to those around him. He saw no need to connect socially or creatively with his film crew, never buying a single meal for anyone – meanwhile his chauffeur would bring him his cigar and *Times* to enjoy at 11 a.m. every morning. In the end Luke, another assistant and the editor took him to the union for his behaviour, 'the final straw in this instance included screwing us into a completely unreasonable financial package'. Luke doubts even then that they would have taken him to the union 'had he been decent enough not to flaunt his own wealth'.

This contrasts with some very positive experiences at school and in his early professional life where people in positions of authority supported the young Luke in his ambitions. Luke ploughed his O levels, yet people at his school really encouraged him to go on to do A levels in art, history and English. 'They still felt I had something to offer even though I was an abject failure.' Luke talked particularly fondly of his art teacher. When he'd started at school he had been no more than average as an artist, but over time – with the encouragement of the teacher – he became better and better. It was a relationship of mutual respect; Luke respected him as a teacher and the teacher respected Luke's potential and ability. His English teacher who, at times, 'was a bit of a martinet' was also very supportive towards Luke during his A levels.

As he crabbed his way towards his ambition to be a filmmaker – he describes his life as 'a series of sideways steps' to achieving his ambition – he fell into the company of many well-intentioned people in positions of authority who helped and supported him. There was the editor of the British Transport Film Unit, then a great outpost of documentary making, who wanted 'to talk to me about films and wanted me to watch films'. When there was not too much work on Luke would be encouraged to go off and watch films. Within this film unit 'I felt I could hold my own in conversations… I felt I had a talent and they recognised it.'

Later on in our conversation Luke said he could never understand the 'master–servant' framing of authority. Prior to boarding school he had grown up in the Middle East and 'grew to realise that colonialism was pretty revolting', once he reached his teens and 'had met fellow pupils from Africa and the Middle East and related that to my privileged childhood'. When talking of good and bad administrative authority, good meant an administrator who fought the director's corner and supported him in achieving his vision as best as possible – a non-colonial, non-master–servant expression of authority. A bad administrative authority was one that sought to impose the views of the administrator on the director, subjugating the director to the status of servant and imposing an alien colonial authority over native ability.

Sons and fathers

Much as there were times of conflict between Luke and his father – he greatly resented being sent away to boarding school at eight – they are now very close. There was also, for me, a significant supportive habit that existed between them that meant the son felt able to pursue his ambition. Maybe this is why, in part, Luke has his quietly expressed, but hugely felt, self-belief.

When things fell apart during O levels, his father gave him no criticism. When he dropped out of art school, because they couldn't support his pursuit of film studies, he had a big row with his father but it ended with his father saying: 'If that's what you want to do, then find a way of doing it.'

Luke's father comes across as someone who was in touch with his son's ambitions; he was comfortable with his son pursuing his own ambitions in his own way. Luke speculated in our meeting about how his father had also pursued certain unconventional paths in his life. He was of British protestant stock and married Luke's Jewish mother after meeting her in Alexandria during the war. 'I asked my father. How did my maternal grandfather let you marry his daughter?' The shared fight against fascism seemed to be enough of a bond – the maternal side of the family having fled Europe; so it was that Luke's father was welcomed into his mother's family.

Identity and discretion

This reflection on his parents' marriage, which lasted until his mother died when he was eleven, also raised some possible connections to Luke's coexisting qualities of diffidence and steel. 'In later life I realised that my mother had disguised her Jewishness', unsurprising given that she and Luke's father were based in an Arab country. Yet that sense of Jewish identity may well have been strongly felt, especially in the immediate aftermath of the Holocaust. Many years later Luke's father told him the story of how his mother had become distraught when she heard of an Iraqi Jew being lynched in Basra in 1948 – where they lived at the time. The importance of concealing her identity being brought into sharp focus by this event, 'That hidden-ness has come into me. I live in compartments.'

I can relate that statement to Luke's ambiguous and paradoxical relationship to authority. In his work as a director he knew he had to be the lynchpin, he was the one who had to have the vision. There is a real authority to his self-belief that he is the one who owns the story and the film. It was a felt lack of deserved recognition that spurred him on from being an editor to become a director. He has a need to be in that position of visible authority – and yet he will often emphasise his negative attitude to authority. He is able to want it and dislike it – hate it even – at the same time. This may be because of an osmotically acquired capacity to compartmentalise his life, to have an identity and not have one at the same time. It may also be because he holds onto some very strong views about what 'good authority' is – that can be difficult to talk about because the language of authority, leadership and management have been hi-jacked by the practitioners of 'bad authority'.

The nature of creative authority

Creative authority is good authority. It is characterised by environments where the gradations across a hierarchy are small. In his early days at a major broadcasting company he remembers fondly how even if you were the assistant film editor people listened to you – directors and producers would have coffee with you.

The person in a position of creative authority does have some very specific responsibilities. It is 'someone having a vision and a plan of what that vision would look like e.g. a film or documentary'. They also have a duty to go about realising that vision in a very specific way. 'What the director does is utilise other people's talents... pull these talents together to realise the director's vision.' This involves 'listening to the views of others as to how to produce it... getting inside and understanding what someone else wants to do'. In terms of the support required from outside of the filmmaking crew. 'You need a management that understand that the people producing the goods are the best people to do that.'

This last point also leads on to one of the features of 'bad authority'. 'I have a big difficulty seeing managers as being "over" others'. When managers see the craft of management (of exercising authority) as superior to the crafts of the people who do the things that give an organisation its identity and purpose – then that is a management that has lost its grip on its purpose. Talent and responsibility should go together: 'I felt very comfortable being given extra responsibility [at the major broadcasting company]... I was recognised as having talent.' Talent leads to authority, not vice versa.

In a director 'bad authority' can emerge in the form of bossiness. Because there are always many ways to tell a story, a director has to own the vision of how the story will be told. Bossiness is avoided 'when people respect my abilities and I respect theirs'. Bossiness is therefore a function of a lack of mutual respect and mutual respect is, and always has been, of great importance to Luke. Avoiding bossiness, however, is very different from avoiding asserting a director's will – bossiness is when that will spills out beyond its role and stifles the contributory will of others.

Social and emotional connection

As I reflected on our conversation I was struck by what I would label 'connection'; the importance Luke gives to his voice and the voices of those around him being heard, of different perspectives and realities being acknowledged. His practice of authority has an inclusive quality, although not one where inclusivity is allowed to undermine purpose and direction. His disgust at the behaviour of the well-known feature film director and of managers who see themselves as being over others may be a reaction to his sense that they lack connection with the realities and abilities of others.

When we met he told the story of how he learned of the death of his mother. He knew his mother had been ill, so when he discovered that his father was to visit him at school he suspected the worst. That weekend his father broke the news to him away from school and they had an awkward hug – there was very little discussion. When the time came to return to school Luke waited at the bus stop in the dark. The headmaster drove past having picked up the visiting preacher for the Sunday evening chapel service. 'He stopped and picked me up as he was passing and made no mention of my mother's death... he couldn't relate emotionally to the boys.' Maybe for Luke part of his need when in a position of authority is to relate emotionally to those around him.

Luke's concluding reflections

'The way I work reflects my personality. I acknowledge obliquely the need for authority but that authority should not be judgemental or overbearing. If it is then it is at odds with what I believe.

'As a father I'm very suspicious of my authority and want my authority over my kids to be benign. I really don't like telling people what to do, a reaction to being told what to do throughout my school days. My mother was quite soft but I was handed over to the school in the 1950s and people were very bad with children, incredibly insensitive. As a parent I've reacted so that I could not be overbearing. Maybe I was a bit with my eldest child, but not by my last.

'I'm very grateful that I've never had to work in a job completely based on hierarchy. Except domestically, my life has always been routine free. I've got nothing but pleasure from bringing-up children… my work has allowed me to be far more present in their lives, which is such a contrast to my own childhood.'

Reflections on Luke and his authority

Luke has had a number of positive mentoring experiences. People at the major broadcasting company and the British Transport Film Unit supported him in his ambition; there were teachers who kept alive a sense that he had something of value to bring to the world. Even his father, with whom he disagreed so fundamentally on politics and who he spent some years resenting because of the decision to put him into a boarding school, provided support in leaving art school to pursue a career in film.

Many of these mentors were kindly, but some were people with whom he fell out at some stage – although he usually seems to have fallen back in with them later on. He does not feel the need to kowtow to mentors; he can be robust in his relationships with them and they with him.

Luke has had a sustained ambition to make films, particularly documentary films. He has sought out positions of responsibility (of authority, even leadership) because he believes that he is a talented filmmaker. He is clear that it his right and responsibility to assert his talent. 'Good Authority' is therefore a process of stepping into the authority required to realise your talent – and part of realising your own talent is realising the talent of those around you. Authority oversteps its boundaries when it is not in the service of talent but in the service of itself and sees no limit to what it can achieve without reference to the talents of others.

Luke's art teacher used his authority to encourage Luke. Luke's sense of self-worth meant he applied for director training and was generally comfortable taking on responsibility. The good face of managerial authority is when it looks to support the realisation of a vision. Authority when it looks to serve primarily the ego needs of the director – as was the case with the feature film director – is not a healthy expression of authority. Neither is the authority of the apparatchik looking to navigate his or her way up an organisational hierarchy, without reference to the creative purpose of that organisation.

Luke has had the experience of being disrespected and he hated it. He knows what it's like to be treated as less than he is capable of and it is a source of distress to him. His career has been founded on taking his ambitions and abilities seriously and – however crablike – pursuing them. Authority becomes a positive experience when it is leavened with a respect for personal and collective ability.

Luke's initial reaction to the notion of authority has stayed with me. I suspect that for him the word has a number of associations: with formality, hierarchy and the impersonal – hangovers probably from his school days. In his working life he has sought out the informal, the personal and the non-hierarchical, where people with a common interest (in making good films) talk and socialise and create together. Formal roles do have a place but they are in the service of the collective creative endeavour, not in the service of a hierarchy per se. In Luke's language of authority, words such as 'talent', 'creativity', 'vision', 'respect' and 'support' stand out.

Luke's reflections on this story

It's a strange feeling; reading about oneself, my attitudes, prejudices and life experiences, condensed and perceptively interpreted by another.

I read it several times through and then left it, to give a chance for anything to float to the surface – and then read it a couple of times more. Apart for some slight factual inaccuracies [now corrected] I can't fault it.

I thought of our conversation and the resulting document the other day. This year I've been doing a fair bit of tutoring at the National Film School. The students are all post-grad, intelligent and motivated. My authority is in no way "managerial", I'm pleased to say. It's an authority that is based purely on my experience of making films; I can pass on what I have learnt and advise. My "authority" as such, is to try and understand what a student is trying to do, and within their own terms, help, even if I don't necessarily agree. Because I value the control I have over my work, I value theirs over their work. If that makes sense!

That's it basically.

ID # CHAPTER 9

Thomas: Management writer, coach and refugee from authority

Thomas has been working with, and writing about, leaders for many years. He describes himself as 'a refugee from authority... until I was 38 I was a potential authority figure and then gave in.' He has a particular view about the effects that holding power has on people who take on positions of authority: 'It's damaging for their health'.

He sees this in a particular senior health-sector executive who nine years ago was full of bounce and winning engagement – but who has most definitely lost that bounce now. He sees a macro pattern, played out in public figures such as Blair and Brown, of authority turning into a celebrity game in which we – the public – build people up so we can knock them down. People who hold positions of authority have immense amounts of 'crap thrown at them and it wears them down'. This opinion not only comes from his research but from the work he does with senior managers throughout the NHS and beyond.

Using secrecy to contain crap

One particular client, let me call him K, has developed a particular way of coping – although one that has its cost. 'I have a sense of him performing below his potential. He retreats from crap by being secretive and manipulative. He's much lauded and respected but behaviourally secretive. He has a pattern of playing his cards close to his chest... not having any open dialogue... it's very clever in one way [as it allows him to] judiciously steer his way through the issues. He never talks openly', or rather when he does it is always 'one on one and behind closed doors'. This can result in everyone wondering what he is saying to everyone else when they're not there.

Living with personal attack

In a competitive and highly politicised world such as the UK health sector, being the leader of revolutionary change is a high-profile activity. Thomas's client M is involved in such a role where he is at the very top of his area of speciality, used to dealing with the most senior ministers, civil servants and health colleagues. The 'toughest bit [for M] are the relentless personal attacks by two or three senior others'. One in particular 'always wants a fight... he likes a battle' and it is a 'very personal battle where he will tell ministers that M is incompetent' and lacks the necessary academic qualifications. In this situation it is 'as much as anyone can do to think clearly'.

Thomas comes to a paradoxical conclusion based upon M and the death of his bounce. 'It seems like the only leaders who can survive are those who keep emotional distance'. In order to be an effective leader 'you need to foster connection and personal attachment. But it is those who don't develop connection who survive.'

M has also developed some unpleasant patterns that allow him to cope with his invidious position. Thomas has been asked, for instance, by a number of people to mention to M 'his Margaret Thatcher tendency', which shows itself in his need to 'always be right' and a habit of denigrating others. This denigration of others can be seen as going as far as always having a scapegoat in the team – there is always a 'so and so' who is 'useless'. Thomas sees this as 'a way of processing all the crap. Crap [that] is too much for sensible, reasonable human beings.'

M is not alone in experiencing personal attack. Y is the head of a prestigious scientific institution. In her case 'what got to her was the defeated candidate for the presidency'. She believed that 'they're out to get me… and they were'. Y has not really learnt to deal with the attacks. She has her friends but her personal 'processing has never got beyond "they think I'm shite and I think they're shite"'. Thomas has provided her 'with sticking plaster support' but has never been asked to provide more.

The nature of ambition

Thomas strongly advocates the opinion that 'people wouldn't be ambitious to be leaders unless they were trying to fix something in themselves'. He is aware that attackers become difficult to deal with when they latch onto the other person's demons. In his own life Thomas recalls a finance guy at a textile firm he used to work in. He hated Thomas and 'knew instinctively where my real vulnerability was… he was loathsome'.

Making it work

Some people do seem able to make leadership work for them. Thomas has observed the head of a European business school who 'seems reasonably oblivious to the mayhem and distress he causes… he leaves it with the individual. Others' distress washes off him.'

M copes by 'taking his holidays, doing other stuff and [having] a tremendous network. There are lots of people he talks to for support… [he's] constantly triangulating other views.' Another client, K, 'has retreated from the highest stakes and taken a lower place'. K has a 'very strong relationship with his wife' who he can talk things through with – it stands out that he has 'external sources who can give him perspective'.

In the case of one senior research scientist it is the quality of his relationship with his number two that makes him able to handle the pressures of being in a senior position. Thomas compares the two of them to 'a good married couple. They rely on each other and they survived a very testing period when the finances went wrong when he was in his first leadership position.' This experience meant he 'began to see his number two as being "there for him"'.

M also has this ability to rely on others, a capacity Thomas describes as an ability to 'negotiate your way through to really relying on people around you'. M has 'people around him committed to him and to the vision'. He also has a 'fantastic partner [who is] an extraordinary voice of reason', able to be 'calming and thoughtful'.

Popular delusions and glimpses of humanity

These people do not live in a vacuum but are caught up in the wider fantasies of our age. 'Our expectations [for leaders] are ludicrous.' Thomas likens it to the 'football manager syndrome'. We'd met a few days after Kevin Keegan had been reappointed as manager of Newcastle United. 'How is Kevin Keegan going to transform Newcastle in a few weeks? We love the idea… we know it's a fantasy and [we] love it.'

On a wider front our current culture has 'lost religion and we don't take politicians seriously'. Which throws up the question, 'Who do we respect?' Thomas has seen M able to engender respect from others, 'It works for him when he stakes his authority… [when] he speaks personally.' The moments when he 'really grabs authority are when he is talking personally'.

Thomas has seen the power of the personal in the CEO of a consumer electronics company. Thomas had seen H talk with many groups of thirty or so at workshops where 'he'd parroted clichés'. Then came a magic session when he was full of thoughtfulness, spontaneity and personal disclosure. He talked of a time when he'd been coming up through the ranks and how 'he'd deluded himself he'd rescue the US operations. How he'd kidded himself about how easy it would be to sack half the workforce.' Without being self-abasing 'he talked through the shittiness' of his time in the US, 'breaking up people's futures and families'. He talked about 'what it meant' and gave those who were present a 'glimpse of humanity'.

Does knowledge of personal history matter?

Thomas has been involved in many coaching relationships with senior executives and has found that 'senior people in the first meeting will tell something personal from their childhood'. There was one week when Thomas was starting work with three separate managing directors. 'One was abandoned by his parents in New York at the age of eleven for twenty-four hours.' An experience that left him with a burning desire to show the world just how tough he was. The second, who runs a software business, told Thomas about coming home when he was thirteen to find his mother had committed suicide. The third had another horror story that Thomas did not want to talk about. In his line of work it is 'very normal for people to indicate serious engagement [by] sharing something personal that has marked them in their leadership role', whether it's the experience of being 'the odd one out' or having an 'adored mother'.

There are any 'number of leaders who want to earn their dead father's approbation. History is enormously present. You only have to create the opportunity and people identify these moments as important and critical.'

Being informed rather than consumed by personal history

The process of becoming informed by personal history is not one of epiphany, of blinding light on the way to Damascus. M is dealing with some strong meat in his past and, in response to it, has been able to develop an attitude of 'better make the most of it'.

Y, the head of the scientific institute, is a 'woman in a man's world' who comes from the 'wrong side of the tracks. She deals with the snobbish male environment by adapting to it. She learnt this early on in' her days of working in hospitals. She learned not to get 'annoyed by the Oxbridge Consultants'. Instead she got on side with them.

For Y and M 'informed' is not the right word to use when describing the power of the personal past: it is about demons. These demons are 'lived with' and they also 'provide potency. It is what drives people on.'

When Thomas reflects on 'the level of energy' that M and others have 'it leaves me completely winded. M is out most nights after a very full day.' He comes home 'to read papers and starts again'. Shifting onto a wider political sphere Thomas noted, '[Prime Minister] Brown must be very disturbed to be that ambitious.'

The issue for these people is 'how do you hold your demons[1] in their place?' Another client continues to be driven by the need 'to do it for daddy' and 'they'll take on another thing and another thing'. Getting driven people to admit limits is very difficult. One Cambridge client of Thomas's did one day blurt out 'I'm nearly at my limit' and this was an incredible statement for him. He is doing his enormous job for his disabled sister, to 'make good for this damaged sibling'. This person is 'scared witless of the notion of limits' although Thomas sees it 'as very good for him to explore and understand his limits'.

This mania for work plays out in a cancer specialist. He has 'four half-time jobs'. For six months Thomas worked with him to see if he 'wanted to change this'. With 'a damaged child, part of this is escaping the hand he and his wife have been dealt and putting the world to rights'. After six months they 'got nowhere'. Maybe the answer was to 'stop fretting about this'. There has to be the risk that he'll keel over, but this is not just about him working hard for the money, this man – and his ilk – are 'saving humanity'. These people are 'so committed and so competitive', and the drive comes from demons such as damaged siblings.

The cost of ambition

These very driven people are frequently not that aware of the impact they are having on others around them. They are also probably not that aware of the

---

[1] Thomas sometimes refers to daemons rather than demons, using the word to evoke the meaning Philip Pullman has for it in *Northern Lights* – as some manifestation of character. For simplicity I use the word 'demon' throughout, but allow for this 'daemon' meaning to coexist.

impact they're having on themselves. They kid themselves that 'I'm okay... I'm still holding it together. Sadly it's at a huge cost.' But the whole endeavour is 'utterly seductive' and they can't stop themselves 'recruiting people to the cause'.

It is of course no accident that Thomas hooks up with and gets on with these types of people. Like them 'nothing is ever good enough' for Thomas and he admits to being 'hopelessly idealistic'. He finds himself attracted to these people 'because I have an empathy with them and they can smell it'. Not only does he have empathy, he can join them in their flaws. There he is telling one client to get a more manageable grip on his life, while at the same time Thomas is cancelling meetings because he has triple booked himself. Working with these people is a shared endeavour because Thomas is 'in the same mire'. Perversely this is what makes him able to work with them; 'I feel inadequate because I share their phenomenon but that's what's useful.' He also has a huge admiration for them.

But despite this empathy and admiration he cannot but notice, 'they don't look happy. The great things they're doing don't seem that rewarding. What is uppermost is the stress, the strain, the battles.' They exude an 'oh god this [is] hard' attitude. In 'my idealism, wouldn't it be nice if leaders could enjoy what they're achieving'. Because so much of his work touches on government circles he has noticed 'the higher you go up in Whitehall, the nastier it gets. People are doing very serious jobs' in a 'very nasty' environment. One client, S, has asked 'Is it possible to behave honourably at very senior levels of the medical establishment?' In the cut and thrust of this environment 'some very raw stuff comes out [and it is] very hard to hold onto decent values'. Thomas wonders if 'it's the same at the top of Nokia or Shell?'

Thomas decided when he was 37 or 38 that 'I didn't have the emotional resilience to be in a senior position. If people shaft me, I feel it. That's where I part company with the people I work with.'

One last story from the front line

Thomas reflected at the end on what it is like to be in 'a world where people will leap on your every false move'. He saw the consequences in a senior woman client in the private sector. She has 'a huge ability to engage in the here and now. She takes care of her team, looks after you in a very personal and anticipatory way.' The other side of this quality is the brutality with which she drops those who she feels have 'let her down'. 'People are either brilliant or useless. She can't bear any sense of betrayal or of people letting her down.' Thomas has tried to push back on her but she refuses to acknowledge that she has any people 'who aren't stars'. The team has to be perfect because she is perfect; the team has no weaknesses that can be jumped on and she has no weaknesses that can be jumped on. A state of affairs I experience as exhausting and inhuman.

A short story about creativity, anxiety and metabolising shit

I once gave a friend a book as a birthday present, noting that reading it was like kissing an electric snake. These stories have that quality for me, they speak of an energy and excitement – which plays out in both malevolent and benevolent ways. They touch on a sense of self-destruction that comes with being in a position of authority. They also provide a balm, an indication of what is needed to take on great endeavours. The madness of authority is laid bare, as is its lure.

There are four themes that I have found myself returning to when I look at the stories of Sam, Luke and Thomas:

- Yes there are shitty people and shitty situations
- Work with your personality
- Value others
- Take care of yourself

Yes there are shitty people and shitty situations

All three of them have had difficult moments in their lives; they have had to deal with the lottery of genetic inheritance, narcissism in high places and personal vulnerabilities that rule out the practical possibility of pursuing certain careers. In Thomas's story there is the recurring drumbeat of political nastiness, of people scrabbling at each other's professional eyes as they try to promote themselves. There is no opportunity for calm reason or mutual inquiry – these are people who are having to live with a viciously competitive culture where self-advancement (for whatever reason) occurs at the expense of others. Thomas finds himself addicted to working with people who are dealing with these all-but-impossible settings; Luke chooses settings where he doesn't have to deal with people who feel that taking chunks out of each other is an acceptable way of behaving – although he's had his moments of eating shit, when he chose to follow the money and found himself working for a well-known and deeply self-regarding feature film director.

Sam speaks to another form of shit; he's faced it down throughout his life, learnt how to cope with the horror stories of teaching and the corrosive disappointment of his mother for his father. More than either of the others he spends time with the shit, dealing with the unprocessed rage and confusion of troubled teenagers. His organisation exists to attract shit and that is what it gets – but these days he knows that if you're going to engage with the so often unacknowledged underbelly of reality, be prepared. Thomas and Sam in particular live in a world where people in authority seem to act as lightning rods, attracting highly charged reactions from all directions. Within themselves, and the people they work with, these charged encounters also evoke a charged response. To be in authority, or close to authority, is to live in a maelstrom of often unprocessed and un-owned emotions – and to live with this shit day after day is tough; especially when it connects straight through to the mother lode of some personal demon (which is why what counts as shit differs so much from person to person).

Work with your personality

All three of them appear to have a robust and realistic understanding of themselves – and have established working lives that are informed by that understanding. Sam is an intense man, capable of feeling deeply and connecting with the rawest aspects of the human condition. He is also able to go out into the world to promote what needs to be done to help troubled teenagers. He has a well-integrated masculine and feminine; his reason is infused with his feeling and his feeling is infused with reason.

Luke has established a modus vivendi that sits with his quiet steeliness and his discomfort with hierarchical gradations. He has found a way of marrying his pleasure in family life with his love of filmmaking. He is comfortable telling the stories of others rather than his own, so as a documentary maker he does not feel the need to parade his ego to the detriment of the story. He can live with his learnt distrust of authority so that it doesn't prevent him exercising authority in a way that works for him. He has not tried to dismantle himself or his history, but has sought to find a way of wearing authority that can accommodate values and beliefs that are an indelible part of him. He has integrated an uncomfortable childhood and troubled (but now much loved) father–son relationship into a wholehearted ability to accept people for who they are. His authority is quiet but present, configured to meet both his personal and professional needs.

Thomas seems to be the stormiest in his relationship to authority. He is drawn to the company of those warriors who can do nothing except go out and do battle with the world – so as to heal it or make it in some way better. He's had to step back from the frontline, his capacity to be hurt and disabled by those who know how to fight dirty ruling him out from the rougher end of authority. His gift to authority is his own need to find a way of integrating his knowledge of what goes into healthy authority, with his knowledge of the often-distorted drives that consume people but also enable them to endure and achieve great things.

Value others

They all have a disposition to value others; they see people as talented and capable, but not in some idealised 'other than human' way. They do not see their authority as a way of imposing themselves on others, but as a way of freeing others to do the best they can. This is not about abdicating their responsibility, but about understanding its limits – they are not there to live other people's lives for them or do their jobs. Their authority is about a habit of constructive engagement with others, with ears and eyes open.

All three of them hold to certain beliefs about what makes for generative relationships between people and this is at the heart of how they approach others. Authority for them is enmeshed in reciprocal relationships – there is nothing unilateral about it. Authority is part of a negotiation between people who need to play different roles in a common cause. Of course differences in weight of voice exist, but those who have greater voice (i.e. have more authority) do not use this voice to unvoice, belittle or drown out those around them. Thomas in particular has to live with the tension between his personal values and the lived forms of authority he encounters with those he works with – and Thomas models particularly well his ability to value others, even when he believes they should be exercising their authority differently. His ability to value others seems to be rooted in an ability to empathise with, and walk in the shoes of, people who exercise authority in a world where authority sets them apart from others and sets them up in the eyes of others.

Take care of yourself

The care of the self comes from engaging with an ambition that sits well with you, having a lived philosophy that informs how you act, having in place the support you need and a healthy appreciation of your foibles and habits.

Sam's ambition for a long time fuelled his attempt to be a 'man alone', while at the same time avoiding being at the front of stage with his authority – the deputy head rather than the head. He has only been able to step into his current ambition, one that seems to draw on his more integrated sense of self, in recent times and subsequent to an extensive process of psychoanalysis. Luke's ambition has been a more defining part of him from earlier in his life; his need for creative expression was an informing part of his life and he was able to pursue it thanks to some benign authority, some doggedness and the experience of what it felt like when he was not doing it. Thomas has also found a way of promoting better leadership, although not through its direct practice. It took him a while to realise he was too sensitive to those who knew how to, and wanted to, fight dirty.

I have already touched on their way of operating; I would like to add some words about the nature of the support they seek out or have in place. Sam is the most comprehensively supported; the emotional storm that he and his colleagues live in means that they must take good emotional care of themselves if they are going to be able to be good enough containers for their clients. Luke's support seems to come from working with like-minded people who are skilled at their craft. Thomas's support is more opaque – his story is primarily about how he supports others, which he does by joining them in their reality (which sometimes almost teeters into the madness of unprocessed psychological habits and fantasies) and working with an assumption and appreciation of their good intent. It is not clear to me how he is supported in processing what he exposes himself to – although his writing would seem to be a useful way for him to make sense of what is going on for those he works with.

In all three stories, and in my memory of meeting the three of them, I am left with a sense of men comfortable in their own skin. They live their passions and contradictions, while at the same time being cognizant of them. I doubt they surprise themselves too often or find themselves engaged in an activity, or way of being, that doesn't fit with their sense of self.

section three

Hanging tough

Chapter 11
Adrian: Combative authority — 81

Chapter 12
Michaela: Refugee from the malign — 89

Chapter 13
Giles: An ounce of ruthlessness — 97

Chapter 14
A short story about hanging tough — 105

CHAPTER 11

Adrian: Combative authority

A stormy family. An alcoholic, non-functioning father – a man of huge intellectual capacity, with limited emotional intelligence – who liked making scenes. A tradition of politically engaged argument. A mother who died when Adrian was fourteen. An absence of all but eight to ten memories before that age.

Piecing together Adrian's history and how it informs his current-day authority is tricky; there's a lot there but he mentions things briefly, almost in shorthand.

Current responsibility

As we walked down Brick Lane to a coffee shop he knew, Adrian seemed doubtful that his experience was relevant to an inquiry into authority; I may also have hamstrung him a little by saying that I wasn't interested in the narcissism that I saw being portrayed in many inquiries in this area. It took a while for him to be able to admit to his self-confidence and sense of self-creation when it came to his authority.

Adrian founded and runs a theatre company with a difference. It works with people who are homeless or have been homeless, as well as asylum seekers and refugees. The company also looks to employ people from these parts of our society as well as holding performances and workshops in hostels and theatres. Adrian is 'responsible for the leadership of the organisation', which includes fifteen full-time staff and a broad stakeholder community. 'A lot of people are affected by this organisation… and feel they have a stake in it', be it as freelancers or participants.

The meat and drink of the company is Forum Theatre; a participative, political and argumentative theatrical tradition that comes from Augusto Boal – author of books such as *Theatre of the Oppressed*. Adrian has both translated Boal's books and worked with him. Within the company Adrian has always been the artistic director 'deciding the artistic content of what we do' while also being co-CEO for most of the company's 15 or so years of existence. For part of this year a sole managing director was in place; now, however, Adrian is the sole CEO.

Adrian experiences himself as having a lot of responsibility. The work of the company 'means a lot to a lot of people' and Adrian 'wants to get it [the work] right'. This work involves delivering six to seven workshops a week for homeless people as well as putting on large scale productions every couple of years with a staff of a dozen or more. These bigger events have also included collaborations with the likes of the Royal Shakespeare Company. In recent years he has been approached by a mutual friend of ours, Howell Schroeder, who has 'seduced me into working with people in management positions' where Adrian seeks to develop self-awareness within the context of organisational leadership. This builds on Adrian's considerable experience of teaching the practice of Forum Theatre in the UK and overseas, for NGOs as well as theatre and non-theatre groups.

Memories of authority

Adrian was 'born into a posh little family… [and] I experienced myself having authority from a young age'. There was an au pair at home who Adrian felt he had some authority over, particularly as his parents were both away a lot travelling. 'From ten I had a sense of having authority.'

Having made that point Adrian very quickly made the observation that he was 'not very comfortable with the notion of privilege', a point he highlighted with one of his few childhood memories where he 'remembers telling kids from the village to get off a wall of ours'. Maybe Adrian's early doubt about the relevance of his experience to my inquiry is informed by a sense that in many walks of life authority and privilege have become interchangeable terms, authority bringing with it an assumption of privilege. Adrian has a very clear understanding about his own authority and the authority of others. 'I've always had a problem with other people's authority… [I've] never been very good at recognising the authority of others. Maybe this is because I've never experienced other people's authority. My father was an alcoholic and had no authority. My mother died when I was 14. I ran my own life from then.'

These teenage experiences have left him with a 'sense of loss, abandonment… which has coloured – unconsciously – the way I've gone'. For many years he 'hung out with hippies and did the hippy thing', which included taking copious amounts of drugs. He has always been drawn to 'outsidery people'.

With regard to his current organisation he is aware that it has a very definite hierarchy, one that he would not have come up with if 'I had solely been responsible for setting it up'. But there is a worldliness to Adrian, an acknowledgement that while he may dislike and distrust hierarchies, his organisation operates in a hierarchical world. He has also had some negative experiences in working in the organisation when the hierarchy was a site of conflict, responsibilities were divided and the non-executive board were ineffective in resolving these conflicts or recognising what was actually happening – which included being bullied by his co-chief executive. There were three years of conflict between him and the co-CEO and the board played out the role of ineffectual parental figure (familiar enough to Adrian). 'Now having regained authority I'm not going to let go of it because life was too unpleasant for those years. I started this company and I know how to run it.'

Authentic authority

I asked Adrian how he ran his company.

'I listen to people. I like to talk about things. I like to delay decisions as long as humanly possible.' Adrian's commitment is to 'getting things right'.

'People experience me as quite stern and/or demanding. Some people experience me as authoritarian. When I'm directing this is a persona I don't discourage. It's my character; I'm deeply opinionated.' These reflections led him to recall how he came to start working with Howell Schroeder in the arena of leadership development and how the word 'authentic' was so popular. At first Adrian experienced the request to train people in authenticity as oxymoronic – you are either authentic i.e. true to your self, or you aren't. Authenticity is not a trick to be learnt or a piece of clothing that can be put on or taken off as the mood takes. On reflection he did see some purpose in authenticity training, if its purpose was about 'being the best you' – so long as it was not about pretending to be someone else.

The authentic Adrian is not an easy character. On the rehearsal room floor he say's 'I'm surprisingly horrible. I get very passionate. I shout.' He gets away with this, he reckons, because 'I love them [the cast].' These days 'I tell people about myself before we start.' He is aware that in the past he has been perceived as being 'very angry'. To prepare new employees for who he is 'I give them instructions of use about me', which explains that his default expression is a frown, something that his physiognomy simply falls into – and this doesn't mean he's angry. Another part of the user's manual he now provides is his love of debate: 'I will debate vigorously with most people.' Adrian believes this can present problems because most 'people are not used to vigorous debate'.

The purpose of vigorous debate

Vigorous debate really matters to Adrian and was something he and his brother grew up with. 'It helps me crystallise my thoughts.' There are two points about Adrian's attitude to debate that stand out for me. The first one concerns creativity and a particular understanding about where ideas come from. Adrian explains this with reference to the theatre. 'Theatre is a collaborative art. I don't go into the rehearsal space with many ideas; ideas come from others and from the synergy [between those rehearsing].'

The second feature of vigorous debate is that it is real. 'I don't like unreal debate… I don't like 'consultation' processes involving presentations. I'm all for people's voices being heard but these voices must be going somewhere; something must be done.' He is very dismissive of faux consultation when nothing is done with the opinions and information collected – when there is no debate to digest and make sense of what has been said. He made specific reference to an Arts Council-launched 'great debate' that he experienced as nothing more than a bloggers paradise. For him a parade of opinions is not a discussion. This is in accord with the principles of Forum Theatre which is a theatrical debate, not a theatrical presentation – an involving rather than a distancing activity.

Role models

When I asked him who had influenced him in his practice of authority nobody leapt out. He politely, rather than passionately, mentioned a number of famous theatrical names, noting how he had 'learnt a few tricks from them'. He was at pains not to be dismissive of the skills that these others had shared with him, such as Boal's demonstration of 'how non-defence is the best defence.' But he was keen to point out that Boal was not a father figure to him: 'I've invented who I am' is how he put it. 'To be honest I was already pretty well formed [by the time he met these theatrical names]. I'm 51; the way I can do things is [in place]. I'm not a great one for role models.'

It took some time after our meeting to make sense of this; in all my other interviews to date very specific people had stood out as having an informing role in people's lives. Adrian doesn't deny his history, but he is not defined by it. He sees his own character and way of being as central to his authority – what others bring are certain techniques that may help with specific situations. They cannot however touch his core, his authentic expression of himself in the moment.

Being vigorous but uncertain

Adrian debates vigorously, even confrontationally. I note how anxious I am about how he will want to debate what I have written here about our meeting. He is stimulated by being challenged although he is aware that he has an unfortunate tendency (which he attributes lightly to 'negative early life things') of 'saying "no" before I say "yes". When I'm in debate with people I might say "no" and then think about it overnight and say "you're right" the next day.'

Adrian's strength is his willingness to change his mind and not be tied to the heat of his original – frequently negative – position. I can see a difficult shadow for this strength. As someone who dislikes confrontation I could imagine being frightened of him, particularly if I were part of a hierarchy that had him at the top. Sometimes I suspect he may not see how his positional authority may give his critical voice a dangerous power – a critical voice that led his wife to say, after spending a couple of evenings with him being dismissive of various TV programmes, 'All you do is tear things apart.'

On bullying

In my first draft of Adrian's story I wrote of someone who could be – in my words – 'a bit of a bully'. His response was heartfelt and vigorous when he read it. 'I hate and refute [what you have written].' I had put him in the same camp as Alan Sugar and the macho 'big clunking fist' of Gordon Brown. 'I will admit to anger, dissatisfaction, a sometimes bleak negativity – but I am not a bully.'

'I am surprised if I said that about bullying.' I claimed he'd told me he had once overstepped the mark from passionate argument to bullying. 'I do not believe I have ever been a bully. A bully is someone who abuses their power, to belittle or threaten others. It is a weak thing. I have never done that. It is possible that I have been experienced as bullying. I think that is slightly different.'

'I am pretty resolute about this. I do not like bullies, never have.'

'The persona I occupy in the rehearsal room is the persona of a patient but pushy person, with very high expectations of everyone. And it works. This is why I enjoy the respect of a lot of people who have been through the company. Bullies do not earn respect. I challenge you to find more than one person (an accuser – there is one) who would call me a bully.'

CEO and theatre director

'Everything I do stem's from being a theatre director. [That is what] gives me pleasure.' Over the years Adrian has 'learnt more about management… [but I] usually approach management the same way I approach directing a play. I've learnt [some management] processes and procedures but I'm a sceptic about much management training.'

For Adrian there is one particular form of development that he values for all people. He has a 'belief [that] there is value in people having experiences that promote self-awareness'. He has been seeing an analyst every week for one and a half years. But for Adrian this is in addition to the core of his development: 'my self-awareness comes from rehearsing'. This is a complex environment for self-discovery because he is always 'aware of the presence of others. In the rehearsal room casts can turn against you… there are lots of feelings… a lot of vulnerability… if people can kill the father, they kill the father. This hasn't happened to me for a long time.'

Adrian's self-awareness develops in the intense experience of actual work, not in an emotionally detached workshop. Part of the authenticity of his authority is his willingness to exercise it in the emotionally charged reality of the work of his company, not in some impersonal or un-present fashion. Even though he can treat his role as CEO as a performance, he never pretends to be anything he's not. He does wear 'my heart on my sleeve… [though] less so these days.'

He is also aware that he is at odds with another prevailing cultural characteristic. 'People place a value on confidence; uncertainty is not valued, but I believe uncertainty is very healthy. I have a lot of respect for uncertainty – people who are certain are dangerous, fascists.' This worries Adrian, especially in a world where there is 'not a lot to be certain about really'.

My reflections on Adrian and authority

This feels like a very honest, warts and all story. Adrian's presence is authentic, but it does not make for necessarily comfortable reading. His character is combative and political, his life's work in the service of creating authentic engagement between people — and part of what makes an engagement authentic is the emotional and intellectual charge of the engagement.

As both artistic director and CEO he wants to bring people together for a purpose, not to go through the motions of some empty exchange. He is a man driven by what he believes to be right, who puts great value on self-awareness and yet has few memories of his life before fourteen. He sees authority within a dramatic context, where people come together with their vulnerabilities and feelings to explore what it is none of them can be certain about in their going on together.

In the end two points stand out above all others. Firstly the notion that authority is a matter of personal character not a collation of tricks and learned characteristics; 'good' authority is about understanding your character and discovering how to work well with what you've got — rather than trying to be something else. For Adrian this has meant learning how to forewarn and equip people so they can 'use him well', as well as learning how to rein in his passions without denying them. Secondly authority, authenticity and development are social activities; they happen in the presence of others with all the uncertainty and messiness that entails. The nakedness of the rehearsal room is both a metaphor and actuality of Adrian's habits of authority.

CHAPTER 12

Michaela: Refugee from the malign

Michaela sees her current authority in two distinct ways. Firstly there is her authority by position. This comes from being the director of a prestigious national institute in which she has responsibility for a collection of over four million items. Secondly there is the 'authority of what I know'. This is not just to do with the administration of the collection but also her understanding of collections at large and how it can be put to use. Although this second type of authority is 'much less used now than in the past [it] gave me the authority to apply for the current job'.

A preference for the authority of knowing

'I am probably much more comfortable with the authority of knowing rather than position.' This may be because 'the bulk of my experience is in academia where' she experienced much less hierarchy than she does at the institute. She is also very wary of titles carrying authority: 'titles are a ludicrous idea. You can be designated anything. It's the way you carry out the responsibility of the position that gives you authority or not' – an unsurprising attitude for someone who grew up in the grip of post-war Czechoslovakia.

Tooling up

Because of her personal background Michaela's experience of personal authority came later on in life. For her it meant 'the first time I knew something I was able to share and put back out'. Even though she was awkward in the initial stages, it was something 'I wanted myself to do', sharing something 'others didn't know'.

Michaela began her working life as a linguist, but when she 'emigrated from Czechoslovakia to Canada I couldn't use that specialism. As an English major I couldn't compete with all the native speakers. As a Chinese major I couldn't find any interest in late '60s Canada. I had to retool myself', which she did by getting a library master's degree and then taking on the management of a university architecture library. 'I decided I wanted to understand architecture in a more profound way [and] went back to graduate school.' This gave her a PhD in Architectural History and Theory as well as an opportunity to combine the two specialisms (architecture and collections) as a curator and administrator.

Problems in developing personal authority

For Michaela 'authority was embodied in the '60s Czech communist regime'. This was an authority that 'you fled from'. She only knew authority through 'being in dissent to it. I didn't know how to develop any reasonable authority as a person. I didn't understand where it was situated.'

'If the only authority you know is repressive, controlling, [where] somebody else makes all the decisions' it is hard to see authority as a positive force within you or around you. 'It took a while' after she'd gone to Canada in her twenties 'before I learned to believe in authority'.

During her time in Czechoslovakia a 'friend of my family spent time in prison. My father was dismissed from his job for a lack of ideological subservience. I couldn't express anything in school that reflected my personal or family beliefs because it would harm me and my family.' Her 'parents always made a distinction between what could be talked about at home and at school'.

'I grew up as a very hidden person' and it 'took a while to reposition' herself in regard to her relationship to authority. She found for a while that she was unable to distinguish between good and bad authority. She recalls fainting the first time a Montreal policeman came to her door collecting money for the Fireman's Ball. She had 'direct experience of how police at the front door means someone in the family is going to jail'. She couldn't get her mind around the notion of their being a benign authority.

She recovered a more multifaceted understanding of authority 'through continued education'. In Prague there had 'only been one right answer and that had nothing to do with truth'. In Canada there was a 'more relativistic principle' at work, which represented a 'whole new way of thinking about things and how they're represented'. It took a while for Michaela to adjust.

First experience of authority as a force for good

'Self-imposed silence was a terrible thing… a way of life for a long time… to let go of the silence, to have an opinion… to be able to express it and have others value it was a heady experience.' This came about for Michaela for the first time when she was running some workshops in the library at her university in Canada.

Good authority has some very specific characteristics for Michaela. Good authority is 'something that doesn't have to be enforced… a consensual experience between myself and others. [It is] implicit in the way you behave with other people… an acceptance of your ideas and a willingness to carry them out.'

Family experiences

Michaela described her father as 'very authoritarian'. He worked with 'authority by declaration. Like the regime!' It was only later that Michaela 'understood this was for protective reasons'. He'd 'had a very direct experience of what the regime could do to you. He knew that talking about things in public was dangerous.' When Michaela and her brother revolted, it was against their father.

'My mother was authority by consensus… by being part of a team and understanding that each of us [would be] leaders in turn based on knowledge and a unique capacity that others [don't have] to the same degree.'

A legacy of discomfort with confrontation

Michaela finds confrontation 'almost impossible to do… even if there is a cause… anybody challenging me in anger or aggressively, I have a very difficult time dealing with it.' She has learnt to deal with it 'by stepping back', which can actually be 'to re-discuss something later'.

'I used to deal very badly [with confrontation] by withdrawing… a pattern I had appropriated earlier [in life] and returned to.' Michaela has learnt that she needs 'to claim the opportunity, the time, to reflect', when faced with situations 'I find subconsciously threatening'. She is still living with the leftovers of her sixties radicalism which means she can retain a tendency 'to feel I am still on the barricades'.

This experience of being on the barricades is a 'personal trait I don't like and in a broader social context comes from a belief that if you truly believe… you defend it by activism and dissent'. This is a perspective that 'has not been [appropriate] for a long time'.

Sixties activism

'I was part of the Prague Spring movement… there was great enthusiasm for change', especially among the student population. When the Russians invaded Michaela became involved in certain things that may sound silly now 'but were not silly for us'. She 'carried radios around and took down street signs'.

This struck me as immensely courageous and I asked her where she got this quality. 'I truly don't know. It must have been from reading more than anything else. My mother was a very courageous person but very quietly, unobtrusive. Father was a revolutionary anarchist', not the same thing at all.

Michaela described herself as having 'a combination of traits, both inherited' and wrapped up in 'the idealism of the time and the numbers of people in my generation wanting to be part of making the world a better place and seeing how horribly it had failed'. Her experiences from this time were mentally and physically traumatic and left her with this need to make sure 'I'm always standing up to be counted'. Her need to act didn't leave her when she went to Canada, 'when at last in the late '70s/early '80s I was able to go back to visit my family in Prague… I smuggled manuscripts back to the West'. When everything changed with the fall of the communist regime in 1989, Michaela felt a 'little void. There was no need to fight.' Her void was as nothing to the dissidents who had stayed behind in Prague, 'some of whom lost their raison d'etre'.

Michaela still has a 'residual need to ensure I don't stay silent when I feel something is wrong'. This habit of speaking out, of standing up to be counted has caused some difficulties for her since she's come to the UK where the 'rules of argument are substantially different' and she could find herself 'standing out to be counted' when she 'didn't need to'.

Inspirational reading and a cultural inheritance

The reading that inspired Michaela at that time came from the period after the break-up of the Austro-Hungarian Empire, when Czechoslovakia had an independent existence from 1918 to 1938. This period is one that she has kept returning to in her research 'including my PhD'. 'It is a heady opportunity when you first have a chance for independence. How do you construct a different type of state?' How do you work with you historical inheritance? This is a theme she is still mulling over.

She also read, and still reads, a lot of poetry from that era. 'I have a feeling that was a moment I would have liked to live in.' This was a moment that her parents' generation had and she never did. She was the first post-war baby in her family and remembers reading about the 1920s and 1930s as a 'model that seemed so much better than communism'.

What made that period so much better was the emphasis on ability and the opportunity 'to live in a pluralistic state and to have real voice in it. After 1918 this was the first independent voice [the Czechs had] in 300 years of Hapsburg rule. The first Czech president was a very charismatic professor of philosophy who had a great vision for a State and the importance of culture in political life.' Michaela sees this as a 'specifically Czech phenomenon', shown again in 1989 when 'the first post-communist president was a playwright'.

In the Czech tradition of 1918–38 'there was a real validation of the intelligentsia and its role in the state.' There was a 'desire to build something new that hadn't been there for 500 years. That seemed possible in 1968 and then took a detour for twenty years.'

Under the communist regime 'the intelligentsia was the most persecuted and proscribed part of society. Portrayed as parasites on the body of the nation.'

'I was interested in whether culture can lead rather than pure politics. That made me and directed my professional choices, the research I have done and ideals I espouse.'

The ideal of equality

Michaela espouses 'equality and the real role of culture in the political life of the nation… I grew up in a so-called classless society that was anything but. The intelligentsia were excluded and persecuted for not being working class.' There was very little equality, the members of the Communist Party were the ruling class, the working class were meritorious and the intelligentsia were 'in prison or designated as enemies of the people'.

For Michaela consensual authority is built on real not espoused equality. 'Having experienced inequality so acutely' she knows you 'can't teach something like this if you don't feel it'. If you haven't felt it, 'don't think you can elucidate it for a bunch of middle-aged people [in a workshop]'.

Michaela's journey through authority

Michaela has had to think about issues that I suspect many of us who have grown up in the democratic West have only paid cursory attention to. 'I had to think about authority because my understanding was perverted from the word go. The first authority [I experienced] was the authority of the state. [That was] very negative.'

The second stage in Michaela's relationship to authority came 'when I went to Canada. I had to redefine authority… I had to do a lot of thinking… [and it] was not just a matter of going from bad to good government.' A lot of what was going on in Quebec at that time was 'scary'.

Over time she came to the conclusion that 'you personally know whether you have any authority'. This authority 'has to come from a source', and Michaela doesn't 'exclude natural authority', but she does believe 'you have to work it out'. 'I associate authority with that quiet confidence that you're doing something right.' Your authority is 'doing what you need it to do'.

Now in her position of directorial authority 'I envy my curators… in a university it is very easy to combine knowledge and managerial position. Now in my current position, at the end of my career, I come to this fabulous collection and because there is so much management I have very little time to enjoy the content.' She reasons her position thus: 'by being director I enable other people to get that content out… I have ideas of how to do this and do it better.' But this does come at a cost. 'I miss the thrill of discovery from direct contact with books and drawings. So from time to time I run seminars for students. I need to convince myself I still know stuff. I'm a reluctant manager.'

Why is she a good reluctant manager?

'I understand the post, like an orchestra conductor who has played all the parts of my staff of 30. I've been a director of rare books. I have been a librarian, archivist and curator. I understand how the orchestra comes together. I have some ideas that other people might not have because they've only played one or two instruments.'

'I hope that I can understand the big picture. It might help that I have lived in many places and was exposed to different cultures as it gives a sense of perspective.' The staff are the ones 'taking it forward' although 'along the way I have suggestions about what else can be done, where money can be found, who could help us. That's what I bring to the table.'

She also brings her activism, which sleeps but never dies. For over two years she has been campaigning to make the collection more accessible to the wider public. This has succeeded but she was struck by how those refuseniks to greater public access were also the same ones who bemoaned the reputation of the institute for elitism. Combating the privileges of an elite who pretend they are not elitist seems hard-wired in her.

Differences in authority in Canada and the UK

It seemed foolish not to explore national differences in attitudes towards authority with someone who has inhabited so many cultures. Michaela found Canada to have 'a much more relaxed approach to authority. More informal, a lighter touch, less bureaucratic and more direct.' Her UK experience 'could be coloured from being a staff member in a membership organisation' – her Canadian experience comes from inhabiting the world of universities. Her observations still struck home for me. In the UK 'the authority is not the person you're talking to but some third party. A lot of authority is mediated, [which leads to] more bureaucracy and more political correctness than in Canada.'

In recent times she has been working with a mutual professional friend to try and bring about a 'more collegial approach to governance'. As a process she is not sure if they have succeeded; some staff have gone along with it while others remain much more comfortable with a hierarchical and role-governed structure. She recalled how when she first came into her post 'I'd invite people for coffee and some would be like deer in the headlights… being invited by a director for informal coffee was a rather disturbing thing for them.'

My reflections on Michaela's story

An anxiety I have when reflecting on any story is whether I can do it justice. Michaela's story evokes this anxiety more than any other, both because of her academic prowess and also because of the world history that she has taken part in. I have to stop myself being in too much awe of someone who has confronted Russian tanks and so create some impossibly idealised person.

'To do something right' is a rich phrase, combining both technical and ethical considerations. Authority that is grounded in right action requires expertise and an understanding of what constitutes a good way for human beings to engage together. In Michaela's story, her learning and the importance of this learning to her sense of authority is paramount – yet when it came to her first experience of personal (benign) authority in Canada that was not enough. It also involved an act of sharing.

The other quality that stood out for me in her story, and in being with her, was the quietness she brings with her – not in the sense of having no voice, but in having no need to raise her voice. A voice of authority that is quiet can be heard more easily than one that is loud; a quiet voice invites close listening and often makes it possible for other voices to join in. Michaela's story is a celebration of authority grounded in having expertise and an ability to make that expertise available to others, while not drowning out other perspectives.

Hers is the authority of consenting adults, freely choosing to take part in a mutual experience where who does and says what will ebb and flow as the situation unfolds. This is about authority in situations that are not governed by simplistic set procedure or by the parading of pre-thought opinions. I associate the consensual quality of Michaela's authority with the difference between thought and thinking. Thought is what was known before and so can be predicted and controlled. Thinking is the living source where thought came from and is less easily corralled; it requires a greater quality of presence if it is to be engaged with.

I am making a divide here between authority as a mandated experience, where roles and rules are set, with authority as a consensual or negotiated experience, where roles and rules need to be constantly investigated, challenged and recreated. I am assuming that for a real consensus to exist, people need to be able to own and exhibit their authority in a way that works unique to any given situation.

It is impossible for me to reflect on Michaela and her relationship to authority without reference to the great evil that authority can bring. Those early years were played out in an environment where authority was a given not a negotiation. Authority was imposed by those who claimed all truth and virtue to themselves, while demonising that minority who had the greatest wit to challenge that perspective. Authority is malign when it assumes that only those who are in positions of authority can be right; when it becomes dangerous to speak out of turn or say anything that does not comply with what those in authority have already decided should be said; when the title of authority is more important than any expertise or competence. Authority becomes malign when it becomes stupid and it becomes stupid when it cuts itself off from any ability to learn – in short when it becomes self-referencing or solipsistic.

Michaela's reflections

> Not surprisingly it made me feel very self-conscious and to question everything I said as pompous or inadequate. But on the whole, I could recognise myself, warts and all. It also made me think of how lucky I am to have lived this particular life even though a lot of it was about overcoming [challenges, setbacks etc.], or perhaps [it was] because of that. And how lucky I was to have a profession I really love.

CHAPTER 13

Giles: An ounce of ruthlessness

At the moment Giles is vice chairman of a division of one of those huge, international advisory firms. He started the division in 1986 and theoretically retired in 2002 – although he has stayed on 'to do various things'.

His decision to retire came when a 'very good friend in the German practice... was suddenly diagnosed with leukaemia'. The friend 'went through various vicissitudes' and had a bone marrow transplant. This went perfectly up until the moment his body rejected the transplant. 'I was with him for the week of his death. His wife made me promise to spend more time with my wife. As an understanding to her I retired.'

This friend's widow explained her attitude to her husband's work and death. 'I lost him... what do I get from this deal... [his] working 18 hours a day.' Giles now works two days a week providing 'proper opinion' on 'large valuations' of deals that his division is advising on. He also provides impromptu support to the present leader of the division – currently this involves 'sorting out Germany and the Middle East, both areas where I have lots of experience'.

In the past he had a much bigger role within both his division and the wider firm. He was 'instrumental in selecting the current leader of [the firm]' – he played the 'Kingmaker role'.

Realising I could do it

The very first time Giles experienced his authority was 'probably when I was in charge of some field work after I'd qualified [as an accountant]. I suddenly realised I could do it. I could understand the process of an audit and how to get from A to B in a satisfactory way.' This experience was at an armaments firm where Giles remembers, 'On the same day, an Iraqi colonel and an Israeli general both testing shells from the same batch.'

Soon after this realisation of competence came a realisation of personal power. He was 'approached by a firm in Zurich to go [to them] for three months a year to do a specific audit and thereafter act as a senior manager reviewing their other work'. Giles 'negotiated my own contract' which meant coinciding his time there with the winter skiing season, as well as increasing what they'd pay.

Self-assurance in the presence of others

Giles was educated in Germany and speaks German. Back in 1972 he was involved in a deal that involved an Austrian firm, which had been appropriated at the time of the Anschluss, being bought back from the Austrian government and established within a UK public company. The deal went through and all looked fine until a huge loss was found that would have to be reported to the AGM. 'I was asked to go and find out where the loss had come from.' Being able to speak German gave Giles a distinctive 'power and authority'.

'We found the error quite by accident on day two' of the investigation. 'I flew back to London to say what it was.' So Giles, then in his mid-to-late twenties went in front of the main board directors to tell them that firstly: 'You are getting management information from this company and it is rubbish – but I have a sense of what is needed… and I'll come back to you in a month and a half [to tell you what you need].' His second point was more personal. 'My car is still out there and someone needs to go and collect it.'

By the age of 28 he was an adviser to the Emir of Kuwait, 'writing reports which were well received'. He had a complete confidence in his ability to do what he was doing and this gave him authority. 'I was being paid to go all over the world.' These travels, experiences and relationships meant he 'got involved in the nationalisation of the Kuwaiti oil companies' – an exercise that he 'found a breeze. I was doing something no-one had done before. There was no benchmark.' With regard to his sense of authority, 'if you demonstrate a certain type of authority, people follow'.

Confidence that something will turn up

When he was working on these sorts of projects, where the nature of the problem was unknown or the process for going about it not yet defined, Giles would go through 'day one or two feeling my way. After two or three days a clue would come out that would highlight something, give me the kernel to build something around. I'd thrash around in the dark until I hit the kernel… I'd always know when I'd hit it.'

Confidence also comes through being lucky. 'I was lucky in getting on the Kuwait job where I was a junior member of the team.' This experience meant that he was 'asked to review a job in Libya'.

Taking care of boundaries

In Libya Giles 'fell out with Gadaffi's henchmen' who were keen to push Giles and his team around. 'We had to have an environment we could work in without being pushed around.' The henchman pushed their luck, purloined Giles' bedroom and Giles 'turned the job down', demonstrating the confidence to turn something down if the conditions were not right.

At this point in his life Giles got married which 'gave me an enhanced level of confidence'. His marriage did not prevent him continuing to work around the world. 'Within five minutes of getting married I went on a job in the Far East for three weeks. On the back of this we won a huge job… implementing the nationalisation of oil companies'.

Working with complicated authority structures

Giles was working for the independent assessor in this country, who was 'very well connected but knew nothing at all about oil. He'd got his position through birth rather than anything else. I had to act on his behalf [even if] I wasn't going to get any support from him.' Giles' position was further complicated by being 'appointed underneath a senior manager in a local office' – the responsible partner for the work being based in London.

The work was difficult with 'nobody taking any prisoners. The government was taking and the oil companies weren't giving.' As regards support for Giles, 'within two weeks out there I realised I'd get no support from the independent assessor as his social position would be threatened if anything went wrong'. Meanwhile the 'local office senior manager chap never turned up and never gave any help in the early stages'. He was 'bright… [but] clearly wanted to remain in the background because he felt he was out of his depth'.

I asked Giles if he'd felt out of his depth at that time. 'Sort of,' he said, but 'I felt if anyone could do it I had a sporting chance. I didn't want to get on the next plane home. I wasn't confident I could do it [but there were] enough clues.' In his characteristically forthright manner he phoned up the partner in London and told him what he wanted. 'I want the local office bloke taken off the job. I will run it in his stead. I want a proven assistant manager in Special Assignments sent from London… someone I can rely on. Twenty-four hours later he'd removed the local office bloke (who still speaks to me) and gave me someone I knew to act as my number two.' And they set to it.

Dealing with a potential international incident

At one point in the work Giles uncovered something going on that could readily have been interpreted as questionable or even fraudulent; it could even have been enough to bring about an international incident (for reasons Giles and I agreed still could not be divulged).

Giles went to the CEO of one of the parties involved 'laid out what I'd found and asked him what he was going to do.' It was clear the man was deeply shocked, and was unaware of how some may choose to interpret the activities that concerned Giles. He agreed with Giles that they had to prove that his organisation was whiter than white and asked Giles what could be done.

'I want your people working 24 hours a day to prove my [benign] hypothesis. If I'm happy [we can categorically prove] nothing has occurred I will say nothing. I will record the incident but not go to the government. Because if I go to the government I know what will happen.'

One week later the necessary reconciliations were done and it was proved beyond a shadow of a doubt that there was nothing to worry about. Giles felt the right thing had been done. 'If there was one incident that made me feel I had a level of authority' this was it – this incident 'and one other led to me becoming a partner'.

The prime minister brought an end to the talks and one key clause was rushed. It meant the oil companies were going into an agreement with a pricing mechanism 'that was unworkable'. After this premature conclusion 'I spent the next couple of weeks rewriting the clause and calculating the mechanism for pricing' oil as it was bought and sold between government and the oil company. After travelling widely around the region and talking to oil people Giles came up with a mechanism that linked the price to a 'basket of crudes around the world'. This was workable and Giles assumed it would then be more thoroughly revised after a year. The mechanism he devised stayed in place for nineteen years.

Giles' firm 'got out well from what could have been a sticky time' in that country and Giles was made a deputy manager, which meant 'I was in line to become a partner'.

Focusing on what needed to be done

'At the time' of this complicated work Giles 'didn't go around with the personal confidence that I could do this. It was about looking for a solution to fit this particular set of problems. Maybe luck… maybe a bit of bravery. [It was] not a function of personal confidence.'

'I was no high flyer at school or in work before then. My secondary education had been in Germany and I did four-year articles because I didn't have a UK degree. If you go back to see where I first got my confidence… it was passing my accounting finals and being chosen to go on the Kuwait job.' Giles built his career by 'building on each job in turn and doing a good job'. The 'size and importance of the jobs didn't strike me until later'.

Running his own department – free hand Giles

Back in London Giles was made a senior manger with his own department of forty people. This was 'an administrative job allied with some technical input and I absolutely loved it'. It was 'the right combination of work, supervising the work of others and meeting senior clients'. This position was one of huge power, which the firm has since got rid of – Giles could 'choose what job he wanted to do' and 'I could turn away work given to the department by partners.'

'I adored the combination of work… absolutely loved it… I worked very hard… but was never bored by admin. I wasn't governed by regulation or rules. I could make my own… I could express myself as I wanted (and I had the confidence to do this).'

'I got huge loyalty from' the department and 'I wanted them… to win', whether it was the departmental rugby or squash team. 'We were winning together', and Giles' reputation helped ensure that lots of good work came their way.

Last negotiation for himself

'After three years I was approached to deal with a problem in the Middle East. Would I go out and rescue the practice?' Giles agreed to go for three to four months but 'my price was partnership. I want you to confirm my partnership before I go.' There were some grumbles but it was agreed. For Giles this was a matter of logic rather than threat: 'I don't approve of people advancing through threat.' He knew he was well on track for partnership and 'didn't want the most important decision [of his career] being made about me when I was working round the clock to dig the firm out of a hole in Dubai.' His only mistake at the end of this time was to mishear who he was going to work with in setting up a new department. He thought he'd be working with a much-respected friend and colleague; instead he found himself 'working with an unguided missile', who other partners thought Giles 'would be good at keeping in check'.

Ambition and ruthlessness

'You've got to have a slight streak of ambition,' Giles said when we stepped back to consider the role of ambition. He caveated this straight away by saying that it was 'the ambition to find a solution rather than the ambition to find a position'.

'I don't think any of my acquaintances would have seen me as ambitious. I've been kingmaker rather than the king. I've stepped back from positions of authority.' So recently he had helped recruit a new head of his department rather than step in and take the job for himself. 'I peaked in my forties.'

As for ruthlessness, you 'need a streak' of it – 'an ounce of ruthlessness that gives you the bravery to carry things through'. It is this small piece of steel that allows you to say to yourself, 'I might as well try it.' Giles' ruthlessness seems to be concerned with the determination to address a particular problem, find an elusive solution. There are two or three times in his life when 'I've gone to sleep without a solution and woken up with it. It's clear what I have to do.' I'm wondering if a better way of describing this attribute is tenacity rather than ruthlessness – although sometimes the 'right course' can appear ruthless, as was the case with the sidelining of the local office senior manager.

Giles put it like this: 'When you make the best of it you follow a course of action that sets you apart.' In Giles' case this is based upon an ability 'to sort the wood from the trees' combined with an easy ability to explain what needs to be done. This can result in some unusual moments. At one point Giles was working for Richard Branson, who is a famed negotiator, and 'I became convinced that I should represent Branson as his negotiator'. Somehow Giles won his client to this point of view and things went well.

Around him Giles has 'seen utterly ruthless people rise up'. This is not to his taste. 'How many CEOs of FTSE 100 firms would you wish to invite to dinner?' He asked. 'The answer is very few in my case – which is why I didn't wind up leading the firm or being a CEO or chairman of a public company. I only have an ounce of ruthlessness. To get to those positions you have to tread on so many people. Some are mega ruthless and ambitious... [and] only want to talk about themselves. Hence the paucity of their quality as dining companions.'

These reflections led him to suggest that there are two forms of success in life: 'one is measured by the position you achieve' while the other is 'what you get out of life'.

Balance

'I have achieved a work–life balance that works for me. I've achieved far more than I expected in my work. I have managed to combine it with softer issues I thoroughly enjoy. [I've been] dead, dead lucky. I'm healthy. Family's healthy... I'm enjoying family life.'

My reflections on Giles' story

I experienced Giles as a man very comfortable in his own skin, someone who enjoyed what he was, and what he had been, in the world. He certainly had ambition and was good at what he did, but I got the sense with him that at some level he felt that fate had given him a good hand – even if he'd then had to play it.

Giles has a well-developed confidence in his ability to see a way through things. In his work all around the world, often working in uncharted territories, he has a knack for seeing how to get from A to B. Without this sense, authority can turn into bravado as it is not grounded in a tangible sense of purpose. By being able to provide this sense of direction Giles can help contain the anxieties of those around him and so allow them to relax enough to get on with getting on – rather than worrying about things. It is around the course of action that a sense of purpose and direction can emerge that allow a coherent course to be followed.

When he told the story of his trip to Asia and the removal of the senior manager from the local office, my antennae were alert for any sense of grandstanding or political manoeuvring. I never got any indication that this was the case. Giles was focused on behaving in the only way that he believed made it possible for the job to have a chance of success. This clear-headed calculation was also evident in his engagement with the CEO of the company whose activities appeared so potentially suspicious. Authority that is grounded in the right thing for the job will be readily accepted by people around it, even when difficult decisions have to be made – it legitimises those who use their authority.

Giles has a touch of the charismatic – there is a bit of 'pixie dust' to him. This little bit of magic seems to me to come from an easy impishness – a willingness to tell a board what to do while also asking that they help get his car back from a foreign country. He wears his authority with some charm and lightness – without denying that on occasion there has to be some steel. I think he can exhibit this chutzpah because it comes on top of some deep-rooted competence, a track record of ability to deal with problems that many others may find daunting.

He is that rare beast, a man who is comfortable going into places without a route map; he has a sincerely held inner belief that what he needs to know will make itself apparent, because it has done so on so many occasions in his life. His is an authority that does not need to jump to premature conclusions, but is willing to wait for what needs to be done to become apparent. It is grounded in a very well attuned connection to the reality of what is and what that makes possible. This contrasts to the authority that comes from claiming to know ahead of time what and how things need to be dealt with.

His authority is not naïve – on a number of occasions he has quite explicitly ensured that he does not lose out on what he believes to be his just desserts. He also looks to ensure that he has in place the support that he needs to succeed. This is not self-aggrandisement, but comes from a healthy sense of self-preservation – while also being about getting the job done.

He has also ensured that he has taken care of his life in the whole, stepping back from those opportunities to take the top spot, preferring instead to support others who are hungrier for the all-absorbing requirements of certain posts. His wife and family were mentioned a number of times in our meeting, and of course family concerns are touched on in the first and last paragraph of his story. He enjoys being in a position of authority but he has a well-developed sense of the limits of its importance. I could not imagine him sacrificing his identity and personal priorities for any organisational need.

A short story about hanging tough

These are three strong-minded individuals, whose lives touch on significant points of cultural and economic crisis in modern history. None of them are apparatchiks, they are all mavericks of a sort, who have learnt how both to challenge and take up authority. Despite having a tenacity, a touch of steel to their personalities, their strong-mindedness does not fall over into a love of strength for its own sake – there is an absence of fascism in their authority.

There is a worldliness to them; they have lived and drawn on influences from around the world – North Africa, Asia, Latin America, North America, Eastern and Central Europe and the Middle East. They are citizens of the world who have had to engage with a flux of cultural norms about what is an acceptable expression of authority. This worldliness and breadth of experience may be one of the reasons that their authority rests within their character and competence, factors which can cross borders and divisions in society, whereas titles and hierarchies move less easily.

The features of the three stories that I want to reflect on are:

- Standing up to be counted
- Personal freedom and autonomy
- Self-made authority

Standing up to be counted

None of them will put up with what they believe to be unacceptable or wrong. Adrian has a wonderful fire of justice and integrity that seems to make him constitutionally incapable of not pursuing what he believes to be the right course. From a different world, Giles puts in place what is needed for him to get the job done. He seems to walk with princes and with commoners with equal ease and is not in awe of people of position – indeed these days he seems to hold a modicum of personal disgust towards the corporate elite and their self-regard. Michaela is a quieter voice, but has been tempered by the harsh consequences of malign authority and still finds herself heading to the barricades when there is injustice in the air.

They are all three infused by a spirit of doing what is right, not what is customary or will give them an easy life. Because there is a cause behind their prominence, I sense that they are inoculated from narcissism and idolatry. They stand up to be counted not to draw attention to themselves but because there is something that needs to be paid attention. They are the messenger not the subject of the story – this can require a certain grittiness, a toughness, when the message is hard to swallow.

Personal freedom and autonomy

These are people who appear to me not to like being in the thrall of others; their attraction to authority is more to do with living without the interfering (incompetent or malign) authority of others. Through Michaela's academic pedigree and range of experience, she is intent on living with a sense of collegial authority – even within the setting of a traditional hierarchical institution. She wishes to have the freedom that she feels her knowledge gives her and to encourage this sense of freedom in others. This freedom being informed by a felt sense of equality, which she wants to see play out in an equality of voice. This desire both to speak out and for others to speak out is also a tenet of Adrian's life and work. Forum Theatre is a philosophy of expression that comes from actual lived experience, not the words that others would like to put into the mouths of those who've had the experience. As a theatre director, Adrian has to be able to join in the creative process and speak freely.

Giles has spent much of his professional life working in uncharted territories; his satisfaction with management comes from a time before personal autonomy and responsibility were so horribly reduced by an excess of administrative regulation. To have the freedom to shape your working life and the way you exercise authority was an important part of the pleasure of authority.

The three of them, with their differently expressed maverick habits, appeal greatly to me – with my distrust of formal authority. These are people who personalise the formal and who do not seek to hide behind role and function. Their authority is about being a free-thinking human being in a position of responsibility, not a functionary following the rules for their own sake.

Self-made authority

These are lives created as much as given. There has been little passive acceptance of how things should be; all three of them in their different milieus have sought out a distinctive path. Michaela had to step out of the shadow of an authoritarian father and a malign state, where she had to hide herself and where her intelligence ruled her out of authority (unless she surrendered to the self-denying requirements of party orthodoxy). Through her intellectual diligence and habits of character, her expression of authority has emerged; an authority based upon knowledge, equality and a willingness to stand up for what she believes in.

Adrian came from a background of privilege but has spent his life on the outside of the orthodox. For whatever reasons – and his disconnection with his early history is extreme – Adrian's authority is the authority of the outsider. To be outside of established conventions demands that you have to think things through for yourself, there are no easy models or pre-set ways for knowing yourself and how to be in society. I find myself thinking about the difference between authority in the service of inclusion contrasted with authority in the service of exclusion – and how Adrian's world inhabits both. He is seeking to have people included, who are excluded. His work coexists in a world where both inclusion and exclusion are a permanent reality.

Giles was also an outsider, German educated in an English world. Like Adrian and Michaela, he has a certain derring-do that enables him to pursue his own line. Unlike Adrian and Michaela he is more comfortable in making established authority work for him – he is an insider who is able to make custom and practice his tools rather than his master. Giles is also an example of tempered ambition – having a knowledge of how far he is willing to go in the pursuit of his ambition. His story highlights a sense that knowing your limits, as well as your ambition, is a crucial factor if you're not to be consumed by an ambition for authority.

section four

Gods, elders and liberating mothers

Chapter 15
Lesley: Tough love   111

Chapter 16
Bob: Burdened with responsibility   121

Chapter 17
Marie: Working with authority from a Freudian angle   131

Chapter 18
A short story about gods, elders and liberating mothers   141

CHAPTER 15

Lesley: Tough love

Lesley is head of a well-known consulting firm. While she likes to think of herself as attached to the Peter Block notion of 'distributed leadership', at the time of our conversation her leadership has 'never been less distributed'. The established leadership team has stood down and prior to the installation of the new one there is 'an awful lot resting on me. I feel I'm responsible for the whole of' the firm. 'I feel I'm on my own with it.' With new job descriptions in place, that should result in directors being 'really accountable', she 'can't wait to have a leadership team with people who will share the workload'.

She walked into an old leadership setup where there 'were generic roles and tasks were allocated on an ad-hoc basis. I just accepted that this was how the unit was managed.' Outside of the leadership team people didn't know who was responsible for what. The 'collective [accountability] didn't really work'. After a six-month period of consultation it became clear that 'people wanted to see more accountability and responsibility'.

First sense of authority

Lesley can't 'remember not having it'. She recalled 'being seven years old and being given responsibility for my two younger brothers by my mother'. Her terms of reference were to 'take them out of my hair' and 'you're responsible'. The young Lesley remembers 'dragging them off round the parks or to the pictures or being at home with them'.

There was good reason for her mother turning to Lesley. 'Mum and Dad had a pub and were very busy.' Then 'when I was eight, my father became very seriously ill (coronary thrombosis) and was pretty much paralysed for five years. Mum had a pub, four children and a dog' to look after.

Gender attitudes also played a part. 'My mum always thought girls did the work and boys were looked after'. Lesley's mum was the youngest of eight children and when growing up 'the men ate first, then the girls and grandmother ate what was left over'. A woman's place was most certainly in the home.

A tough mother

Lesley's 'mum was a very strong woman'. She not only kept the family and business together for the five years of her husband's crippling illness, she 'made it work for her'. She was 'not a martyr and she wasn't miserable. She was tough and found a way of having a good time.'

Lesley's job in this demanding setting was 'to look after the two younger brothers. I had an elder brother whose job it wasn't.' In Lesley's words he was 'obviously destined for greater things'. From that time on Lesley 'was quick to pick up responsibility'. Indeed, picking up responsibility became her job and it was something she took seriously. Some years later, when her two little brothers were grown adults, they told her the tale of how when they were six and eight they'd 'escaped from the house and gone around the town in their pyjamas'. When the adult Lesley heard this 'I felt shocked because I'd have been in trouble' if this escapade had come to light at the time.

'Occasionally I can look back and see it as fun.' She recalled 'returning from the pond with a bowl full of ducklings'. This light memory was immediately shaded by the horror of responsibility that emerged when her 'younger brother broke his arm playing at being in the cavalry'. 'By the time I got to be 14 or 15 it was just a burden.' There was 'no escaping. I'd be invited to the pictures by a boy and I'd have to take my younger brothers with me.'

Drawing a line in the sand

Prior to her father's death, Lesley went to a convent school so that she could 'become a young lady', something her mother wanted for her. Although Lesley seemed to rock the boat, at one time being the spokesperson and organiser of a petition to have something done about the disgusting school food – a campaign that led to the mother superior witheringly ripping the petition to pieces in front of Lesley.

Her father's death created an hiatus in the family fortunes and the family was no longer able to afford the convent fees. She went to the local secondary modern that she hated so much she refused to go to school. 'I was a school refuser.' Before this could become a major problem, the school leaving age was lowered and Lesley was able to slip out of the education system and at 15 found a job in a handbag shop. A year later she went to work in a bank as an office junior: 'it was very much a job… a grinding job', although bits were okay. She stayed there for two years, realising by the end that they were 'never going to let me do anything interesting… only the boring stuff'. The next move was to an accounts department in a newspaper and by 19 she was 'married and responsible for my son' and had discovered that being a mother was much more interesting than anything else she'd done.

Being a subject of study

By this time Lesley, her husband and newborn son were living in St John's Wood in London. Her health visitor asked Lesley if she'd 'have a Tavistock student observe me for a year'. Lesley agreed and the student came to visit Lesley and son at home for a couple of hours every week while Lesley 'did what I did'. This was Lesley's first introduction to the idea of psychology and 'I was fascinated by it and by child development'. The student observed Lesley and her son and then 'talked about what had changed in the week… what was different in our relationship'. This experience 'led me into doing something interesting with my life. I decided I needed to do some studying and I did some courses on working with kids in London.'

Alongside this studying Lesley got heavily involved in all sorts of activities 'that fitted in with being a mum at home'. She couldn't afford to go out to work. This meant running playgroups, after school clubs and summer schools. She also ran a charity shop, managing an entirely volunteer-run MIND shop – 'one of the first where you could sell your clothes'. Lesley describes how she wound up doing this as a matter of 'putting my hand up' when MIND was looking for someone to run a free shop they'd been given.

Getting qualified

'By 28 I decided I was in a bit of a rut and would never get anywhere without some qualifications.' She also had a sense of what she wanted to be, 'a psychologist like Maureen the Tavistock lady'. She found out about a new development at the Paddington College that was 'just starting an access course for mature, unqualified students'. Lesley 'went and enrolled and had the most wonderful year discovering education' of a very different character and process to that of her childhood. She studied all sorts of subjects and did some very useful remedial maths. From there she went on to do three years studying psychology at the City of London Polytechnic where she was one of only three mature students and felt 'very old'.

'My big plan was to be an educational psychologist' but the rules changed and 'I couldn't join teacher training without O levels in Maths and English. I didn't have them and didn't plan to get them.' With that route closed, Lesley 'decided to be a clinical psychologist instead' and went off to 'work in a hospital as a trainee psychologist prior to getting a master's'. She got a 'job working in a terrible hospital and left after seven months it was so awful. It wasn't the patients. The staff and the institution were horrendous.'

Moving into management

'That's when I picked up my management career.' Lesley 'got a job as an assistant manager on a government scheme to help the long-term unemployed return to work'. The job required 'someone to do all the recruitment in finding people jobs in the community, such as local charities, that didn't replace proper jobs. I had twenty-five people in all sorts of places.' Lesley got the job because of her degree and because of her 'experience from all the things she did as a mum – [such as] running after-school clubs'.

The key to success in this work was identifying 'those who could really benefit [and] support them in returning to mainstream employment'. Lesley really enjoyed the work – and there was plenty of it, given that this was taking place in the early 1980s when unemployment was up around the 20 per cent level. She also had her political antennae up: 'I was concerned that it could be just a sop… but the scheme grew and after three years there were 200 on it.' Growth led to restructuring and 'I carved out the niche I enjoyed most'.

This generative experience came to an end when 'a new manager came in, in the last year... nearly driving me mad, wanting to control things; wanting to control me'. Lesley does not respond well to others controlling her, as her scores on the Firo-B instrument demonstrate. 'I have a real rebel profile. If people don't give me enough room I find it very irritating.' So Lesley had to move on.

By a process of networking she found a position in Barwent County Council setting up health and welfare schemes for a population of 45,000. Her first job was to get rid of the one very poor doctor who was dedicated to Occupational Health, a drunk with an addiction to one-armed bandits. She also had to set up the organisation from scratch. 'When I first arrived there was no desk or office. I had to find space and beg, borrow and steal lights etc.... then begin to develop the team.'

Falling into a career

While finding this satisfying she was 'worried about where my career was going', she didn't seem to fit easily into any particular slot or label. She 'fell in with Colin, an Organisational Development [OD] consultant in Barwent, [who was] responsible for some senior management programmes'.

Barwent was a 'very good place to learn the ropes', experience she supplemented by also taking an MSc in Organisational Psychology at Hertfordshire – this was in addition to a Diploma in Management Studies she'd also picked up by then. These courses not only gave Lesley 'fascinating information' they also provided 'great networks' and 'a sense of having some knowledge that might be useful'.

She spent five years working with Colin in Barwent which not only exposed her to all sorts of OD experiences and practices it also 'helped me understand what it is to be a client'.

Sparking ambition

She and Colin were also being worked with to explore how they worked together. Then came a show-stopping question from their coach, asked of Lesley in private: 'what was I going to do when I was better than Colin?' It provoked all sorts of questions for her. 'Was I in a subservient position? Was I carrying on being a disciple too long?' It didn't feel like this to Lesley as she and Colin worked as equals. The questions she was finally left with were, 'what do I have to do to be better than Colin? Can I be? Do I want to be?' The result of this self-examination was a spark to 'further ambition', a further sense of more growth – and with this sense of further opportunity so Lesley was shaken out of her groove and began to ask 'If not here, then where?'

She joined her current organisation in order 'to work outside of the public sector and the UK' and as a mission 'to prove that five years OD work in the public sector was very good experience'.

This was not how she was received. After a very long time the consultancy agreed to give her a job as a 'consultant-under-development'. Lesley was 'bitter that my experience didn't count'. There was also a gender split within the group she joined. There was a small but exclusive group of people who were business directors – who were mostly men.

'I felt totally discounted… [I] couldn't influence anything and I hated it. I didn't leave because Alastair [the MD] gave me some responsibility. Then I got onto the leadership team.' This came about when the 'the whole leadership team stood down' and everyone could apply to join. Up until then Lesley and two other women had felt like 'the fairies who did all the work… with no sense of being able to influence anything'.

Lesley 'felt angry and things had to change'. The establishment of the new leadership team was cathartic.

Becoming managing director

Lesley had been on the leadership team for five years before she became MD. This time gave her an understanding of what leadership meant in this particular organisation. The key question within the organisation concerned 'what is legitimate authority?' For Lesley this became the question 'did I have the authority to do the job?'

In her time as a member of the leadership team 'I took on most of the HR stuff… [and] felt it had worked well'. The then MD, Alastair, was 'also very good at giving you a sense of being useful'. In Lesley's case telling her '"you're the keel of the ship". [He] suggested I had a way of helping the organisation stay on track.' When Alastair told her he was leaving she was shocked and 'didn't believe it'. She wondered who would do his job, 'I didn't know who I wanted to lead' the organisation. 'I couldn't see anyone.' Then two or three people 'came up and asked me if I was going to apply'. This prompted a reaction in her, 'maybe I am'. This discovery 'felt like a huge surprise at the time'. Her ambition was steeled because 'I felt I had support', thus addressing the issue of whether she had legitimate authority to lead. In terms of her life and her career it 'felt like the right time to discover an ambition to do this'.

Lesley on Lesley

I asked Lesley to reflect on what she saw in her life and her relationship to authority. She could see one pattern immediately: 'I have periods of contentment followed by ambition'. There are times when she can simply enjoy the job in hand and then there will come a point where the job in hand is not enough.

In terms of her external persona she is 'very adaptable', although this does not mean she simply bends in the wind. 'There is a point where I won't adapt any more – there are lines in the sand.

She sees her life and the way she lives it as 'my choice. I make my life. I choose to make things work or not work. This is within my power to decide.' When she was studying she came across the 'learned helplessness model' and was shocked to discover this existed. 'My children say I have brought them up to be very independent. I can't bear unreasonable dependency.' Linking this back to her early experience of looking after her two little brothers she observed, 'the only way to deal with my brothers was to get them to learn to be independent'. This philosophy of self-actualisation fits with the pleasure she gets from being in a position of authority. 'My greatest enjoyment is seeing other people acting with authority and independence. I don't like taking all the responsibility.' Indeed if she is taking all the responsibility then it's 'a sign that it's not working'.

She recalled her time with the Occupational Health teams where there was 'a woman who could do nothing unless everything was really spelled out. For goodness sake,' Lesley thought, 'this is your opportunity to make it the job you want'. In contrast the people Lesley most enjoys working with are 'free agents who want to make their own ideas come about'.

My reflections on Lesley's story

The phrase 'tough love' comes to the fore when I reflect on Lesley and her story of authority. To meet her it is easy to experience a gentleness, she is thoughtful and softly spoken – but this coexists with a steel, even a harshness, that can appear when she talks of difficult decisions or people she feels have not taken responsibility for themselves.

Authority can be used defensively as well as proactively. In Lesley's story I was struck by a sense that she often stepped into authority in order to ensure that no-one filled a position who got in her way. She seems to have little interest in more than lightly directing people and her attraction to positions of authority may reflect her take on the old medical instruction 'to first do no harm'. She is the rebel who doesn't want to prevent others from being rebels, but wants to keep the forces of control and regimentation at arms length. Authority meets a need for her and she seems to be well aware of what that need is. There is nothing apologetic in the way she talks about how and why she leads, her practice of authority is a logical extension of her own values. This should mean that people know where they stand with her, so making her authority transparent and comprehensible to those around her – even if it doesn't necessarily make them comfortable.

Authority needs legitimacy and this legitimacy can come from many sources. Sometimes it is a matter of situation, sometimes a matter of personal ambition and sometimes it arises from the support of those around you. In Lesley's early life her authority was mandated by her mother and the situation the family found itself in. There are times in all walks of life when authority sticks to whoever is around at the time – someone needs to be labelled, so someone gets labelled. Authority in those circumstances is not so much about the person as about the situation per se. The catch with this is that once someone has acquired the habit of being given authority, they learn to expect it and/or exercise it – this would certainly be the case when looking at Lesley the eldest daughter.

In Lesley's story there were moments when her ambition came to the fore and she was willing to put herself forward, either out of a desire for personal growth or because of frustration with the status quo. Authority is something she wanted and I would claim that part of the authority of authority comes with the desire of someone to take it on. Ego and ambition play a role and that is no bad thing – it is only when they are taken to excess, or are the sole motivators, that their shadow may emerge in the form of narcissism. Lastly authority can be a function of colleagues and peers inviting you into a position of authority – this can be problematic when people are invited to take on roles that don't match their own ambitions and feel honour bound to step into the breach. In my dealings with a number of senior women I have felt this to be the case – they will hide their own needs in the service of the wider 'family'. In Lesley's case her ambition and the invitation of peers provided a 'perfect storm', allowing her to step forward in a way that met the needs of the situation, her own wants and the desires of those around her.

Lesley steps into positions of authority when she wants to grow, when it fits with her personal development agenda. Her practice of authority is about her own self-actualisation (or at least the preventing of others using authority to block it). This self-actualisation agenda is then used in how she engages with people around her, she is unashamedly ideological – self-actualisation is generally good, self-denying compliance with authority is generally not so good. This puts her in stark contrast to the part of Marie's story where a leader uses his authority to seek out adoration and dependency in those around them.

I suspect that it takes a high degree of self and group awareness to avoid falling into the pitfalls of others' dependency. Lesley can draw on an upbringing that demanded personal resourcefulness and a character that never wanted to have others hanging on her coat-tails (especially when there were boys to go to the pictures with). Others who had more compliant upbringings may find it more of a struggle to experience people in authority as potentially liberating rather than restricting or worse.

Lesley's story is a proactive and conscious one. Circumstances were as random and unpredictable as in any life but she maintains a strong sense of her own agency throughout. When things are not going well or something changes in what had been up until then a comfortable situation, Lesley responds in ways that will work for her. She has no interest in living her life through others or of using her authority to bolster her self-esteem or sense of self. Exercising authority is something she chooses to do and I sense she expects others around her to choose their relationship to their own and her authority. This is not an easy authority, that invites people to slip into unconscious or un-owned patterns where someone else can 'be in charge' of their lives. Lesley's authority insists on the conscious personal presence of everyone around her – this is the antithesis of a pacifying authority, her ambition I believe is to exercise an energising authority and an energising engagement with the self.

A second conversation

'What I recognised in the story was my mother!' Lesley observed when we met for a follow-up conversation. 'What a wonderful role model she was… you might have a difficult time [in life but you] just get on with it.' For Lesley there is no alternative to 'just getting on with it', although the other day – for the first time – she let herself think that there might be an alternative; such as not doing it, or running away or staying in bed and letting others pick up the pieces.

When we first met she was in a buttoned-down mood. Against her advice and earnest pleadings, her old leadership team had stepped down leaving her with the unpleasant task of choosing a new one. With the new team in place she was able to look more directly at the pressures this process had put her under.

'I did have mentoring in the last six months… I chose someone who would be tough with me.' Prior to this 'I had someone who was gentle, supportive and developmental'. To cope with the transition in leadership she found a mentor who would 'hold me to account'. He gave her 'a bit of tough love back'. Compared to the contained Lesley I'd met two months previously, this Lesley could acknowledge 'how awful it is to make these sorts of decisions about close colleagues… [and] not just colleagues… [these] people were friends'. She summed up her experience of leadership thus: 'I can do the tough love, but I still want people to love me.'

More self-awareness

Lesley had recently completed a refined version of the Myers Briggs instrument. This revealed that she has some very strong yet contradictory impulses in her nature. On the instrument she was 'very strong in logic and questioning', as well as having a strong disposition towards feeling. She holds within her the capacity to know what a right course of action is, and to feel the consequences for herself and those around her. So when she appointed the new leadership team she knew the reasons for appointing the three she did, but she felt most keenly the damage that had been dealt to her relationship with the other five who'd applied and not been chosen. She knows that 'I can't please everyone' but that doesn't stop her being 'very sensitive to criticism'.

Gender was another feature of our conversation. Lesley saw 'the gendered nature of my story… the expectations of being a woman' playing out in both professional and personal spheres.

Last comments on Lesley

Conversations are, as I well know, greatly influenced by context. In the story Lesley told there is a steely grip, almost a remorselessness – a sense of a capable and resourceful woman who has made her way in the world by making the best of things. When we met to review her story the worst was over; relationships had been inevitably damaged but the tough choices had been made. I could almost see her shoulders were looser and less set than when we'd last met. With the grim necessity of a logical course of action now out of the way, she felt able to acknowledge what she had been unable (or unwilling) to acknowledge before.

From a professional point of view she is going to be much less gung-ho about recommending 'green field' organisational choices to her clients; choices that 'don't take account of [the] dedication, loyalty [etc.]… that people give'.

So Lesley's authority is one of 'tough love' – but that doesn't mean she doesn't appreciate the need for a little tenderness now and again.

CHAPTER 16

Bob: Burdened with responsibility

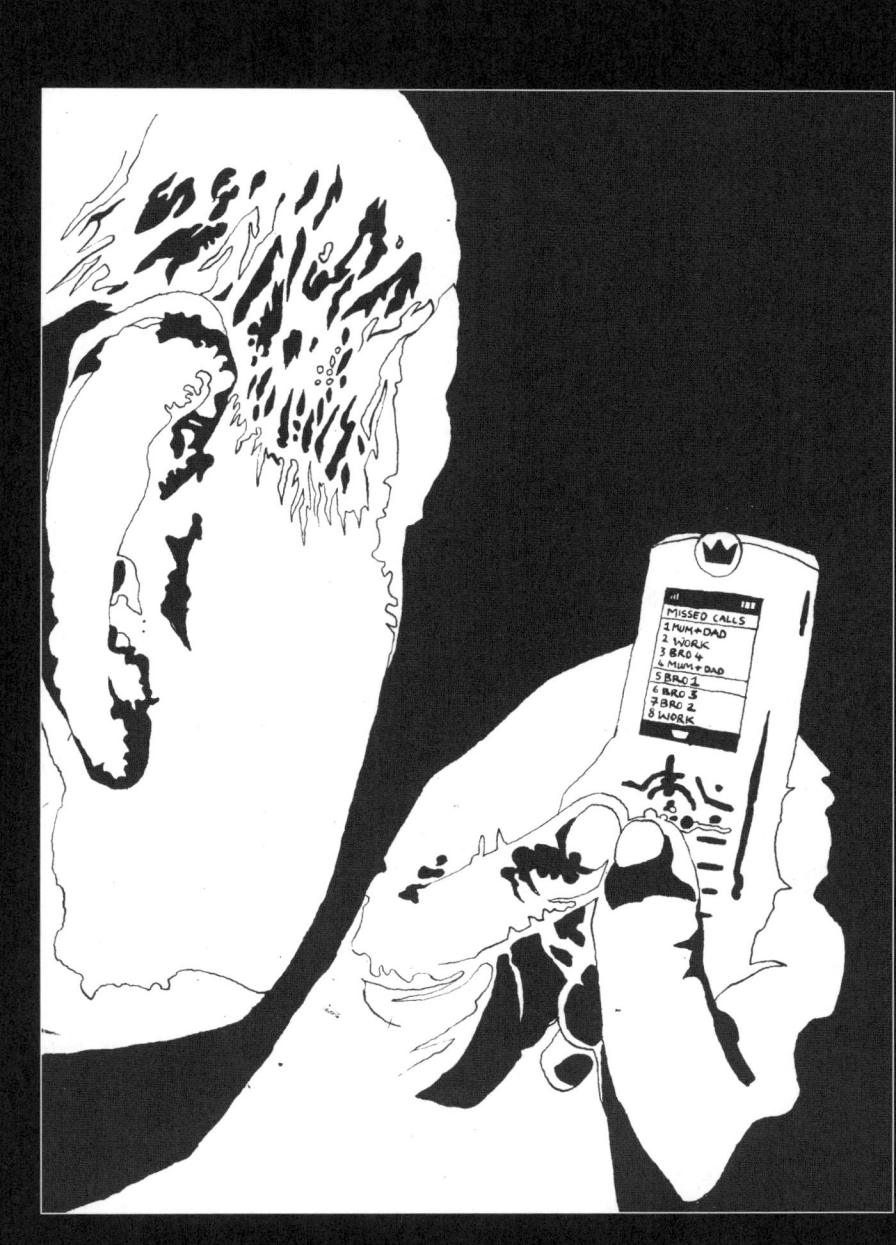

For Bob authority is responsibility. That's 'how I'd measure it' and its scope is 'both family and corporate'. Bob is co-owner of a small event management business, father of five daughters, eldest of four brothers and has 'responsibility for the company, the staff and how it all fits together… to clients and also… to family, brothers, parents etc.'

Bob is 'at the point of my life [where] I have maximum responsibility in just about every area. Business wise [I] have responsibility for everything… I have a business partner [but] I shoulder most of the day-to-day responsibility. This provides a big pressure for me… almost crushing… [We've] had a very difficult couple of years. [We were] left holding the baby to the tune of £100,000', two years ago. 'Things are getting better but it has been hard to come back from such a deficit.'

The company has 'just taken over another business [which] is going to give us more organic growth. [It also] gives us the possibility of an exit route'.

Bob, born and living in the North, had gone into business in the first place to get 'financial security… have enough money to fulfil my responsibilities and not have to worry'. His plan has always been to 'ultimately sell the business for capital gain'. The business is now 15 years old 'and right now the value of the business is in' his business partner and himself. Things are tough at the moment, 'for the last six months I've worked 90 per cent of weekends… trying to catch up on the financials'.

Bob is 'not wishing to be heroic. [I've] tried to employ people', to do the work on the financials he's currently clearing up, 'but they haven't delivered. I have to do this myself'. This monumental task is at last paying dividends, 'I feel I am at [or] close to feeling that I'm back in control'. He paused to reflect on what he meant by 'being in control', musing that it has an elusive quality. He concluded that he was 'back in control in terms of vision'. For a long time he's felt like he's been a 'captain of a ship in the fog'. The day-to-day demands of running a small business 'does mean that sometimes you take your eye off the ball'. His attention is on the coalface; 'if the toilet needs unblocking, you do it [and] I feel even worse because I know what I should be doing'. He could excuse himself if he were 'just bumbling through' but he 'feels worse because I feel I should have done better'.

His subconscious is also keeping up the pressure on him. 'I don't really dream very much. [But] there was one day when I did dream… it showed "me" talking to "me"… I was kind of appraising myself'. One Bob was saying to the other Bob, 'You said you'd be a millionaire in ten years, ten years ago. What are you playing at?' The other Bob replied, rather pathetically, 'You're right… but I've been trying really hard.'

'I probably drive myself harder than anyone else… [I'm] my own task master.'

Growing up with responsibility

Bob has 'never not had responsibility'. He was born in 1955 and is the eldest of four brothers. 'My father was a GP and my mother was a nurse, who would do the receptionist role and was therefore tied to the house.'

Bob, being three years older than the others, would take the younger brothers to school three-quarters of a mile away and 'do Saturday errands from the age of six or seven'.

'I've always felt responsibility… never known not having it.' These days he has five daughters ranging in age from twenty-two to ten and 'I have responsibility there'. He lives near his parents who are both in their early eighties. They still live in the old family house, '[There are] problems of safety and [my] mother gets worried about the lack of facilities'. She's asked Bob to help sort out the bathroom as she finds it difficult to get in and out of the bath. 'My father was always into DIY but never really finished anything and will never pay someone to do a job.' His father also hoards things, never throwing anything away – keeping 'newspapers from twenty years ago'. Bob has 'found things I'd thrown away when I was a teenager which he's retrieved from the dustbin'.

When the phone goes, 'I subconsciously think "Is this the call?… An accident?" I know I'd have to sort it out'. He knows his father will 'have left a mess… he's such a nightmare'.

A responsibility magnet

Responsibility is 'not all negative', for Bob, 'there's just a lot of it'. This volume of responsibility may also be a function of his personality. 'I'm often accused by those closest to me of attracting responsibility… [meeting] my own secret need to be wanted. I would strongly deny this, but I am impatient and want to get things done. This is I am sure a reaction to my father who started lots of projects but rarely completed any of them.'

'I accept I attract responsibility.' If he's with 'a group of people sitting around, I'll sit waiting for someone to take a lead'. His patience will run out and he'll find himself saying (in part to himself), 'Okay I'll do it because I want to get something done, moving, under way'. It's not only in these group situations that he puts himself forward.

'If someone asks me to do something, if I think they're worthy, I'll try to make time. This willingness to seek out more responsibility is in part because 'If I just stick with drudgery [life will] become very dull'.

Enjoying responsibility

'At school [I was] not very academic… [I] found academics hard. I went to a grammar school so I must have been quite bright. [But] exams didn't agree with me… I found them tough. I'm much more practically oriented.' He wondered at that stage whether he'd 'possibly been doing the wrong job all my life'.

'I enjoyed the cadet force... I became head of [it]. I was proud of that and also passing my accountancy exams', which he found very tough. He enjoyed being head of the cadet force because 'I didn't think it would happen [as] I wasn't a prefect'. Bob enjoyed the camps, one of which involved 'a yearly four days of arduous training in Wales, [where] you survived on what you could carry'. The sense of endurance and improvement spoke to him, as did 'firing guns and traditional boys stuff'.

'Possibly I should have joined the army. I enjoyed working in teams.' In the cadet force he 'enjoyed getting raw recruits and moulding them'. He got a kick from getting people to do better than they thought they could. He told the story of three groups competing over an assault course. 'I got the dross and my team won.' He inspired them, asking his group 'everybody thinks you lot are going to come last. Are you going to let them beat you?'

'I've always had a fascination with small elite teams working and punching way above their weight... people overcoming difficulties.'

Overcoming difficulties

Bob has had to struggle in many situations when young, particularly in the field of his academic prowess. He tried for medical school but was rejected after interview. 'Probably a good thing in hindsight.' He failed one of his three A levels and after a thorough review of the alternatives had to stay at home for another year to retake Physics at a time when 'I couldn't wait to leave home'.

At university he read Chemistry and got a third class degree. 'I want to tell you I'd pissed away my time on hockey' and other fun activities. 'But I really did work hard.' He taught for three years and ironically wound up 'teaching more physics than chemistry. Then I went into chartered accountancy', passing his final exams after taking them three times 'during the course of being made redundant and the birth of my first daughter'.

Bob 'got divorced in my late thirties [and] I gave everything away. [I] realised that all that crap didn't matter... [I] left the marriage with my tools and clothes'.

The 'positive from this gruesome experience [came when I realised] that all those material things didn't matter. Realising that was a great sense of relief. I had been tested and I wasn't going to be defined by my material possessions. There was an immense feeling of liberation.' This realisation was not instant however. 'It took me five years to get over the divorce.'

Personal freedom

I asked Bob how this perspective on material needs not mattering fitted with his persecutory dream, where he criticised himself for not being a millionaire yet.

He reframed what the material meant to him. It is 'not so much the money [as] a sense of achieving some level of personal freedom'. This freedom has to include 'being able to satisfy and discharge my responsibilities, [so that] no-one who is relying on me is disadvantaged'. Money has a very specific meaning in this context, it 'gives me the freedom not to eat so much of the crap, relax a bit, be more content, achieve something I'm proud of'.

'I feel I've been struggling most of my adult life.' His business, which started with two of them, peaked at 20 people and now has a staff of ten. He remembers that sense of there being a dream when the business started with 'just the two of them in a room with two phones, a pile of money and just buying in and managing the services that were required to fulfil the client contract'. Since that moment 'work has taken over'. There was 'one year we made a reasonable profit… [we] got more staff but profits [were] flat'. The extra hands were simply 'feeding activity'. It is 'very hard to stay on top of this'.

'I'm responsible for the administration side.' The challenge for Bob is 'finding a good assistant', finding the right help has always been 'very, very hard', and continues to be so. By its nature the business is administratively complex with some of the events they organise having a lead time of over a year. The work is 'all about long-term stuff with a huge administrative tale'. Bob finds he doesn't have the time to support people in this task and they frequently go, leaving a 'mess behind'. A mess he is determined to sort out himself now.

A habit of sorting things out

'Even my brothers, if we're together', skiing for instance, 'they'll look to me to order things, speak the local language etc. I would be happy if they'd say "we'll sort it out".' Within his family he can see that 'my eldest daughter exhibits these traits. Being the eldest is very important to her.'

'I've always known I'm the eldest… it's been my earliest cogent memory of having to look after someone else.' Bob is three years older than his next brother and 'three years was a big difference when I was a teenager. When I was 16 or 17 I wanted time on my own. [I didn't] want some little oik ruining things (I could do that on my own!)'

Living in a female environment

Bob had talked of having five daughters. He also observed that of the 12 children he and his brothers had, only two were boys. Bob can now 'understand how my mother must have felt' living in an all-male environment. 'It can be quite lonely at times.' It's not that he feels left out; for Bob, it is a function of being 'very male. [I] like doing traditional male things. I'm into DIY, tools etc. [I] have all the stuff… [it's] an antidote to the crap I put up with.

Gives me the ability to indulge in one of my luxuries... doing a job on my own. The rest of the time I feel like a server [with] energy being drained off from me.'

At home, doing a job on his own means he can get on with doing things his way and at a decent pace. 'I enjoy making and fixing things.'

His girls 'are not girly girls', but they 'like the things girls like... shopping, chatting, make-up etc.' This means Bob can feel lonely, not because of them but there are 'only so many chick flicks I can watch. On a Friday night I need a film with some gratuitous violence.' In terms of fantasy Bob 'would like to be a Clint Eastwood-style character, righting some wrongs in an old-fashioned way. Ridiculous I know but sometimes...'

This sense of being whatever people need him to be plays out at work. 'I'll do everything, sorting out tears etc.' His business partner leaves this sort of thing to him. In addition to picking up this social responsibility, Bob is also there with all the fine print of contracts and paper work. 'When it requires attention to detail, that's my bag. The skills of checking and reviewing the quality of your own work just don't seem to be taught any more.'

Learning not to go with the crowd

'In a group you can get a loudmouth, someone who wants to be the "leader". I'm not that person. I'd be looking at the group and assessing their skills.' Bob would not describe himself as 'naturally a group person'. The importance of 'not going with the crowd was drilled into me, from both my mother and father'.

He recalled a time when he was at the local school. To get to it you had to walk 'down a lane with a church on the opposite side'. One day, one of his group of school friends said, 'let's go in and sign the visitors book'. They went in and one boy wrote, 'Fuck' in the book 'and then we all ran away. I felt really guilty about this... I felt this was fundamentally wrong.'

The next day 'I went back to rub it out or tear the page out'. But Bob was found by the priest and both school and parents were informed. From this, and prompted by the intervention of a wise adult, 'I learnt "don't go with the crowd"'. 'Not going with the crowd' also shows itself in the friends he has. 'I don't really do friends. I have three or four... I'm close to my brothers... they give me male company.'

Hatred of being let down

After a brief pause Bob went on to speak with considerable intensity, inspired by his reflections on friendship and groups. 'One thing I can't stand is being let down. One of my brothers is full of crap sometimes. "I'm going to help you," he'll say... he believes it at the point of utterance, but you know it won't happen. I can't cope with people who'll let me down.' What Bob aspires to in friendship are 'jungle mates. People who I'll trust to watch my back whatever the situation.'

Bob takes his own promises and commitments seriously. 'If I say "yes", I'll be there even if it's subsequently inconvenient.' This dislike of being let down has a number of roots. 'I'd rather not ask for help than be let down. I can deal with a "no" because there's certainty, you know where you stand. But I can't deal with the hope because when help is offered and I really need it, I tend to relax. It's then much harder to raise your energy to do the task when the offer of help is withdrawn, usually at the last minute when the chances of getting a replacement are minimal. I don't trust people very much as in my experience they are often unreliable. And I can't see the point in investing in friendship on a superficial level.'

Bob makes fast judgements about people. 'I sum people up in thirty seconds. I do make mistakes… I can be harsh, but usually my gut is right.' He returned again to the sensation of being let down. 'I hate it… I never want to let others down. I can only operate on a level of full commitment for someone to be a friend.'

The mistakes of others

Bob does not go very far when it comes to letting others make a mistake. 'If it becomes catastrophic, then it hurts me and our company's reputation.' Should he let someone run with their mistake he is 'not even certain they'll learn from the experience. Nobody benefits, the company loses reputation and the staff member will make the same mistake again.'

'Delegation is not a problem', so Bob says. 'But I want the job done to the correct standard. If the work standard is sloppy you have to say "this is not good enough". When something is consistently wrong, you can't let it go to the client. Because it's my company, anything that goes out of the door says something about my standards.'

My reflections on Bob's story

Walking in Bob's shoes is a disturbing experience. The sheer volume of responsibility in every dimension of his life feels quite overwhelming, even before you compound it with his deeply ingrained habits of stepping into the line of fire when something needs taking care of. I caught myself getting quite directive towards him in my head, wanting to serve up platitudinous recipes for building trust and becoming a more effective delegator – but then I'd step back and look at his life in the whole and think that at least he's found a way of keeping it together, although heaven knows at what cost.

If I were thinking of the stereotype of what being the eldest child means, Bob is it. He's the one that his parents turn to first, having been expected to grow up fastest in order to fulfil a role they still need him to fill. This is not a matter of choice or free will; this is the brute reality of the eldest child fitting into the un-chosen structures and rhythms of family and working life. Throughout his life Bob has looked after others; he takes 'taking responsibility' seriously. It's not about grandstanding or drawing attention to himself, it's about ensuring that what needs to happen gets done. Bob as the eldest child is practical and self-reliant, wiping the metaphorical noses of those around him and making sure everyone is properly dressed and fed. Authority in this context is not something you choose; it chooses you. This is being born into authority — not with a silver spoon in your mouth, but a shovel in your hand and a never-ending supply of muck to be shifted.

Bob is not just the eldest son in his family, he is something of a universal eldest son — available to everyone. He has learnt to accept responsibility and that makes him a most desirable companion, both professionally and personally. If you want something sorted, Bob's a man you can turn to — someone who seemingly won't say 'no' if he can see any way at all of making a difference. This comes at considerable personal cost. His energy is a public (and free) resource, not a private one — so I suspect the one person he does not take enough responsibility for is himself. But then I look at his situation and think 'how could it be different?' At his age, with his type of business, with his sort of family — he has responsibilities being thrown at him from every direction. Authority is about accepting the reality of these demands, knuckling down and dealing with them.

Bob is a man doubly alone. Firstly he is at the top of at least two hierarchies, home and work — bucks stop with him. Secondly there is his wariness towards others, a fearsome burden of allegiance that rules out easy friendship — there are high barriers of entry to Bob's world. Authority and aloneness, maybe even loneliness, go together. I got no sense of him having someone he could turn to nor any wish or ability to explore any vulnerability — I can imagine him wincing as he reads that word. I don't think Bob does 'vulnerability'; he's too busy getting on with the business of life for such indulgence. I also get a sense that he has to sit on his hands — that he would prefer to adopt a more robust, masculine form of authority, but he's denied the opportunity to do this because of the types of issues he has to deal with. Sometimes our personal preference may be for exercising authority in one way, but our situation demands that we adopt another.

Bob has learnt to struggle; he does not give up easily and can stick at a task — even if he is not suited to it. He has learnt to accept and work with things he does not find easy, which means he can work with all the challenges that being in a position of authority throw at him. He can cope with whatever life throws at him and I think this gives his authority a distinctive, resilient quality. I can see why people turn to him — they see a man who can cope, come what may, and they feel able to draw on this in order to bolster themselves. He is the ultimate backstop in the lives of people around him because he knows how to deal with (or struggle through) things and carry the burden of responsibility for both well-known and new situations.

Bob's practice of authority is an extension of his identity; it is about his values and standards playing out in the world. It is about being true to your word, honouring your responsibilities, doing what needs to be done. How he exercises his authority is not a technical exercise or learned skill – it is an expression of how he wants to be in the world. This should give him a terrific constancy and well-grounded sense of what the right thing to do is. It should also mean that those around him are not surprised by his behaviour or actions. Consistent authority allows others to have a sense of what is expected of them and what authority can and can't give. It may not be appreciated or wanted, but it is certain.

The shadow of having authority so closely tied into identity comes when it is challenged, misunderstood or unwelcome – these responses will be felt personally by Bob. It is impossible in this setting to separate the professional and the personal. When authority is part of who you are, everything becomes personal.

CHAPTER 17

Marie: Working with authority from a Freudian angle

Marie works in organisations as a behavioural consultant; she has recently qualified as a Freudian-informed psychoanalyst. I spoke to her for a perspective that blended the two – the organisational and the psychoanalytical.

Her first consideration was centred around 'where authority lies'. How much sense do people have of their own authority and how much are people underneath them willing to give? There is 'the person, the systematic pattern within the organisation and how people are using the organisation as a whole'.

Organisations as useful dumping grounds

'Thinking from a psychological/systematic' perspective, there is a need to pay attention to 'how people unconsciously use organisations to manage a sense of wellbeing'. Working from that point of view 'people can often split off those aspects of themselves that cause them discomfort or anxiety and project them onto the organisation, thereby giving away what makes them feel bad and keeping what makes them feel good'.

'In order to create a healthy environment, the organisation then has the task of noticing what has been given to it, making sense of it and ultimately giving it back to the individual in a way that the individual can take responsibility for and work with. The difficulty is that these processes are often not explicit, so for example an individual may complain about a lack of communication, and this may be responded to at an explicit level by improving communication processes. However, what may underlie it may be a feeling of not being valued, or fears about personal competency – the organisation becomes the focus for these anxieties, and people in authority in particular.'

'The challenge for people in positions of authority is how they are able to accept and make sense of these projections, and ultimately give them back in digestible form. In some organisations anxiety gets magnified and not contained by people in authority, and when anxiety is not contained people feel exposed, isolated and on show.'

When organisations are not experienced as a container, then Bion talks of 'how leaders get set up in certain ways… when groups become dysfunctional they put the leader into a particular role'.

Leader as god

'The one I'm fascinated by' is informed by Freud's thinking around 'what having a god does' for people. This translates into Bion's notion of the basic assumption of dependency. 'You put everything onto the leader… the leader is your saviour [and] all your hope rests on [them].' This positioning of the leader/authority figure 'takes away responsibility and a sense of agency from people in the group and gives it to the leader'. The upshot of which is that 'the group has bonded cohesively together', although at the cost of its individual members being able to act as adults.

'If I look at BigCo over the last year, the organisation has not been robust.' Marie has been working as a consultant for BigCo for nearly a year as it went through a complex and protracted takeover. She has been working closely with K, a senior man at BigCo. With her psychoanalytic hat on she can see that during this time he had been having the saviour role thrust upon him by the wider organisation and 'he took on godlike characteristics'. The consequences for him were that, on the upside, he was 'enabled to lead the organisation'. On the 'downside, he put aside his own needs in making a number of decisions. [It] cost him his own sense of agency. At one level he felt all-powerful but only as part of a group... as an individual he felt disempowered.'

An industry of naughty schoolboys

With the hiatus of the merger behind him and with a new role, 'he's now avoiding what he really wants and avoids thinking about his own emotional needs'. But then, he is in a very macho industry where people 'don't talk about emotions'. What they do talk about are 'bonuses and money. Otherwise they become like naughty schoolboys.' Marie the woman 'they treat like mother, telling naughtier and naughtier jokes to see when I'll react'. This provides some relief from the uncertainties of their situation, 'but it is not grown-up relief'. It is more akin to 'hysterical laughter'.

K is not a typical senior player in his industry; he is a man with a lot of integrity in an industry that is much more concerned with the next big thing. He explains his decision to take on his new role in the merged organisation as a matter of integrity; Marie 'thinks it's about power. He still has power but much less than he did... and what does that mean for him?'

Currently 'he's searching for a way of feeling powerful', a situation that wouldn't 'happen to an egomaniac'. The 'Basic Assumption Dependency' that Bion describes and K played out, 'can go to your head'. In her role as a behavioural consultant Marie would record many of his speeches and the only way she could describe the relationship between the audience and K was one of love. He has been adulated by the mass and it has turned his head – and I cannot see how it would not turn the head of nearly any person.

Learning to thrive again

I wanted to know how Marie saw this man being able to thrive again. Currently 'he's disillusioned [and] doesn't see that he can contain anyone, let alone himself'. He's engaging in behaviours and actions that I would interpret as signs that he has yet to learn how to thrive again, and simply wants to recreate that wonderful – but self-denying – world of before.

Marie's prescription for his thriving starts with him 'understanding why he took the role he did in the merged organisation'. He will say 'he was pressured by others to take the job and keep giving hope'. Marie thinks he took it because he 'needed to be worshipped – [and it's] not healthy for a human being to want to be worshipped'.

Currently Marie feels like one of the advisors who surround President Bartlett in *The West Wing* TV series. She is one of a small number of mothers to him who 'alternate between feeling like mum, picking up his socks, making his tea etc. so he can go out and be this fabulous chap OR we feel like his corporate wives, who do all the picking up after him and get given the odd showering of gifts' as a thank you.

It's not just the women – 'all the people operate around him like this. His old COO said 'I just want to be with K' and moved with him into the new organisation.'

When we met to work on the first draft of this story, Marie wanted to delete the two paragraphs above, describing their observations as 'naff'. I reassured her that this role of 'corporate wife' is well documented (see Huff 1990) and suggested she was mirroring the habits of the industry she's currently working in – denying those aspects of herself that don't 'make it look like I'm a powerful woman, full of authority'.

Fear of the non-rational

'By being godlike, K keeps a distance from his people and he has been given a huge emotional power'. I wonder if this is in part about the avoidance of intimacy that means he not only keeps his distance from others – and so can function more easily as a god – but also allows him not to 'acknowledge his own needs'.

'This man generates love… [he's] a magnet'. As Marie reflected on his personality and his atypical industry behaviours she came to the conclusion that his identity is wrapped up in 'being different in the organisation', and that while he's 'not addicted to the job, he's addicted to the emotional power that comes with the job'.

J's story – a robust male

Some years ago Marie worked with the CEO of an offshore distribution company. He was a big fish in a small pond. His story was very different to K's. 'He was loved and adored by everyone in the business but retained a sense of self.' His way of being with people was as a very traditional male. 'He'd go outside with the smokers (he didn't smoke), chat and slap people on the back. He knew everyone and their families.' He was a traditional, hearty male. Compared to K he 'felt more real and kept his boundaries. [This was] safer for him and for his workforce.'

The company was heavily unionised and there was 'lots of conflict. People in the organisation were very able to express vociferously how pissed off they were. He could take it and work with it. It was okay to be pissed off.' At BigCo being pissed off was not okay.

J was, in Freudian terms, a man with a well-developed ego. One that was 'able to face and deal with reality'. This contrasted with K who was being consumed by an id of love and passion and a superego that said he must look after his followers – this left very little room for an ego to deal with the reality in the middle of the id and the superego. 'Yet to listen to him you'd think his ego was very strong.'

Knowing reality well

A conclusion to come to is that in order to exercise authority well, in the sense of meeting the needs of the self and the organisation in which that authority is being exercised, a person in a position of authority needs to be well connected to the reality of what is actually going on within them and around them.

What stops people knowing reality well are two very personal and basic fears: 'The fear of being invaded and the fear of being abandoned. Relationships are either too distant or too intrusive and overwhelming.' The challenge for any human being is how, in the midst of these basic fears, to retain a sense of personal separateness.

'The only way people can deal with reality [is] if they can separate out their own needs and what's driving them from the business or primary task of the organisation.' In Marie's opinion, if you fail to make this separation then 'I don't think you can make choices. The organisation invades you and your relationship with the organisation becomes all consuming because you're afraid of losing it.'

At the other extreme it is possible for an organisation to exist solely in the service of personal need. There was 'a woman I used to work for… she headed up an organisation that was all about her. So she couldn't bear anyone leaving the organisation.' The act of anyone leaving was 'traumatic'. 'When someone left after working closely for her for ten years she called him into her office and screamed at him and told him to get out.'

'The organisation was founded on the belief that the organisation was fantastic.' S – the founder – had to know about your family and your life. 'Clients who left were phoned up and cried at. It was the most paranoid and stifling organisation I've been in. Nothing could be wrong with the organisation or with S. When I left she sent lots of abusive emails at five a.m. on the Saturday morning. She couldn't face the reality of an organisation where people come and go and have their own agendas. She was very narcissistic and couldn't bear anyone to be different to her.'

Narcissism

'Narcissism must feature so hugely in leadership. You say you want people to get on and do things, take accountability, but do you?' From a narcissistic perspective 'you want them to be doing what you're doing'.

'S was a very split woman. It was either very good or evil. You were evil or ideal. There was no middle ground, no depressive reality. Yet to meet her she'd be charming.'

This story highlights the difference between being self-obsessed and true to yourself. This difference came to Marie when she recently 'went to a Jungian lecture on individuation'. The question she had was 'so you individuate and what does that do for you?' The answer she heard was that the individuated person knows that 'whenever they say something, do something or make a decision they know they're being true to themselves'. It is based around a 'sense of being so centred that you can integrate the needs of an organisation, others and yourself'. It is no longer a matter of 'me versus the organisation', it becomes about 'me in the organisation and the organisation in me'.

'Ultimately [it's about] your own ability to contain and make sense of the anxieties in you and around you', although this must be difficult when 'you've got thousands of people projecting anxiety onto you [as in K's case]. Just to bounce it back is not leadership.' The responsibility of leadership is 'to assist in the sense making... show people reality'.

Having reached a seemingly neat end point, Marie raised a question whose answer I don't know, but whose implications seem enormous. 'How much do we envy those in authority?'

Reflections and conclusions

We met again some weeks after our initial meeting to revise the story so far and for Marie to speak to her conclusions as an expert — a term I used that sat uncomfortably with her. Her conclusions spoke to the following themes:

- Love and identity
- Masculine authority and the fear of intimacy
- Holding the tension between personal and organisational needs
- Don't be fooled by conscious models of change
- Envy, love, authority and aggression
- Projection is a two way street

Love and identity

Marie's reflections started with the question of 'what is any particular organisation doing for an individual in a position of authority?' Or, in other words, what is it that people are getting out of a particular experience — because people are always getting something out of a situation, whether consciously or unconsciously.

'Authority brings [in certain settings] adoration and love', but this can 'come at the expense of your own sense of self'. This means that the loved sense of self that the organisation provides for the authority figure is actually a false one – in the sense that it is an externally rather than internally generated identity, one with insufficient ego.

'If this "false" self develops' unchecked then the need for that organisationally mandated and provided adoration can 'become too much and the individual in authority will merge with the organisation'. They become addicted to this 'false' love – as contrasted with a true love developed out of mutually felt and owned emotions. For those who otherwise do not have sufficient love in their lives, this organisational love is a useful pain relief for that lack. 'Like a paracetemol after a hangover it keeps you ticking over', but it doesn't address the root of the problem.

On further reflection Marie moved on from the comforting conclusion of that simile and began to think in terms of what need this 'false' love meets and what makes it attractive. 'If you can get love in a falsely safe way, you don't need to get close to people.'

Masculine authority and the fear of intimacy

This attraction of the 'false' love that organisations offer could be about a 'fear of intimacy. [People] want love but fear intimacy because with intimacy comes the potential for loss.' If a person gets close to another person then there is a cost when that closeness ends.

This intimacy issue may well be bound up with gender. 'I know it's a patriarchal society… is there a gender issue playing out' in terms of how men in authority 'search out for intimacy?' The intimacy that can be experienced between an organisation and a person in authority can be described in terms of a one-night stand; it is an intimacy of a very contained nature that does not touch the person in authority too deeply. It is intimacy of short duration and no significant attachment, and so any loss felt is marginal or irrelevant.

This analysis does not, however, fit well with Marie's experience of K's authority. For K, the organisation seemed to be a safe way for him to be a powerful father. 'Many of the men I know who are in power have children, but don't spend much time with them… organisations become surrogate children for them. Secretaries [and the wider support network] create an entire family experience, but one that is safe because people don't ask too much.'

Authority can, in conclusion, provide people with what is perceived as a safe experience of intimacy that won't touch them too deeply and awaken denied longings for love.

Holding the tension between personal and organisational needs

A person in a position of authority needs to 'pay attention to their own needs in equal weight to the needs of the organisation'. This attention comes from being 'cognizant of this tension and understanding why you're doing what you're doing;' the importance of this being 'if you're not paying attention and containing your own needs, how can you contain and pay attention to the needs of others?'

If the personal and organisational are not kept separate, they become one – a fusion that can play out in two ways. Firstly in the form of narcissism, when the organisation is no more than an extension of the self and its needs. Secondly, when there is insufficient attention to the self, 'you merge yourself and become open to the unconscious processes that drive a lot of organisational activity. You become open to the id, the instincts, the aggression and so on of the organisation. You're not maintaining boundaries and making sense of what is going on.'

'The reflective habit to be encouraged in people in authority is the continuous asking of two questions. Firstly, how are you using this organisation? And secondly, how is this organisation using you?'

Don't be fooled by conscious models of change

In the story of K, 'the really interesting thing is the shift from being powerful to being taken over. [There's] lots of discussion about what it feels like to be in an organisation that is being taken over.' Talking from her position as an experienced behavioural consultant Marie said 'our response is to come up with the Kubler Ross change curve [based on grieving] and turn it into a tool. All you need to do is understand the change curve and it'll all be fine.'

'This approach is deeply disturbing and doesn't pay attention to the places [mergers] take people to emotionally. Most organisations can't talk about this.'

This presents a challenge to the practice of authority, if part of the role of people in authority is to help with the personal and collective sense making. How can these difficult and often quite basic emotions be acknowledged, and worked with, rather than buried or denied so that they seep or surge out in unexpected and even more destructive ways?

Envy, love, authority and aggression

'Envy is a destructive emotion. We want to destroy, murder what we envy. If you are filled with envy then you will want to attack something.'

People in authority, 'who may want authority to get power and love from or over others', may be setting up a situation in which they unconsciously want to be attacked. They inspire envy in others and so they will set up a situation in which aggression becomes the dominant form of interaction. In our workplace culture aggression is an acceptable form of interaction, whereas love and intimacy are not.

Again the responsibility for those in authority is to pay attention to this reality and work with it.

Projection is a two way street

'People so easily give up their hopes and pin them on someone else – what a burden that must be. Why do we do that? Give up our own authority and agency, is it too much for us to bear? We want someone else to be responsible so we don't have to deal with the bad, or things gone wrong. We're so afraid of it we give the good things about ourselves to others, so we don't have to deal with the bad things. It is difficult to bear the depressive position, the one that is grounded in the reality of life – the good and the bad – so we split, sometimes giving up the good and sometimes the bad to people in authority. And being in groups or organisations enables us to do this. This puts a huge responsibility on leaders to reconnect what has been split for employees; it is also a huge parental role. And maybe this is what people in organisational authority do not want – they come to work to escape the children, or at least children who have unbounded needs and an inescapable demand for intimacy.'

A short story about gods, elders and liberating mothers

These are stories of individuals taking on authority in difficult circumstances. With Bob and Lesley there is the lifelong commitment to responsibility, starting with the family and then spilling into the organisational. They have different ways of executing this responsibility: one looks to get others to step-up while the other is more willing to step-in. In Marie's story there is K, absorbing the tensions and pressures of thousands, living through a brutal merger as an emblem of hope. There are no smooth rides in these stories and few moments of reprieve; I am left with a sense of 'one bloody thing after another'. There is a romantic notion of authority as decisive decision making; I remember reading about Tito in Fitzroy Maclean's book *Eastern Approaches*, where Tito's name is approvingly explained – he was a man who told people to 'do this' and 'do that' and that is how the name Tito evolved.

In the three stories, decision making is much less romantically decisive; it's about the long haul, keeping oneself sane and in touch with reality (or not, as the case may be).

I want to reflect on three themes that are inspired by these stories:

- Getting put into roles
- Making your own life
- Fantasy and reality

Getting put into roles

K is obviously the most extreme; a man who had joined the deity and acquired enough followers to found his own cult (quite what his tax-exemption status would be in the US I'm not sure). In the story as Marie tells it, the unconscious forces of the group are in full play. With Lesley and Bob things are a little more nuanced; they are both fully aware of their family history and their willingness to pick up responsibility. I wonder if they are actually both trapped into these habits – or rather, I wonder what it would take for them to give up these habits. They talk knowingly of their situation, whereas K seems blind to his, and (however uncomfortable) accept that this is the disposition they must work with. For either of them to seek to lose their orientation to picking up authority would seem perverse; it is what fate has given them, their choice is to find a way of picking up authority in a way that works for them – the choice of not picking up authority doesn't really seem to be there.

Because of circumstance of birth and history, certain roles are demanded of us all – we are all a daughter or son and many of us are brothers, sisters, mothers or fathers. To deny roles is to become enthralled in them; if I bury my head, it doesn't make the reality leave. In organisational settings people in authority live in a sea of invited and uninvited roles, some conscious and some unconscious. The challenge for a person in authority is to be able to work with this reality; sometimes rejecting invitations, sometimes accepting – nearly always negotiating to ensure that the role works well for themselves and the wider group.

Making your own life

However tortured and ensnared (and that's not how he says it feels), Bob is trying to make his life in authority work. He has his ambitions, his responsibilities and his code of conduct; he is in the process of keeping his show on the road. Lesley has consistently made significant changes to her life in response to her sense of ambition or disquiet. Their lives may be informed by their connections with others, but they are not lived at the behest of them. J is also a man who has found his robust, comfortably masculine modus vivendi and wears it well. It is with K that I get my most serious sense of a man living out the needs of others – Christ-like, he is both the powerful god and the one who must be sacrificed (in the sense of giving up his own needs).

I am drawn to Marie's observations about the nature of individuation, that the woman or man who is individuated is one who is always able to act out of a sense of personal truth: 'I act this way because to do otherwise would be a betrayal of myself.' This is not a hymn to sainthood, but a celebration of human uniqueness and its expression. This is the wellspring of the multiple nature of authority; a mature, self-aware and self-guided authority is one that expresses that unique individual – an un-individuated authority is one that is often an expression of unmet historical needs or unconscious group dynamics.

Fantasy and reality

Fantasies are powerful forces; that's why you find middle-aged men paying to wear giant nappies and so much of our culture is populated by fantastic beings, from Superman to Mother Theresa. Bob acknowledges his fantasy in the form of a hankering after a Clint Eastwood-type character, from those films when all it took was a man with a gun to keep the show on the road and cut through the crap to see off the evil doers. Bob can see his fantasy, but he knows his reality. He's the one who has to keep the show on the road, the drains working and the customers happy. His fantasy hero is in reality much closer to George Binney et al.'s work on the dramas of ordinary heroes (see 'Leaders in transition – the dramas of ordinary heroes', Ashridge Report, 2004). The fantasy is that authority can exist out of context and the mess of now; the reality is, it can't. Our love of tidy stories can erode this simple truth – as is seen in the litany of management and self-help books with their little sayings and easy to follow steps to success: these are damaging fantasies because they don't help people connect with now.

In K I can see not only a product of Bion's basic assumption dependency, but possibly a person who takes writings about tough and heroic leadership too much to heart. Part of what I hope this book can help bring about is a much more realistic attitude to authority – one that is not consumed by positive or negative fantasies, but is informed by a sober understanding of what function authority can healthily play in our lives.

Lesley presents a compelling face of sober authority; one that doesn't support people in their fantasies of handing responsibility for their lives over to those in authority. Lesley's authority is about supporting others in authoring their own lives, not in creating some relational fantasy where she is the mother to all.

section five

Taking care of the self and others

Chapter 19
Eve: Authority without a title   147

Chapter 20
Lucy: Connected authority   155

Chapter 21
Diana: Authority as authoring   163

Chapter 22
A short story about taking care of the self and others   171

CHAPTER 19

Eve: Authority without a title

Until four years ago Eve was the legal director at a well-known regulatory body. The title meant a lot to her because it 'defined my authority'. Now her own name denotes her authority as she has moved on to a pluralistic career where she has become one of 'the great and the good' in the British establishment.

This experience of stepping into her own authority was stimulated by defeat; she worked closely with the chief executive of this regulatory body, a man she experienced as 'a guy with a huge ego… charming but utterly single-minded'. Unable to get him to temper his ways she decided she had to let go of the comfort of a title and go self-employed; she also had the hard task of admitting defeat in her dealings with the gentleman in question.

Seeds of change

A few years ago, before this defeat, Eve had gone to a reunion of her primary school in New York where she made two discoveries. Firstly the most popular girl in the class talked with her and remembered 'wanting to be like me'. Secondly she found out something about the school. 'I'd always known the school was considered to be the best state primary… classes were streamed… and I was top in the top stream.' But there was more to it than that. 'Actually I was in a programme for intellectually gifted children.' This had been a complete secret to her and finding out about it made a big difference.

Prior to this school reunion Eve had participated in a workshop I was running, where Paul Robertson, a renowned musician and thinker about the relationship between music and the mind, joined us. Paul had made a comment when talking about his own gift (or talent) that had stayed with Eve. 'If you have a gift it's not a gift if you don't give it.'

Eve recalls telling herself on her return from New York, 'Eve you've been a lazy bugger. I have a brain, I really ought to use it and feel comfortable using it.' Up until this moment 'I'd held back… I'd been ambitious but scared of achieving. Somehow realising that as a child I'd been identified as having all this potential gave me the freedom to feel comfortable with my brain's ability and to use it.'

Lots of things changed as a result, including the end of her marriage. Her level of comfort at work changed and she began to work to a wider canvas 'feeling I do have the ability to make a difference and effect change' through a combination of brain power and the fact people tended to like her ('And I like being liked').

That wider canvas

The scope of her current authority is impressive and includes being the wise counsel for a director of a high-profile media company. The director is a very private person who is poor at giving her attention to her team or revealing her feelings. At times Eve has become 'the mother to the team', seemingly the only one who can get both the intellectual and emotional attention of the director. While she does not see herself as a maternal mother to the team, she does enjoy 'seeing people work well together, being as good as they can be'.

Outside of this nitty-gritty of being an advisor to an organisation she sits on three public commissions, all highly visible, as well as carrying out a range of international media-related consulting. Her work encompasses not only the commercial aspects of the media, but also the complex arenas of policy and regulation that involve Westminster, Strasbourg and beyond.

When she describes her behaviours on these various commissions she comes across as a very skilled operator, being able to fit in and also hold to contentious or minority views. Throughout her life, certainly since primary school, if she felt strongly about something 'I was persuasive at getting people to do what I wanted to do'. She also has 'no recollection of… being in a group and being forced to do something I didn't want to do'.

Her authority comes in part then from this ability to belong to a group and be an individual voice in a group, a form of 'connected authority'. In the stories she told of joining one of the more rumbustious and macho commissions, the other thing that stood out for me was that she really knew her stuff. Her willingness to pursue a particular argument was informed by rigorous understanding of the issues involved. So her 'connected authority' is combined with her 'expert authority'.

Family demographics

It took a long time for Eve to step into 'authority without a title'. I asked about her family background to see how that might have held her back as well as giving her attributes that were now flourishing.

'Both my parents have international backgrounds. My father is German Jewish and a hero.' At the age of 17 he got both his parents out of detention camps and away into Spain. From there he got them first to Cuba and then into the USA. He is now a 'very successful businessman living in Japan'. Eve's mother was born in the USA to a Russian Jewish mother and a Northern Irish Protestant father. Eve was born in Japan.

Her parents split when she was three and she went to live in the US with her mother. She was glad she didn't have to live with her father, much as she was also glad she hadn't been a boy. She feels that there would have simply been too much expectation on her. She has one brother, eighteen months older than her, who is learning disabled.

Much as she feels relieved to have escaped paternal expectations, maternal relations were more than difficult. 'My mother is extremely difficult… she's a deeply bitter, unhappy and frustrated woman. Very unloving; an archetypal old fashioned headmistress', forever arching a questioning or disapproving eyebrow.

In terms of Eve's 'authority without a title' years, 'the big thing that ties in… I was never good enough for my mother. I'd come home with a straight A report card and she'd ask me why not A+? I'd tell her they don't give an A+ grade. I only expect A+', was the ending response.

There soon came a time when Eve gave up trying to use her brain. She had a major academic achievement when she came top in a noteworthy public exam when transferring to secondary school in New York. Her mother reacted to the news with a very understated 'oh, well done', and Eve decided she could either work very hard to be at the top, or coast along and be in the top quartile. 'I stopped working at 12.' It was only ten years ago that she started trying to use her brain again.

As an adult she had a slightly drunken conversation with her mother. Eve said, 'I felt you expected me to make up for my brother. I felt I'd never be good enough.' 'You were right,' her mother replied.

Light in the dark

In the context of the relationship with her mother, Eve learnt how to be rebellious and found the steel not to be afraid to say what she thinks – a quality that serves her well in her work on the various commissions, especially when combined with a sophisticated sense of what it takes for a minority or dissenting voice to be heard. Her home life taught her how to stand-up for herself as well as accept responsibility. While growing-up she always felt very responsible for her brother, always looking out for him, seeing that he was happy and including him in what was going on. These days he's in a home and Eve is his guardian.

In addition to these attributes of self-assertion and caring for others, Eve is also fired by a burning sense of justice – for her authority must be a 'just authority'. She did not experience her mother as practising a 'just authority'; she was deeply inconsistent in her parenting and would 'lose it a lot… beating me with a belt and a belt buckle'. Eve has vivid memories of sitting in her room 'crying at the injustice' of her treatment. She remembers vowing never to be like this and much as it has taken many years for her to deal with the experience of not being good enough, she has always had a burning desire to promote justice. This may well explain why her professional qualifications and roots are in law.

Being taken seriously

Her international work 'is fun and good for the soul'. Much of this work involves her visiting or reporting back to Strasbourg. Her name badge when she visits the monumental European offices there reads 'Eve X, Expert'. She really enjoys being an expert; it gives her a sense of validation and she treats it as a big responsibility. She has a sense that 'what I will say will be taken seriously'. At last in her life Eve is able to experience her authority as being good enough to be taken seriously because she can feel herself to be good enough to be taken seriously. Not in some narcissistic, self-serving way, but in the service of something important in the world – in this case the freedom of speech in Europe.

Her authority is, of course, meeting needs within her but it is also in the service of something outside of her. I see her authority as self-expression connected to the needs of others. It is not a self-referencing, or solipsistic, form of authority.

Not needing a title

Eve has just finished working on the review of a major government agency with three others. As they came to the point of finalising their report the person doing the drafting needed to name and title the authors of the review. The other three reviewers were all well-titled chief executives or of similar ilk. 'What should I put for Eve?' asked the drafter. 'Leave it as Eve,' replied the other reviewers, 'her name speaks for itself'. After two weeks of working together 'they didn't feel I needed a title. That feels good. I'm seen as being good.'

Reflections on Eve and authority

Eve's authority bleeds history. She can see how her authority has evolved as both a positive and negative reaction to her upbringing. The need for justice in response to the arbitrary behaviours of her mother; the need to nurture and include others as she learnt with her brother; the consequences of ignoring or taking seriously one's gifts; the need to be taken seriously and seen as good enough. Her authority is shot through with sensitivity to the relational context within which she finds herself; but this relational context is not about Eve disappearing herself, but about how she can be a powerful and visible presence within a relationally informed setting.

Until four years ago Eve's authority rested upon whatever title she had. I suspect this limited her. She has now grounded her sense of authority within herself; it is an expression of her own personality and history – which includes her professional competence as well as maternal scars. Authority has both professional and personal qualities. It is both something about the individual and something about the wider world in which that individual operates and grew up.

Eve described herself to me as 'a regulatory anorak'. She knows about regulation and she invests a lot of her life in it. She has not simply happened upon the strands of work that make up her portfolio career. She emphasises the social dimensions of her work with the media company director, but her contribution also includes much hard-headed understanding of the commercial and regulatory reality of the media. It may be an historic need to be recognised as 'good enough' that in part drives Eve, but it also ensures that there is rigour and intelligence behind her contributions to the work of others. Her authority arrives with content, not just with some claimed right to influence.

Eve has a strong sense of self and a more strongly expressed ego than when I first met her six or seven years ago. Yet the potential for arrogance or self-love that can sometimes come with this were not qualities I experienced when I was with her. When Eve talks about her work and her authority, the other is always present. She does not stride through the regulatory world as some isolated heroine or warrior, but as a very adept connector. She can see herself, she can see others and how she and others need to connect to work well together.

On the commissions on which she sits are many people of strong beliefs and opinions, who are used to getting their own way. There have been times when she has had to accept that she will not sway the majority, even if events have turned out to prove her position correct. Authority is about judgement, holding on to what you believe to be true and working with the reality of what can be accepted or achieved within the context of a specific group addressing a particular situation.

Eve seems to have found a way of being able to express unpopular views, without becoming a scapegoat of the group or the irritating (and discounted) lone voice. To express the minority view requires skill if it is to be heard by others. Authority and social expertise go together in Eve as much as authority and technical expertise.

Eve's authority exists for a purpose and not as an end in itself; in particular her authority is about 'doing the right thing'. This right thing may be about enabling the media company director to hear the opinions of her team so she can make good decisions or it may be about supporting the development of better approaches to regulation or the promotion of free speech in Eastern Europe. I have more often than not seen authority through the lens of power; I find seeing authority as an expression of justice a most compelling alternative.

Eve's reaction to this story

'It is a bizarre experience to spend an hour chatting about one's life and find it accurately translated onto a few pages. I recognise myself, but feel uncomfortable with the portrayal of someone who appears strong. Still, after so many years of success, I struggle to step fully into my power. I have a deep sense of being able to effect change in the world around me, to be able to do good; to make a real difference. But the challenge is to embrace my authority fully without overstepping into hubris.'

A further round of reflection

We met in a café in Victoria to reflect further. When I asked her about her response to the story, she said she 'felt pretty good' about herself. We then moved onto her further reflections about her relationship to authority.

'A lot of my success in exercising authority is linked to the fact people like me, that I'm a nice person.' Eve seeks to make her work relationships personal, although not in the sense of becoming friends, but as in 'pleasant and nice'.

'A really important thing when dealing with people who I don't think are nice... is to really try not to fall out with [them]. [You] never know when you'll see people again or in what context.'

'I find it wrong when I see people exert their authority by being rude, looking down on people... making people feel bad about themselves. I disapprove of this so make a big effort not to do this.'

A few years ago Eve was having a lot of difficulties with her peers, in particular 'there was an engineer... [he was] very technical and he couldn't communicate. No-one understood him so he became diffident.' Following on from a workshop of mine that she'd attended, Eve 'tried a different tack. When I had something of his to review, I praised the bits I understood. Over a few months he changed completely. I was not blaming him for my lack of understanding. [I'd] get him to talk things through until I understood them.' Up until this time 'we'd all been stuck', dreading 'another paper from P'.

Eve was able to see P's experience through his eyes. 'What he was saying wasn't being heard and no-one was taking the trouble to help him.'

She had a similar experience when working on a major project recently. Eve had 'to corral many people to write their bits'. There was 'one guy who was responsible for a major piece of work. He was a real high flyer but I couldn't get anything from him. He never delivered. Then I realised that he couldn't write... beyond a few bullet points. It wouldn't do me any favours to "blow his cover", so I sat down with him and I wrote it and he checked it.'

Prior to this realisation and resolution, Eve had tied herself up in knots wondering why he was not delivering. 'As I was getting more frustrated I thought he was undermining my authority.' An opinion that was fuelled as he started avoiding Eve and Eve began missing deadlines. 'Then I realised he wasn't [undermining my authority]. Yes he was avoiding me, but it was about him not me.'

'We can think other people's reactions are something to do with us... [we can be] very solipsistic. We have to remember, it might be them.'

What enabled Eve to change?

When she was at this workshop of mine, something clicked for Eve. She was able to see that 'when she was stuck' she should 'step back and try something different. At the time I was going through a tricky time in my personal life...

[I'd] fallen in love with someone while still married. [I] had to look at myself differently.'

Unsurprisingly old habits don't completely disappear and Eve is 'sometimes slow to remember that when hitting your head against a brick wall, step back'. The 'brick wall is because my expectations of what I want from someone are unrealistic… and I have to think of a new way to achieve [my required] outcome'.

The ability to recognise the reality of the other

Having grown up with responsibility for her brother Eve 'always had the ability to recognise what's going on with others'. When she was young she was not only sensitive to this, she also found herself taking responsibility for the experience of others. At university 'all the waifs and strays came to my shoulder. I had some draw [to these people] but I didn't want it in my everyday life. So I became a Samaritan at 20 – the youngest in my university town… [I] felt like I was doing good, using skills I had, without it becoming my [whole] life. [I] did my shifts and that meant I felt good about then drawing boundaries around myself.'

While this boundary drawing is something she has learnt to do, it 'is something I could improve on'.

Eve's final reflections on what makes for good authority

Eve summed it up as doing 'all this relational business… understanding where you are in relation to the other [and] bringing the other with you in that relational context. Not in the [sense of] forcing people to come with my vision… where possible [seeking] to develop consciousness.'

There are other times that you have to 'recognise that someone has the authority and you have to go with it… [this] can be painless if there is an understanding of where the other is in the process and being explicit about that'.

'When I've been with a boss who wants me to do something I think is wrong [I'll say] I disagree with you but I'll do it. The boss says "But I want you to think it's the right thing." My response is, "No. You're the boss. I'll do it – even though I think it's not right."'

CHAPTER 20

Lucy: Connected authority

Lucy works in a management role in the language department of a university, which includes significant commercial activity. In her division she is one of five directors who report directly to the CEO. She has direct managerial responsibility for 35 to 40 staff and within the organisation is 'perceived as having a lot of authority'. This authority stems, in part, from responsibilities 'for relationships which provide a huge percentage of the business activity'.

'Our organisation is not very hierarchical… [it is] flat in terms of how people talk to each other.' She sees her authority as a 'force for good', in that she uses it to 'empower others'. While much of the decision making is quite centralised, 'in many ways our organisation is particularly good in delegating authority'.

First memory of authority

Lucy's parents were 'very benign' and the first memory Lucy spoke to was of a 'mini backlash against authority at the age of five'. She 'comes from a very normal family, very average… [one that] has huge respect for people in authority. Police, doctors [and so on] were a 'force for good'. Her parents were people who accepted things and when she was growing up they would 'never complain in a restaurant. Although they would now.'

When she was five Lucy was shocked 'to find someone who wasn't a force for good… a cruel teacher. She was physically very intimidating, middle-aged and married to the local vicar.' Lucy recalled her as a complete disciplinarian who 'forced me to sit and eat prunes and cold custard over a couple of hours', until the dish was finished 'despite me crying'.

'I wasn't hit by her… she would show her anger verbally. Very unpleasant. She scared me into learning.' In particular Lucy recalled the ruler that she used to intimidate the class by 'whacking [it] on a desk'.

Power and authority

'I don't know the distinction between power and authority… I began to feel power as I realised I was quite bright and it gave me an advantage.' This intelligence meant she was able to go to the local grammar school where she became head girl, a position that was voted for 'by the staff and sixth formers'. Lucy recalled 'quite enjoying this power thing… enjoying the whole role, representing the school, making speeches. [It was a] very pleasant taste of being in authority.'

She believes that people voted for her because 'I wasn't very threatening… [and I was] liked and fun to be around'. She was also sporty, which had cachet in the school, as well as being reasonably bright. 'I wasn't bossy (as I've become). I was sufficiently tentative and collaborative not to alienate anybody.' From the teacher's point of view she ticked the good pupil boxes: 'I did my homework, did stuff for the school and was not likely to bring it into disrepute.'

There was an interesting wrinkle to her appointment. The school she was at was a convent and 'I was the first non-Catholic head girl they'd had.' On reflection she sees that it was 'unusual for the sisters to vote' for a non-Catholic. At the time it was 'not made a big thing of... [although] some Catholic parents questioned' her appointment.

Setting up a women's co-operative

On 'leaving university I went to teach English in Spain for a year. At the end of that year I met some young women and we decided to set up our own school.' So at around the age of 21 or 22 Lucy helped set up 'a women's co-operative'.

There was one 'woman [Bev] I looked up to (now my best friend)' and she had a 'magnetic' quality to her. She was 25 and the moving force behind this new school. She approached Lucy and 'said "I'm thinking of setting up a school, would you like to be in on it?"' In all there were five of them and they each put up £500.

'It was a completely flat structure and we all moved jobs each month. [There was] no overt authority', although 'there were two clear leaders – me and my friend' – who Lucy describes as being 'the lead lead'. As a system it worked fine in the first year and it stayed fine 'until we started making money'. She recalls that first year as being a time when they 'all pulled together... eating cheap cuts of meat'.

A pecking order did exist, or emerged. 'It was not as if Bev and myself conspired together... we probably did that tacitly. Somehow a form of respect and pecking order had emerged which meant people deferred. Bev and I concurred [then] Bev carried the others [with us].'

'Bev was able to be more confrontational... she has a very strong sense of "what is right" and can be very persuasive. The force of her personality could sweep objections aside. [With] me backing her up it made it hard to resist.'

'As [we became] more successful we divided more, argued more and spilt two and two with one floating person. People began to think about ways of not being involved [with the co-operative]. We'd all committed to two years and towards the end of the second year people began to look elsewhere. Bev became a sleeping partner and I went off to China for a year.'

'After about five or six years Bev and I sold out to the remaining three [and the] school then ran for another 15 to 20 years.'

Reflections from this time

'What made me feel uncomfortable [was] elements of ganging up once [we were] successful. Two against three was not very pleasant, especially for those who were ganged up on.' Then there was the experience of 'working with friends (we socialised together) in a small and insular town. Three of us lived together', so they were together 'full on, for 24 hours a day'. It was impossible 'to separate work and what else you were thinking of that person'. Despite the frictions that arose the group are still loosely in contact, Lucy is directly in contact with two and hears of the other two. 'The network is still in place.'

'The decisions we made were very intuitive rather than reasoned... [we] didn't have the experience' to draw on. But 'we got it right a lot of the time'. They'd make decisions about whether to proceed or not without the necessary regulatory clearance with 'no real analysis. We knew no better.' Lucy doesn't regret this way of working, but 'she'd do it differently' now – take a more 'strategic view'.

Working with a sense of freedom and security

I asked Lucy where she got the courage to dive into this entrepreneurial venture. She talked of the influence of her childhood; she was 'an only child of very benign, non-authoritarian parents... [who] were very supportive'. She also 'didn't have any ties or anything to lose'.

'I come from a fairly working/lower-middle class background.' Between the 'ages of 20 and 30 I loved the idea of having everything I had in a suitcase'. So getting nine-month teaching contracts around the world appealed to this footloose and unburdened person. She also demonstrated a capacity to look after herself, 'holding down four jobs to pay for my master's when I went to the US'.

There is also 'much to be said for blind ignorance'; not knowing what you're getting yourself into means 'you don't freeze'. The other key thing about her time at the co-operative was 'I didn't do it on my own. Other people were involved.'

Lucy has a very clear idea about the type of authority she's comfortable with. 'I'm a team player... I don't think I like to be on my own "up there". I like to have others around I can share the experience with. I'm not a kind of visionary leader, like a Bill Gates. I'm much more [of a] deputy chief executive, not a chief executive.' The deputy role 'gives me some safety or protection'. She's also aware that this view of herself may change over time.

For now though, 'I like it because I like working with people... I don't like being lonely "up there". My style of management is very relaxed... although [I'm] quite opinionated. My staff have no doubt about what I think about something.'

'[I] don't want to be a CEO where I didn't have access to people with whom I could discuss ideas. I just like sharing authority.' She considered explaining this in terms of 'some kind of insecurity... but that's not how it feels on the inside. Inside I feel confident and outgoing.'

'A superficial answer' to why she doesn't want to be a CEO could also be 'I like talking and having fun... [this] diminishes as you go up.' She also thought 'it's nice to be able to put trust in an authority figure. If you're at the top you can't do this.'

Having authority thrust upon her

By her mid-to-late twenties she'd finished her master's in the US and was keen to apply for a role as an academic director at a school in Egypt. During the interview process she was made a different offer. How would she like to be the overall manager of a school in another country – rather than just an academic director in Egypt? 'They were very persuasive and I was flattered into taking it. They thought I'd run a school before.'

Lucy found herself in charge of fifteen staff and 'did it very successfully', becoming 'known as a bright young thing'. She quite enjoyed it and it was a significant 'step to where I am now'. If she'd gone the academic route life would probably be very different, giving papers on the conference circuit.

During this time 'I discovered I had an ego that could be flattered, that I was quite bossy and that I could persuade people to do things in a good way. People liked me and the way I did things. I wasn't a textbook manager. I didn't do a business plan for the school, I received a budget and then' improvised. 'On the people-management side, I managed very well' and this 'got me through any crisis'.

Moving up the educational hierarchy

After her time running this school she 'moved into the most prestigious organisation in the profession as one of three assistant directors with 60 staff. I was in charge of Personnel and during the first year we had a downturn and I had to lay off six staff. That was a very good exercise for someone like me to do… I had to think things through more strategically, less intuitively.' She had to be very mindful of working in an environment that was 'very prone to strikes'.

Her goal was to find out 'how to do this without the school going on strike? It made me think about my style.' Lucy 'couldn't rely on people knowing I was alright really. [I] had no track record… no bank of trust with the staff or unions. I had to find other ways of showing I was reasonable.'

She adopted a very collaborative approach – which is not what she'd do now. 'I engaged with the union representatives asking them to help me think things through. Some of these conversations were useful, some not.' One suggestion she got was 'to sack herself'. She then 'presented back to the staff the results following the consultation'.

Being other than collaborative

Lucy is not so collaborative now. 'Now I've got more experience, more options to pull on. There might be different ways of approaching the problem. I was overly solicitous... I didn't want not to be liked... I needed some emotional feedback [in the form of] respect or liking. I'm more measured now, I can live with the fact not everything I do will make people love me. It's the arrogance of old age. I have other things in my life... when you're 28... it's much more important that people like you.'

Lucy has 'more confidence, self-belief in my own opinions... the strength of character to carry the day... caring less about being liked all the time. I have always been very aware of what others think of me. When I was younger this made me vulnerable, [now] I'm older I'm less vulnerable. I can afford to occasionally say: "I'm sorry; I don't care. Just do it."'

'[I've] become less tolerant of certain traits in people... suffering fools in a sense... years ago I'd spend hours negotiating with someone who was going nowhere... these days I cut to the chase. "We're not going to agree. This is the way it has to be."'

This abruptness 'doesn't make me feel good... I get no kick from it. I try (and I have to try harder) not to show irritation. If I cared more what the other thought, then [maybe] I'd try harder.'

What Lucy's current authority gives and costs

'It validates me as a person... tells me I can be successful in the workplace... I can overcome certain hurdles. It gives me a certain amount of personal strength... this then permeates through other parts of my life.' It also 'helps define who I am', acts as a source of confidence. Lucy has been with her current organisation for ten years and 'there was one point where my career went sideways. [This was] the first non-forward move in my career. It began to make me doubt all my self-belief.'

Her current authority has cost her something. 'Time with my daughter... to keep up with what I want to be at work' she has had to sacrifice time from elsewhere. This 'occasionally pricks my conscience'. She tries 'to be aware of where [her authority] is taking me. [I] don't want to turn into a "do it my way" all the time [person] or begin to get a kick from it. [I need to] stay aware of my bossiness, keep in check my willingness to steamroll. I need to develop strategies to ensure the quiet people are heard. It does cost me a bit of soul-searching.'

My reflections on Lucy

Lucy's story is about someone who has a very comfortable relationship with authority – both her own and others. She has a very active relationship with it, not treating 'it' as a thing or as a given, but something living and in ongoing transition. In her story I am struck by how she has become less tentative and more visible in how she exercises authority – moving out from the shadows and into the spotlight (although never yet to be found standing solely on her own).

Her belief is that the top position in an organisation brings with it a profound isolation and separateness – this is something she is not willing to have in her life at present. She wants so much authority and no more for now. I am very struck – 'impressed' would be more accurate – by her understanding of how far she can go in her life and keep in place those things that matter to her, in terms of relationship, connection and conversation. She is clear that by moving into the top job there would be a qualitative change in how she was with others; it would result in her feeling isolated and unable to exercise authority in a way that sits comfortably with her present sense of self. She does not say that such a position should not or does not need to exist; she is simply self-aware enough to know the limits to her own current ambition when it comes to exercising positional authority. Authority sits comfortably on her, but only when it does not compromise the quality of her connections with others.

There is a lovely trajectory to Lucy's story as she moves from self-effacing modesty to the comfortable bossiness of who she is now. The mature woman has a very different authority to the younger Lucy, striking out into the world without enough knowledge to know quite what she's taking on. She has transitioned from naïve to knowing authority and with this has grown a greater belief in her own ability and willingness to put that informed ability to work.

She is also aware that as she has let go of her dependence on collaboration and the need to be liked, so she needs to watch a new shadow. Whereas before her shadow was an understatement of her ability, now her shadow is a potentially unhealthy intolerance of those whose opinions she doesn't value. Her trajectory highlights the need to be constantly reappraising how an individual's practice of authority needs to be monitored, so that its shifting strengths and weaknesses can be monitored. By not realising how your authority is changing it is quite possible to keep your eye on an historic problem, which has now been superseded. Lucy has increased the authority that has come with a sense of personal agency and is keeping a watching eye on not losing her relational contact that has served her so well throughout her life.

Lucy can be quite negatively judgemental towards her younger, more intuitive self – valuing more highly the strategic being she has become. By 'strategic' I assume she meant she possessed a more reasoned and calculating judgement. Intuitive and strategic authority are different but complementary forms. Intuitive authority is one that springs forward in the moment – it is a spontaneous authority and can therefore be absolutely grounded in the moment and also be an expression of authentic self. Its shadow can be that intuitive authority is simply an acting out of personal history in the present. Strategic authority can be one that is rooted in a wide appreciation of the data of the moment, connected to a sense of desired outcome. It can also come across as calculating, impersonal and even manipulative. Authority that blends the two can allow for the possibility of well-informed, spontaneous and personally believable authority being exercised in the moment.

Doing the right thing matters to Lucy – she is not without ambition or a willingness to step into positions of authority, but I get no sense from meeting her, or from the story she told, of her being driven by a need to bend the world solely to meet her own needs. Her authority is connected into both her needs and the needs of the wider organisation – a healthy marriage of self and other. This practice of authority is to me a highly mature expression of 'being a force for good'; a less mature expression would be one that denied the self and subjugated personal needs altogether – turning her into a collectively visible but personally invisible form of authority. So 'doing good' is about being in the service of the self as well as the service of those around you – and being in service in an active, and not simply a pacifying or compliant, way.

CHAPTER 21

Diana: Authority as authoring

Diana retired five years ago when she was 65. At that time she was working for Cancer Research UK, based at Guy's hospital where she was the head of the research side of the breast cancer histopathology laboratory. She is a biochemist who was awarded her PhD for carrying out research into the biology of breast cancer and has been working in this area all her professional life, publishing in the region of 150 papers in scientific journals.

Before Guy's she had responsibility for running a laboratory at the Christie Hospital in Manchester and had been happy to go to Guy's 'to once more just do the research'. Her responsibility for running the laboratory at Guy's was more accident than intention; a consultant became ill and Diana 'took more responsibility because I was the continuity'.

Diana's best work came between 1990 and 2000, which was the golden era for Immuno-histopathology, a field now superseded by gene analysis.

Some background to the scientist

Diana is the eldest of three daughters whose father wanted a boy. Despite this, or maybe because of it, her father always said 'I was as good as anyone else' and she never felt inferior. At school she would have been head girl but for someone staying on after failing their A levels.

She had no ambition for a career and in the mid-1950s it was very unusual for a girl to go to university, while a girl studying science there was even stranger. Originally she planned to study dietetics at Queen Elizabeth College London. This required her to have three A levels but she would only get a diploma after three years work. 'But that's daft,' she thought, 'I'd much prefer to have a degree rather than a diploma.' Diana decided 'I'll be a biochemist' and she told the school she wanted to study that rather than dietetics. They gave her the option of three colleges, all of them for women only! She chose Bedford College and went there to study Chemistry with Physiology. If she had gone to a mixed college such as King's or University College then she could have studied straight Biochemistry – but she wasn't to know this until some time later.

From Bedford she went to the Hammersmith Hospital where she did her PhD, before going to work in a hospital in Birmingham where she was in charge of running the Clinical Chemistry laboratory. She stayed only six months before leaving to get married – soon after she was back at the Hammersmith doing some research only for her to become pregnant. She gave up work and had 'no thought of working any more' as was 'normal of the era'.

Going mad

Within 18 months Diana had two children and then the whole family moved to Canada with Martin's work. In Canada Diana was 'very isolated… stuck in the house with the children. I felt as if I was going mad', the whole setting was 'very un-stimulating and I got myself into a bit of state'. There came a time when her son became ill, or so she thought. She took him to the local doctor to be examined. The doctor's assessment was that there 'was nothing wrong with him', but he forced me to 'look in the mirror'. He prescribed Valium, which she took and then slept for a long time.

Diana and Martin 'decided I needed to exercise my brain', so they advertised for an 'English grandmother to look after the kids' and Diana went to work. The episode 'taught us that I needed to do something as well as being wife and mother'.

Finding something to do

The family returned to England where Martin did his PhD and then started a business in the UK. It 'was obvious I should make a contribution to our finances'. So Diana 'learnt to type' but she was 'very bad' at it. Given that typing was not her thing 'I got a job as a school teacher' teaching secondary science for 12- to 14-year-olds. It was 'absolutely ghastly… [It was] very arrogant for me to think I could' teach without a teaching diploma (which was not required in those days). 'I just couldn't keep control.'

Her next attempt to find something to do was 'teaching A levels at a technical college'. At this time 'I thought it was impossible to go back to laboratory work'. Diana held on to this belief until an Indian friend told her to 'Get a proper job' doing what she was good at i.e. in a scientific laboratory setting. Diana was still convinced that she couldn't find something that would fit in with the kids so she applied for a job as a technician at the University of Manchester. At the interview she was told 'you're too well qualified for this'. However, she learnt that the Christie Hospital were looking for people. During her PhD Diana had learnt that 'some breast cancers need female hormones to grow and some are hormone independent'.

The consultant at the Christie wanted to measure oestrogen receptors in breast tumour samples and Diana was offered the job – a job virtually no-one knew how to do. With the help of her boss they got a method going. This work was of major significance to breast cancer treatment – at that time the removal of all hormone producing areas, such as ovaries, was standard practice in the treatment of recurrent disease. Her work at the Christie made it possible 'to find out if surgery would be worthwhile or not'. At the same time Tamoxifen was being produced by ICI (later Astra Zeneca) as a not very good contraceptive but it was capable of antagonising the activity of oestrogen. Now it was discovered at the Christie that women with oestrogen positive receptors responded much better than others to the drug. This discovery was 'the basis of my work'.

Diana's drive

As someone who combines childcare with a professional career I am very sensitive to the demands that this puts on people and am curious about why people put themselves through these stresses. For Diana, her drive comes from a liking for achieving things. 'I'm happier when I'm achieving something.' It was not just about achieving any old thing though; it was about achieving 'what I wanted to do'.

'When I was working the two children were at primary then secondary school. I was on the PTA and did all the administration for Martin's business.' She was able to make this work for her through the availability of annual flexitime – 'I did thirty hours a week Monday to Thursday in the school term and ten hours a week in the school holidays... [I] never had any paid help.' There was a cost to this, however: 'I used to get migraines on Friday night.'

Success in context

Diana describes herself as being 'not really ambitious'. She has 'enjoyed the success [but] never had a burning ambition to be anything particular'. It strikes me that her focus has been on making her life work as a whole, paying attention to all the parts so that she is able to be a researcher, a mother, an administrator and a wife.

One of the things that made this work was the attention she paid to maintaining some separation between the parts of her life. There was a time when she was 'doing all this administration for Martin' that she considered giving up her research work and working with him. She describes the idea of doing this as 'barmy. If we were working together the ups and downs would be too synchronised'.

She also believes that Martin learnt from her experience of being a working mother. 'He knew the difficulties... this made him much more sympathetic to part-time women.' He also knew that 'if you're sympathetic and flexible they repay you with loyalty and hard work'.

Changing authority at the Christie

Her work at the Christie met not only Diana's love of research but also gave her the chance to interact with people in the laboratory – not that life was without its resentments. 'My boss was a very annoying man', although she now knows he was 'much nicer than I gave him credit for'. Even with this caveat she still describes him in robust terms: 'He was very lazy... I would do the work and his name was on it.' Then he retired and Diana stepped into authority; she ran the laboratory, supervising the work of young researchers. 'I knew I had something to offer. I knew how to do this test [for Oestrogen Receptors].'

Her reputation extended beyond the hospital and she became a member of the British Breast Group, a society for the top people involved in breast research. This national and international reputation made Diana much more visible and it was 'nice being famous and [enjoying] the camaraderie of those who [worked in this area].' When she moved to Guy's she became part of the European Cancer Research Organisation, which was 'important in terms of scientific contribution'.

As regards the taking of formal authority roles, Diana 'accepted the responsibility for running laboratories, but never sought it out'.

An early sense of personal possibility

As we drew to the end of our conversation I asked Diana about how significant her father had been in her life. 'He didn't make me feel "by golly I can" [but] he must have given me confidence.'

This sense of self-confidence came out for me in the story she then told of what she did just after finishing her PhD. 'A Greek woman at the Hammersmith Hospital arranged for me to work in a lab in Greece. My mother helped me buy a car and I drove to Greece on my own in 1962.' She drove to Lydd and 'put the car on a plane to fly to Geneva. Then drove through Italy' and on to Greece. She tells the story in a very matter of fact way as something 'I just did' because 'I thought it would be nice to have a car in Athens'. She did have some prior experience to this. Her father was in the motor trade and Diana spent two university vacations working for the firm's car hire company delivering and collecting cars all around the UK. 'I knew how to find my way around. All went smoothly until I got to Athens and found that all the street names were written in the Greek alphabet!'

Martin on Diana

Martin is very proud of Diana. When he left the room for me to interview her on her own he reminded her not to be too modest. When he rejoined us he immediately put Diana's achievements in context. 'By the time she retired [she was] an international leader in the field of breast cancer research and treatment. All the others she's on a par with have worked full time, very hard. She's reached the same position part time, while bringing up children. Most of her peers are aggressive, full-time men.' He summarised Diana's reputation as being 'through achievement not the pursuit of position'.

'At no part of our middle careers did we expect to reach the heights we did. Diana had no burning zeal to reach the top. We've never been ruthless. We're both intelligent and educated. We've both got a middle-class duty ethic. We've had opportunities and made the best of the opportunities that have come along. Neither of us had a career target.'

For both of them 'authority [has been] thrust upon us'. They've 'not resisted it [but] never measured our success by our authority'. Martin then talked directly to the results of Diana's work. 'What she doesn't point to are the thousands of women' who've survived breast cancer as a result of the research she's done – Diana was quick to intervene at this point to highlight that 'I didn't do that on my own'.

My reflections of Diana's story

I can understand why Martin was concerned that Diana would underplay her achievements – she wears them lightly. The one moment where I really experienced a sense of pride in her life's work was when she got down the folder of all her published papers to show me. She certainly enjoys the recognition of her peers but it does not come across as a consuming need; her work and her authority sit within a more complicated setting – one that marries the domestic and professional spheres.

To understand authority in Diana's life I have to see it in the context of all of her life – within the setting of a wider weave. She has lived her life in such a way that she has been able to be present in the bringing up of her children; she has been able to support her husband practically and emotionally as he has pursued his career; she has ensured that she has an existence that is her own apart from the family; and she has stepped into whatever role needed to be played to ensure that the infrastructure around her research work was kept in good enough order. She established a modus operandi that worked for her and for those she cared about. If this meant taking formal authority, then so be it.

I came across a book some years ago that talked of people being the author of their own lives. I experience Diana as someone who has been able to author her own life, working with social norms and also being able to challenge them enough to support her own identity. Her story is both the story of her achievements in the field of breast cancer research and also the story of her being able to create a life that meant she was able to be a multifaceted, rather than single-faceted, human being.

There were times when Diana tried to deny her abilities – when she applied for jobs that she was over-qualified for or when she tried to live life solely as a housewife and stay-at-home mother. She also tried and failed at doing jobs that, while fitting well with family schedules, did nothing for her sense of achievement – her time as a typist and a teacher stand out in this regard. She was obviously a gifted researcher and it is in coming home to this calling that she finds satisfaction – this is where her work gets its meaning. The running of labs she talks of lightly, something that had to be done if the research were not to be compromised. At no time was there any sense of her wanting to be in charge of budgets or significant numbers of people. The practice of formal authority was the carrying out of necessary tasks; the ensuring of adequate institutional hygiene in terms of meeting the requirements of funding agencies, co-ordinating scientific and medical research and providing sufficient support to those involved in the work. Authority outside of the context of the authority of the researcher seems to be of no more importance than ensuring the rubbish is emptied at home and the fridge kept full.

The only point of edge in our conversation came when she talked of her boss at the Christie. She was annoyed at having her work published under someone else's name – the curse of all neophyte or junior researchers. It mattered to her that she was able to claim what she knew to be hers. The authority of the author comes from being the true writer, of owning what is yours and being able to stand by it in the wider world. It is her published research and the reputation this has supported that underpin her standing in the world outside of the family. When she has tried to deny her voice she has been unhappy, even ill, and when the man at the Christie tried to claim her voice she became angry. Authority in this case is about speaking with your own voice, using words and knowledge that are uniquely yours. It is not about wearing other people's words or claiming for yourself what does not belong to you.

The trappings of authority do not seem to appeal to Diana. At no time did she seek out positions of authority and she never defined her life in terms of achieving status and position. As with Martin, status and position were accidental by-products. I suspect that much of the popular definition of ambition requires a mono-focal approach to life; it is associated with the driven and often slightly unhinged behaviours of people who are willing to sacrifice everything else except their one ambition. Diana has lived a multi-focal life, which has never been about sacrificing one aspect of her being to further another, but about finding something that works in the whole. The responsibilities of authority come and go, but Diana seems to be able to stay quite detached from the meaning of authority apart from its responsibilities.

Authority without ambition means you can take it up and put it down as you need to. Authority is a useful tool in the service of something else, rather than an end in itself. Like money, authority is a useful friend but a lousy master.

Diana's reflections

> I think that I have had an incredibly lucky life. I had a happy but unspectacular childhood. We moved house when I was ten and I then went to boarding school because I failed my 11+ exam and there was not a suitable school for me nearby. I did not know many young people in the area and my two sisters were younger than me so I was a bit lonely at home during the holidays. The luckiest thing for me was to meet Martin whilst I was at university and to marry him five years after I left. We now have two children and six grandchildren and we all enjoy being together. Fortunately both families live less than an hour's drive away from us so

we see them quite often, which is a great joy, and we chat frequently on the phone.

I was a bit apprehensive about what life would be like after work, but I was able to reduce my hours gradually so the final cut off was not too much of a shock. I still review some papers and grant requests but these are becoming fewer as my knowledge becomes out of date. I was slow to get involved with specific things in the village but now my time is fairly fully occupied. I am treasurer of the Women's Institute and chairman of the Garden Club. I belong to the Kirtlington Investment Club, the Oxford Women's Lunch Club, the Oxford Medical Lecture Club and I organise a 'Ladies' lunch' for a group of friends. Most of these are monthly events and there are always other things going on the rest of the time. For example, I am a member of our Patient Participation Group at our local doctor's group practice and attend meetings of the Oxford PCT Trust on their behalf. I attend a weekly Pilates class and we swim every morning in our own pool usually from May to the beginning of October.

Martin and I have an active social life in the village and outside with family and friends and we go on holiday about four times a year. Luckily we have been able to combine Martin's attendance at meetings and conferences with a holiday to such distant places as South Africa, Australia, India and China. All this activity happens against the background of our happy and contented life together. We pursue our own interests as they occur but the thing that makes everything worthwhile is being able to share the experiences with each other when we get home.

A short story about taking care of the self and others

It seems important to me that each story of this triptych is about a woman; to have an opportunity to listen to three successful people talk with such calm authority about their authority is a rare gift. Trying to put my finger on it, I experience an absence of bravado – the strong meat of difficult circumstances seems to have been processed and made part of them. Any one of them would be fully justified in wearing their achievements more proudly, yet they wear them lightly – but without disappearing themselves. These are women of substance who have achieved great things in worlds dominated by men, but they seem to have done it without trying to imitate a more aggressively male form. Relationships are paid attention to; the self and the other are respected.

Four themes stand out for me when I examine Eve, Diana and Lucy:

- Embracing authority without stepping into hubris
- Developing consciousness
- To be [liked] or not to be [liked]
- Relational ethics

Embracing authority without stepping into hubris

I have done some cripplingly embarrassing things in my professional life – and most of them have happened when I've overestimated my ability, my expertise, or skill to instruct or advise. There is a sense of proportion and connection to others in these stories that I know I can all too easily lose in my own life.

When Lucy decided to set up a woman's co-operative it felt like an act of courage, but she doesn't talk of it in terms of being tested or stretching herself. Her focus is on the relationships of the group and how this closeness made success possible. Diana stepped into authority outside of her research only when there was no-one else to do the job – her pride comes from the research not the authority of institutional leadership. Diana's sense of perspective on the international acclaim for her work may also be because her work is just one strand to her life – hubris is unlikely to happen when you stay connected to other parts of your life outside of the professional field. Diana had what was needed to stay grounded; life outside work and an attitude of reluctant acceptance of authority.

Eve certainly embraces authority; what seems to keep her grounded is a desire to be liked and a capacity for putting herself in the shoes of others. Hubris is in part an individual's belief in their perfect rightness, encapsulated for me in the dreadful phrase: 'My way or the highway.' Authority that believes itself perfect is a dangerous creed – the only inoculation is a capacity to know that you are flawed and that misunderstanding is a mutual, rather than unilateral, experience.

Developing consciousness

In terms of personal consciousness these stories speak to following your calling – that way of life that is most deeply satisfying to yourself. I am very struck by Diana's story; by her attempts to be a full-time wife and mother, then her time as an inadequate teacher before she returns to the laboratory work that is most satisfying to her – and makes best use of her talents. Eve's story is more dramatically punctuated; for years she locked herself down, trying to be a label before she was confident enough to give herself free rein. Both these stories highlight the discomfort that can occur as someone moves from acting from a sense of what they think they ought to be – to what they are.

To be [liked] or not to be [liked]

Eve is quite explicit about liking to be liked. Her authority has an inherently inter-personal, relational quality. This may cost her when she has to confront people, but she seems to be exceptionally skilled at working well with people others find difficult to deal with. It also helps that she is skilled at persuading people to see things her way. She is persuasive and likable. I suspect that one of her compelling qualities is the seriousness with which she works to see the world through the eyes of others – and not just seek to work through her opinion. To be with someone who is able to walk in your shoes is probably going to create a strong affective bond. There are arguments to be made that the need to be liked could make it difficult to exercise authority, but Eve admits her orientation and works with it – rather than trying to be something she is not.

Lucy's need to be liked is less central to her identity; when young it mattered, now in her maturity less so. Diana's affective needs seem to be largely met away from work.

Rather than wondering whether needing to be liked or not liked hinders or enables the exercise of authority, I am more struck by the need to acknowledge one's personal disposition and work with it, rather than trying to be something one painfully obviously isn't.

Relational ethics

These are three ethical people – they pay attention to what they do and how they do it. All three have been or are highly successful in terms of position or reputation. But as Martin observed of Diana, this has been achieved without a ruthless focus or aggressive pursuit of ambition. They have not turned into goddesses of their own lives, believing themselves to be perfect or supreme. They retain a sense of humility in terms of the boundaries to their ambition and they also pay significant attention to their relationships with others. This is an ethics that comes from an understanding of authority as a relational activity – something that involves good interaction between those with more and less power.

section six

Cool passion

Chapter 23
Roy: Authority from a Buddhist perspective   177

Chapter 24
Bill: 'I have of late, and wherefore I know not,
lost all my mirth.'   185

Chapter 25
Mike: Tempered reason   193

Chapter 26
A short story about cool passion   203

Roy: Authority from a Buddhist perspective

Roy is involved in helping out at the International Meditation Centre in Heddington, Wiltshire. The Centre is dedicated to spreading the Buddha's teaching, based upon the practices of Sayagyi U Ba Khin – who as a meditation teacher founded the International Meditation Centre in Rangoon in the 1950s. 'One of the main things the Centre does is help lay people to learn and practise Vipassana (insight) meditation.' Traditionally these practices were the preserve of monks.

He has also been a partner in a large accountancy firm and now runs his own consultancy business. I interviewed him with his Buddhist hat on, wanting to discover how this tradition would inform his understanding of what enables or disables people from thriving in positions of authority.

Being true to purpose

The first enabler that Roy identified was being true to one's purpose and that means 'you constantly act in a consistent manner'. The best example of this at the Centre is the teacher, Mother Sayamagyi, who is 'a living embodiment of the teaching. Everything she does, she tries to do in a perfect way.' She 'inspires people around her to try and emulate these qualities even though we can't keep up to those standards'. She does that supposedly simple thing of 'leading and living by example'.

Roy first met Mother Sayamagyi in 1978 'and since then I've had different exposure to the way she conducts herself both formally and informally. She is consistent – she continually maintains the meditation practice every day.' Despite now being elderly 'she leads the meditation session from 8.00 to 9.00 in the morning and in the evening from 7.30 to 8.30 each and every day, as well as teaching a ten-day meditation course each month. She is present and has an indescribable presence... others may have a day off, she doesn't.'

Her consistency is not only characterised by these habits of meditation, she is also consistent because her message is always the same. What she teaches is 'not a fad, it doesn't change because of what's in the papers. It's a deeper consistency so that the responses you get from questions are the same over time.'

'Part of her consistency is her patience... accepting that you can't do everything at once. People can't cope with too much change.' Looking back over time it is possible to see 'that things could have been done years ago but the time wasn't right'.

Not being proud – ego and purpose

The second enabler Roy identified was 'not being proud' which means 'not letting your ego corrupt your purpose. If you seek out fame then it inevitably diverts you from what you really could be doing.' Drawing on his business experience, Roy saw this playing out in the book *Good to Great* by Jim Collins.

What Roy noticed in the case studies presented there was 'people were quite simple in the way they went about things… they didn't seek out fame and press. They just got on with doing things.'

'There are some situations where you can see what you think the right thing to do is.' The challenge is 'trying to disentangle what you are being guided by… is your view of the right thing really the right thing?'

'There are times when you do something which upsets others, even though you don't intend it. If your volition is caring for the wellbeing of all, you may act in a way which 'in the short term has some negative reaction from people affected, even though in the long term it is for their good'.

'In terms of how you tell if it's your ego driving you forward' or whether you are 'acting in a way consistent with your purpose', that is a 'continual struggle'. To live this struggle, you 'need to be humble' and, for Roy, practise meditation. It is in his meditating that he gets 'a little insight into the way I'm behaving'.

Kamma

Roy then talked of kamma and what determines success. He reflected on 'why people want to be successful', the motive that drives them. 'Say I want to be wealthy, I go about behaving in a way that will make me well off. If you take the view that a large part of why someone is successful is their kamma' the question is 'what is it in their past that has brought about success today?'

Roy believes that part of material success comes from generosity, the 'giving of charity, the result of which is also influenced by the donor's volition and qualities of the recipient'. The result of generosity is material wellbeing. So those who have significant material wellbeing have given generously in the past (including previous lifetimes). 'You see a lot of wealthy people giving to charity… maybe they see this was the basis for their success?'

Kamma is not fatalism. 'Everyone's actions give rise to a force called kamma which goes to the debit or credit of their account according to its good or bad objective. What comes out of that account at any time I can't say, but I can choose how I react in the present. I can act in a good way in the present to encourage the emergence of good things'. The reverse is one bad thing leading to another. For example, two people may experience anger, but react in different ways. One person may roll in the anger and make the situation worse. Another may maintain an equanimous attitude and lift himself out of anger.

You can develop an equanimous attitude through meditation. When you meditate, you experience the arising of resultant kamma as a sensation – for example, anger could be felt as burning or heat. The objective is to 'contemplate the changing nature of sensations – observing with equanimity and not reacting. This results in detachment from the anger which is experienced as changing and insubstantial'.

Buddhist teaching asks that we seek 'to do good, to be good and to purify the mind'. It is 'the long view of your ultimate aspiration that will influence what you choose to do'.

Energy and awareness

Thriving requires 'the putting forth of continual effort'. This is a mental effort that will mean different things in different settings. 'If you're in a position of authority you are in a much better position to influence others. Effort goes into guiding, having conversations to inspire and telling stories. If you're not in such a position your effort would be focused on doing things that need to be done, doing a role in the best way, perfecting what you do to the best of your abilities.'

A complementary quality to mental effort is 'right awareness or mindfulness'. You can never have too much right awareness, but you can have too much effort. Putting too much effort into things can engender agitation, while putting in too little effort leads to laziness.

'Awareness is being in the present... being aware of things as they are and not as you'd like them to be.' It is usually to do with 'inner awareness. It's about being conscious. If you're conscious you're more likely to do good things.' There are however 'no guarantees because until you become enlightened you have to accept your imperfection', although you are 'more likely to do good things if you maintain awareness – in your interactions with others by maintaining awareness of yourself you are less likely to do something that is not beneficial to either yourself or others'.

It is important that the care of yourself comes first because 'by protecting oneself one protects others'. Care 'starts with a sense of loving kindness to yourself and then to others'.

How these insights influence Roy day to day

'At a practical level I'm freer to determine what I want to do.' He is able to 'allocate my time and energy on things I feel are appropriate'. When he was a tax partner at a big global firm he had a 'fair degree of autonomy and choice but still had a lot of boundaries to what I could and couldn't do... ultimately I was being measured by the firm's metrics, ones that I felt were not always appropriate'.

'Did I know something others didn't? Who knows?' Roy is wary of sounding overconfident because 'when you're overconfident you miss things, you don't see clearly'.

Reflecting on the effects of belonging to such a firm he is aware that 'when you're a partner you have this status that the organisation gives you that carries outside the organisation. This can positively support your influence in any given situation, but it can also undermine your relationship with other people.

Firstly you can think you're important and secondly the reaction you get from people reflects their view of your importance – you don't get accurate feedback or data about yourself.'

What the Centre can offer people in authority

'What's being offered is tranquillity and insight. If you want a tranquil mind and to develop insight – that's what the Centre is about.'

The consequences of calm are that you 'feel happy within yourself, feel light rather than heavy, bright rather than dark'. This calm comes from cool rather than hot pleasure. Hot pleasure is driven by a wanting of something and encourages a greater and greater craving for that thing. Coolness is grounded in tranquillity and is aimed at the extinction of craving.

Reflections on Roy

This is a perspective that I have an enormous personal attachment to. I've known Roy for a number of years, coaching him through a turbulent time when he was a partner in a large advisory firm and also providing support as he falteringly and then more robustly established his own business.

I'm slightly embarrassed to admit that I've often had a penchant for Eastern philosophy, dabbling in its esoteric strangeness and being drawn to such books as John Heider's *The Tao of Leadership*. Even more uncomfortably I spent a number of years trying to find a way of marrying the Celtic mystic tradition with mainstream business-school thinking. When I interviewed Roy I suspect that what I wanted from him was the magic answer – some distillation of Buddhist practice that could be readily translated into a bite-sized piece of new thinking about authority and leadership.

In all my dealings with Roy he has refused to connect his religious practice to the world of business, except as it guides his choice of profession and his way of being with people. In this conversation he was as true to his principles as ever and once again my desire for instant Kamma was denied.

I was immensely disappointed in my early conversations with my editors and sponsors at Middlesex when they identified Roy's story as the one that didn't work for them. When I thought about it and reread what I'd written and Roy had edited, I tried to make sense of their reaction.

It occurred to me that what the story lacks is drama – in all the other stories there is a sense of struggle, of magnificent beasts confronted, slain or incorporated. This absence of drama is no accident – in my reading of Roy and other Buddhist writers and teachers, the purpose of their practice is to let go of desire and without desire the human struggles that are at the heart of the dramatic life disappear.

Roy's tract talks of the un-dramatic habits of constancy of purpose, of 'developing an equanimous attitude' so as to free oneself from being consumed by emotions such as anger, lust or envy. This is a world away from the day-to-day habits of much Western culture. I, like many I assume, am readily drawn to what's 'new and different'. I enjoy immersing myself in the court politics of the newspapers and am not immune to the blandishments of the self-help world and its invitation to be a new (and presumably better) you.

I am also aware of how hard it can be to achieve an 'equanimous attitude'; I have spent ten years or so in psychoanalysis and continue to find myself in the thrall of highly charged habits of mind that do anything but promote such an attitude. Yet I know that it is in those moments of equanimity that I am able to see most clearly what I need to do and how I need to be.

Roy's story/essay may be un-dramatic, but that is because it reflects exactly those virtues that Roy's philosophy espouses – it is about calmness and quiet, not drama and excitement; it is about constancy and self-knowledge, rather than the fascination and tragic potential that comes with inconstant or self-ignorant woman or man. I sense that the authority that comes with this attitude will bring about a very different world from the one that is expressed by Mark Anthony in Shakespeare's *Julius Caesar* when he declaims 'Cry "Havoc", and let slip the dogs of war.' Roy's world might rework those words to read 'Whisper "Quiet", and let slip the wisdom of reflection.'

Roy talks of the patience that Mother Sayamagyi has; her willingness to wait for when the time is right. Much of our language of authority and leadership runs utterly counter to this perspective. The focus is on 'forcing the pace', 'breaking the mould' – everything is urgent and frequently all-consuming. When I think of Roy's piece in the context of Sam's story I see a strong resonance. Sam talks of 'metabolising shit', of having the opportunity to process physically the strong emotions that he and his colleagues have been engaging with. This processing cannot be accelerated through intellectual understanding; it is something that takes its own time. Too often, I believe, people behave as if they can short-circuit the time it takes for people to come to terms with changing realities. I suspect that when people use their authority to hector people through their sense-making processes, it stores up trouble for the future.

This paying attention to timeliness, that sense of what can be heard and dealt with now, is not the same as passivity or of denying the need to pay some future cost to avoid some present catastrophe. What it does invite is a realistic appraisal of what can be paid attention to now – there is a role for the conscious ignoring of certain issues, rather than a gung-ho assumption that because something is problematic it needs to be addressed now. Sometimes it is only through the experience of staying with something that it becomes possible to address it.

As someone who has been brought up in the secular-rationalist tradition, the notion of past lives influencing the present is not something that sits easily with me. At best I want to reframe it within the psychoanalytic tradition – making links to Marie's Freudian-inspired story. What I can stay with from Roy's beliefs is the notion that the past has an active presence in the present. The sense of being perfectly free of what has gone before is highly attractive, but wrong. It is a lovely fantasy because it can make available to us the sense of a free future – a fantasy that may actually be very useful in certain circumstances. It's silliness is for me, however, captured by a character from the 1990s drama–comedy series *Ally McBeal*, who would excuse whatever crass mistake he had just made through the simple expedient of saying 'Bygones' and then continuing as if by saying it, so the past had been erased.

This role of the past in the present is most powerfully present in Christina's story, where she observed that as soon as you step into a position of authority people are different with you. The ghosts of all the authority figures people have grown up with and known come out to play. This past has a haunting quality, something that exists outside of traditional reason, as it clings to us (like Stella's sense of amniotic fluid). It has an immaterial presence that materially effects us – like Kamma.

More than any of my other subjects Roy worked on and crafted what was written. It was important for him to check with teachers at the Meditation Centre to make sure his particular interpretations were not incorrect or unnecessarily controversial. This may also have contributed to the lack of enthusiasm for the story in certain quarters; this story represented a more formal, on-the-record expression of a particular philosophy of authority and so felt flatter, less human, more perfect.

Orthodoxy and its expression tend to be carefully thought through and have had their contradictions and shortcomings well camouflaged or defended. These collectively owned beliefs are less open to the public acknowledgement of personal foible, which runs counter to what emerged as one of the central tenets of this book – namely that it is in the informal and the personal that fresh insight lies. Orthodoxies tend not to lay bare the tensions within a philosophy, so in orthodox writings on authority and leadership there is relatively little exploration of what it feels like to live with both personal and institutional responsibilities. As Christina noted, leaders are expected to shine and the literature is about how to shine. In Roy's orthodoxy, his philosophy is about the elimination of tension rather than the living with and within it.

For me the belief that care 'starts with a sense of loving kindness to yourself' is the most important point in Roy's story and is one of the major lessons I would like to highlight in this book. As well as my wife's struggles in a position of formal authority, I have been privy to the inside track of many who have suffered as a consequence of taking on authority. I have seen too many breakdowns, relationship smashes and self-destructive habits not to know that being in authority can cost some people dear. One of the refreshing aspects of talking with the people whose stories make up this book has been to discover people like Martin and Giles who have been able to revel in their authority, while retaining their humanity and humility.

In Roy's expression of Buddhist teaching this primacy of care for the self is wonderfully, uncompromisingly clear. If you don't take care of yourself, how can you be fit to take care of others? If you don't take care of yourself what self-destructive habit are you encouraging those around you to emulate? A healthy expression and practice of authority demands, therefore, that the wellbeing of those in authority is of prime importance.

CHAPTER 24

Bill: 'I have of late, and wherefore I know not, lost all my mirth.'

There was a time when this happened to Bill but, unlike Hamlet, Bill knew why. It was at the time when he was weighed down with the responsibility of his position as senior partner in a City law firm. These days his mirth has returned and life seems full of pleasurable salt, even if responsibility is still a significant part of his life.

Bill is the chair of a Financial Reporting Review Panel, a body charged with 'keeping Britain Enron free'. Through the power that comes to it via the Secretary of State the Panel has the authority to take companies to court to make the directors reissue their accounts if necessary. This has never happened as the Panel seeks to 'always go for consensus' and 'persuade the company to do what is right'.

First memory of authority

'The first thing I really remember – [being] a prefect at school didn't make much of an impact – was… the manager of The Mermaid Theatre being committed under the Mental Health Act.' He was 'a client of mine' and sent a letter to his then law firm instructing them to 'get down here [to the hospital] with a writ for Habeas Corpus'. This letter was then handed to Bill by his partner in the firm with the instruction that he had 'better get down there'.

Bill became aware that 'if we took it seriously we had to marshal the authority of the law… [an] authority that comes through knowledge, training and making the system work… In the end nothing happened [as] by the time I got down there he was happy to stay.'

The next experience of authority of note to Bill came with 'being a partner in a law firm. [This is a] strange life… [you] never boss anyone about – [except] maybe a secretary if [you're being] very daring.' As a partner, 'Yes you have authority [but] in all cases authority comes from knowledge and better experience… being the person most likely to know what to do.' Bill then came out with a strong statement about the source of authority in his life. 'Authority comes from knowledge and honesty.'

The authority and value of honesty

'If [you] always [try to] speak the truth, people will accept what you say and listen carefully – that's the beginning of authority.' He contrasted this with power where 'people have to do what you say', whether you are speaking the truth or not.

If you have a reputation for honesty then 'people listen carefully' to what you have to say. 'They know you're not saying something for personal gain but because you know it to be true.' The 'same [applies] with legal advice. If you push the boundaries… people know immediately. [It's] always better to say "our case is weak"' rather than try and disguise the reality of the situation.

At the Financial Reporting Review Panel he chairs, 'we never bluff', and this a 'source of good authority. If we have three points we don't try and trade off one point for another'. 'People know we mean it', that the Panel has an 'honest belief in our cause' and that they have a real intention in following up this honest belief with action.

He contrasted lawyers to businessmen, drawing on an observation by Julia Middleton in her book *Beyond Authority: Leadership in a Changing World*. 'Lawyers are better at exercising authority than businessmen because they're used to not having [organisational] structures behind them.'

Honesty has been an important part of Bill's life. 'I learnt early on at school that honesty was very powerful.' Following on from school 'I was very lucky with the [legal] firm I went to… [I] worked for two very honest lawyers.' In particular Bill was struck by the 'importance of not speaking for effect' and affected by 'seeing people who will not lie'. These honest lawyers 'never got the staff to say [something like] they were out of the country', to get them out of having to speak to someone.

Facts in a crisis

This power of honesty was also something he saw working in business when he was one of the people brought in to help with the 'Lloyd's [Insurance Market] clean-up of the nineties'. Much as 'you can get caught up a bit', in the drama of the situation, 'experience teaches you [that] if what you say and do is soundly based you can't go far wrong'. Bill has been involved with many very charged situations over his working life and has found this to be true.

His first advice is to 'make sure your base is secure… [establish some] incontrovertible facts then move out with ropes and pitons… don't leap over the edge. So long as [you're] grounded in what is real' you won't go far wrong. 'Of course you can make the wrong judgement' based on these facts, but that judgement wasn't based on 'jumping out for effect'.

'In any crisis, [the] first thing you need is a statement of incontrovertible facts.'

Family roots for honesty

'I always thought that my parents would have known immediately if I was not telling the truth and I wouldn't have liked that.' It was the 'same with teachers'. Bill has 'been told I wear my heart on my sleeve', and since that's the case dissembling is not something to try – because 'if you're not very good at something, don't do it'.

His attachment to honesty was 'something I grew up with'. He recalled 'my grandmother looking at me when I was trying to cover something up and remembering [saying to himself] "I'm not getting away with this one."'

In the spirit of political scandals such as Watergate, Bill noted that 'It was never the break in, it was the cover-up that sank you'.

Having values challenged

There was 'one situation [where it was] very difficult to hold to these beliefs. We were acting for a purchaser of a company' which involved buying 80 per cent of the company and then entering into a joint venture with the seller, who kept the other 20 per cent. In the deal there were 'lots of provisions about subsequent share selling'. Then it became clear that 'my client couldn't raise the money to complete the deal and he sold it on'. The other side had made a mistake – there was 'nothing to stop him passing on the deal vehicle and we weren't allowed to tell them'.

The deal went ahead and once completed a 'complete stranger turned up' in the offices of the acquired firm. There was 'nothing illegal but morally [this was] not good. We could have stopped acting… but that was the dilemma… because we owed him a duty to act in his interest. We [his legal representatives] had a conversation between ourselves about what was the right thing to do… there was no point talking to him, he was "brutally indifferent".' So the deal went ahead, 'We did it… and the other side exploded. In the end we sorted it out over two years later.'

'If faced with it again [I still] wouldn't know what to do.'

Not being able to explain yourself

A while ago 'we had to stop acting for two major banks and couldn't say why. [We'd] come into possession of a piece of information' that made it impossible to continue.

The bank was 'dealing with a client of ours' and to begin with it all 'seemed very straightforward'. Then this piece of information 'came into our possession which our original client said we couldn't pass on'. Bill was summoned and 'asked by the CEOs of two big banks why we'd stopped acting for them. We just had to stick to it' and stay mum. 'They were furious… they thought we were crooked. They could not understand why we couldn't carry on. Six months later I could tell them. I went to see them and they still couldn't get it. I couldn't get inside their heads… they thought some Machiavellian plot [was] going on. We got no credit.'

Fairness is the most deadly weapon

As senior partner, Bill 'had to say goodbye to some partners'. As arrangements stood at that time he 'had no legal power' to bring this about.

'Every senior partner knows they have to respond to the market. Financial pressure etc.' For a long time this legal practice hadn't responded as it should but there came a time when action needed to be taken. This is not a course of action entered into lightly: 'to say to a partner who has been around for 10 to 15 years that they need to go, is a very difficult thing to do. You have to persuade them to go... I had no legal authority to make them go and legal process [would be] too cumbersome anyway. I found honesty and fairness the best thing.'

In this situation you 'didn't move unless you could articulate the reason' for what was being done. It 'had to be very fair in the process. They could bring anyone one in they liked' to their meeting with Bill. Bill also made sure that everything 'would be kept completely confidential by me and they could say what they liked.'

'Fairness is the most deadly weapon. If you're wrong you wouldn't have started down this route' in the first place. 'This applies at the Financial Reporting Review Panel. 'If you expose the weaknesses of your own case, listen to the other side and adapt to anything that is right and are instantly helpful and friendly about anything you can be helpful and friendly about [so that] the other person believes you are fair... they can't complain about the way they're treated. The only complaint is whether the decision is right or wrong.'

'Fairness of process leaves a person exposed to the truth... which as we know sets us free... which is why it's so terrible.' Bill's intention is 'to get people to a position where someone can't say [it's] unfair'.

Making a process believably fair

'You have to mean it' is Bill's injunction when it comes to fair process. 'You mustn't be covert'; fairness has to be seen to be believed. When engaging with his unpleasant duty as senior partner, the process and his role in it had to be visible.

He 'called a meeting of the partners and said profits were not good enough. Those without a current or potential client base will go.' The first response from the partnership body was a request that 'you will tell us when you've spoken to everyone' who is to be asked to go.

Bill 'owned the responsibility for this' course of action. 'I covered my bases' by talking to the heads of department of those who were to be asked to go, 'But I did it... Visibly, I hated it and I didn't hide it.' Those who agreed to go included a 'guy I'd worked with for years... [who'd been] a very good assistant'.

'One of the keys' for Bill was to ensure he was 'acting in the interest of the organisation'.

Care of the self

I asked Bill how he took care of himself during this deeply necessary but unpleasant task. 'I don't think you do... that's the problem really.' From the start

Bill was staking his personal reputation. 'When you convene a meeting of the partnership and say "we've got to fire some partners" if the partners had said "no", I'd have had to quit. That was the way people thought then.'

'I knew from the experience of other senior partners that if I backed down but stayed with the firm… I would have been a lame duck. It was "shit or bust". To lose was not possible.'

'As senior partner if I think someone needs to go, it's him or me. It wears you down. You can only go through this so many times.'

As seems to be so often the case 'the best lawyers think it's going to be them', adding to the general mood of disquiet and anxiety. 'Most senior partners have the bottle to do it once, after that you know it's got to be a really big deal… towards the end of your time [you think] "my successor can do that".'

Authority without fun

Bill found very little to enjoy during his time as senior partner; it was a difficult time for the firm and there was a lot of trouble to deal with. But 'we did it', dealing with the loss of the partners and getting a new partnership agreement in place that allowed for partners to be fired. 'Things got better and I immediately felt bored', which was completely unexpected.

This boredom was a reminder to Bill that he is a lawyer at heart and 'I love work, doing interesting stuff and running a department in my spare time.' Being senior partner had left him less time to be a lawyer and had also been frustrating because 'you have to be so bloody polite'. In the cut and thrust of commercial deals you can find 'so much pleasure [in] being able to be rude to someone on the other side'.

Bill quoted Hamlet to describe what it felt like at the end. 'I have of late, and wherefore I know not, lost all my mirth.' It was a strain for him, his family noticed his mirthless quality and he found himself 'becoming more introverted, more blinkered'. He also found that he 'felt the beginnings of depression… felt the bleakness, when [I] realised what it had taken out of me'.

In his last annual medical as senior partner he 'filled in [the] happiness sheet'. This last one was much better than previous ones. Bill was 'within six months of retiring and knew I wasn't going to stand [as senior partner] again'.

Advice to the next generation

'The most helpful piece of advice I ever got… [from reading] a US Senator [was] "when in doubt, do what's right". Be true to yourself… faced with a difficult decision… do what is right, not what is popular or what will get you by. [The] minute I read it, it struck me – it sounds silly but actually [it's] profound. If you do it (what's right) and it goes wrong [then it's] not the end of the world.'

'If you don't do that you lose yourself.' There's a movie about JFK during the Cuban missile crisis, in which JFK is attributed with saying 'There's something immoral about going against your own judgement.' Going with his own judgement is important to Bill, as is respecting the sensitivities of others – his one concern at the end of our conversation was 'I want to have some sympathy for those who were fired… [that they] don't feel pointed out.' Bill is not a man who walks lightly with his actions, but owns them and is aware that they have consequences, pleasant and painful.

Reflections on Bill's story

Bill carries a wonderful calmness with him – at the end of our meeting he told me that he was training to become a coach to people in senior positions and my instinctive reaction was 'thank goodness'. To be coached by someone with his values and with his seeming ability to set his own interests to one side would be a most enlightening experience.

Bill's authority seems to be built around an invitation to embrace reason rather than polemic, power or deceit. He assumes that by paying attention to the reality of what is, unfurnished by defensiveness or trickery, it is possible to establish an agreement about the nature of the current reality – or at least expose where real differences lie. Only by spending time on establishing the true nature of current reality does it become possible to do the right thing. This is not to say that the course of action followed will be infallibly followed – we are but mortals and our judgements are flawed – but by basing our judgement upon what is agreed to be real we can at least be sure that it is our judgement that was wrong not our understanding of the situation.

Grounding authority in what is, rather than what we want reality to be or those bits of reality we are willing to admit to, gives authority a practicality and believability. It may not send the heart soaring or launch a thousand ships but it will enable decisions to be made that can be understood and acted on – because they are based around the reality of what can be done, given the reality of what is. This is the antithesis of visionary authority, with its appeal to great ambition – that can sometimes realise great things, but can also result in the dark side of charismatic narcissism and the failed monuments to vain ambition.

It is in the combination of knowledge and honesty that this form of authority stands out. Knowledge is widely seen as a source of power, something that gives one party an edge over another. Without the counterweight of honesty knowledge can become a stick with which to beat those who are less knowledgeable.

Honesty leavens knowledge, turns it from something certain into something that can be engaged with. Very little knowledge, certainly in the hurly burly of working and family life, is fixed. Without honesty it is possible for those in positions of authority to claim to know more and know more certainly than they do. Knowledge with honesty is knowledge that will always have a smidgeon of doubt attached to it, making it something that can be engaged with by others and found more believable.

A person who has knowledge but no honesty cannot be trusted. How do I know where the limits of this person's knowledge are? How do I know if they are telling me everything they can? Authority that rests on knowledge without honesty is therefore untrustworthy – it will never be clear whose intentions are being best served. Authority that rests on knowledge and honesty is trustworthy and will give people a peace of mind as to the intentions being served by those in authority. The decisions being taken can still be challenged and the decisions taken may not be welcome, but at least their informing motivation is understood. Knowledge and honesty underpin fair authority.

Fairness, knowledge, honesty and reason do not take away the sting of making difficult decisions. It hurts to ask people you know and respect to leave their jobs. The black dog, that mood of near or actual depression, would seem to be a healthy reminder to those in positions of authority that hurting others is not to be undertaken lightly. To blithely talk of 'the greater good' without having some feeling for those who will bear the cost would speak to an insensitive, even inhumane, authority. So finding authority a burden is probably no bad thing, as it prevents people falling in love with its trappings and ignoring much of the grim reality at its core. The buck does stop with you; difficult decisions do need to be made.

I am left again, as I have been in many of these stories, wondering about the cost to the individual of being in a position of authority. I can see what others get from someone shouldering this responsibility for the collective, but for the person doing the shouldering there seems to be little personal benefit. Authority, practised well, would seem to me to be an altruistic act rather than a selfish one.

CHAPTER 25

Mike: Tempered reason

Mike is the CEO of a heavy industry trade association. He's a man steeped in reason and yet he leavens that love of reason and procedure with a sensitivity for human idiosyncrasies, which is why I have given his story the title 'Tempered reason'. We met in an office environment that he had been instrumental in designing and about which he expressed much personal satisfaction. Mike is a man who I found to be very comfortable in his own skin and at ease with his authority and his abilities; a fascinating mix of modesty, self-belief and a desire to do the right thing.

Introduction

Mike's just one of those guys. If you want something to get organised and get done then he's your man. I've only met him once and I understand completely why he's the one being asked to do himself potentially out of his nicely paid chief executive position. The major industry players have asked him to look at how to merge four trade associations, including his, into one – and he is most certainly not going to be guaranteed, nor would he ask for, any sinecure. It's also obvious to me why he's the one who's been asked by some friends to organise their London to Paris rowing expedition. Responsibility sits easily on him.

What is it about him that stands out and where did these attributes come from?

Serious history

Mike has recently 'clicked sixty' and his life has had a rich mix of experience. The youngest of four boys he was his mother's favourite. His father, with whom he had a difficult relationship, worked away from home during the week as a rep and would appear at weekends with an expectation that the family would reconfigure itself around his needs when he was there.

Mike was expelled from one grammar school and then finished up being school captain at the school he went to after that; not that his path was a direct one from un-model to model student. For a while at the new school he played at being invisible, hiding his intelligence and abilities. From there his life encompassed being a professional architect, a macramé-teaching rope-shop assistant and a slow failing boss of a £50m business that didn't deliver quite enough profit. Outside work he has been twice married and once divorced, fathered five children, got two years of personal counselling under his belt and spent ten years in a variety of serious and less than serious relationships.

He has a distinctive style of leadership, a word he is more comfortable with than authority. For him authority has a connotation of being something that is given to you by others and so can also be taken away. Leadership is more personal to him, something that is part of his DNA. While I am sensitive to this, I am going to use the terms leadership and authority in a largely synonymous fashion in this story.

His leadership is informed by a felt need to do the right thing, rather than pursue his own ego needs as an end in themselves – although he acknowledges that there have been times in his life when he may have known what the right thing to do was and didn't necessarily pursue it. There is a certain humility to him, an acceptance of people – including himself – as they are rather than as others may want them to be.

He can be directive but that is not his preferred style. His preference is to avoid confrontation, although these days he's more aware of the importance of confronting and directing quickly, if that is what the situation requires. He prefers to ask people to contribute to reasoned debate, while at the same time being aware that people have a wide variety of needs that have to be met when they contribute. He identified three people who reported to him to highlight this; all three are highly capable and intelligent people but there is one who needs personal affirmation for their contribution, another who needs to have his ambitions supported and a third who simply wants technical support and challenge. This third individual would appear to have orientated any affirmation and ambition needs around his musical activities that take place outside work.

Mike combines a design engineer's need for clarity with a human being's understanding of the need to contribute in ways that make unique sense to any one individual. He has the human heart that lives comfortably with the organisational leader's responsibility for delivery and performance.

Three formative moments

Mike's life and career have been long and varied, with – I sense – a few twists yet to come. Three moments stood out for me about his life as I tried to make sense of what gives him his authority – an authority that includes not only the internal management of his trade association, but also engaging with a broad range of external stakeholders. This engagement includes participating in, and taking leadership roles on, committees in both Brussels and Westminster.

(a) School days

The first moment concerns his school days. It pivots around a teacher who confronted him about his desire to sit and hide at the back of the class, coming thirty-second out of thirty-two. Mike had come to this school on the back of being expelled from his previous grammar school. His behaviour there had become disruptive and finally unacceptable, something he lightly attributed during our conversation to some form of 'basic attention seeking'.

At the new school he'd returned to his confrontation-avoiding, low-visibility, fourth-son habits which he'd briefly shaken off. One day, however, a teacher told him that he wasn't willing to put up with his lack of effort. The teacher told Mike directly, and plainly, that he could see that Mike had more ability than he was willing to let out. On this particular day when the homework was set, Mike was told by the teacher to really try. This was going to be a major challenge to Mike's established habit, which was usually to do nothing and rely on whatever variation of 'the dog ate it' excuse he could think of for never delivering. His excuses were never convincing.

This time Mike did the homework; he really worked on an essay that went on for an enormous two or more pages. All this was done in a home environment that was not conducive to taking study seriously – remember this is a household of four boys with a frequently absent father, where Mike always had to share a room with one other brother. To work like Mike did on that day was to go against a very well established norm. A short while later the teacher marked the work and distributed it in his own idiosyncratic style, a fashion that would seem to bear a greater resemblance to Little Britain than to serious scholarship. The teacher would walk around the classroom throwing the work back to people, starting with the worst and working his way up to the best. Mike recalled getting crosser and crosser as his book didn't get returned to him and the book throwing began to get to its close, 'how dare this teacher not even bother to mark his work having made such a big issue of it with him?' The teacher continued working his way up to the stratosphere of the very best pieces of work.

Of course, in the end he got his essay back; it had been the best of the lot. In a very public way the teacher let Mike know that he would not accept Mike dropping his standards back to where they had been. From then on Mike stopped being invisible at school and began to move on up through the rankings until he was one of the top-performing students; he went on to take O and A levels and even found himself becoming school captain – a role he enjoyed, even if he notices that he didn't allow as much sympathy for the human frailties of his other prefects as he would now.

From this story I can see points that seem to roll out across much of his later practice of authority (or leadership as he would put it). Time and again he emphasised his facilitative leadership style, predicated upon the belief that asking people to join in the decision-making process is much more effective – in most cases – than directive decision making. I see this belief as stemming from this experience of being asked by the teacher to stop being invisible. Mike knows in his waters that people can be intelligent and resourceful if they are asked to step into the light. He has experienced himself as someone who has discovered his authority – as a present, intelligent schoolboy – and he has experienced what it takes and what it feels like to have someone invite, even demand, that he step into his own authority.

A second point that stands out for me is his expectation of high standards. The teacher got Mike to discover what he was capable of and then demanded that he stay with that level of ability. As Mike showed me how he managed the performance of his direct reports I was struck by what stock he set on his people achieving high standards. In his quiet-voiced way, I saw him as having a paradoxical quality of humane remorselessness. He can empathise with people but he will not tolerate performance he views as less than good. I sense that 'good enough' will not appear 'good enough' to him.

(b) IBM in its heyday

In his professional life, his time at IBM in the 1970s and '80s stands out. Mike loved its systems, procedures and its belief that 'good design is good business'. Prior to joining IBM he'd qualified as an architect and found himself working for a practice that was responsible for much of the redevelopment of the West End and Soho in London – including the iconic Centre Point. These years continued to build his experience of being in a position of authority; the architect's position is contractually the most senior and responsible when it comes to money and delivery.

He did however begin to chafe at the experience of never being allowed to admit fault. Because of issues of liability it was impossible for an architect ever to admit that they had been wrong. Mike knew that this was not how the world worked; cocking up is part of the human condition. His own relationships and experience of his father meant that he didn't cling to any idealised belief in the perfectible nature of people. People get things wrong because that's in the nature of people. Quality assurance, whether at work or play, is not about hiding what is going on but revealing what has actually happened and then doing something about it.

He joined IBM to help them better manage their big building contractors who they employed to deliver IBM buildings. It was his first experience of something called a professional manager, someone whose job was solely to do with managing the performance of others. In the world of architectural practice, management was something that was fitted in around the work of designing buildings and being the prime manager of contracts and clients.

I wonder whether IBM's reasoned and systematic approach to management was a welcome relief from the more chaotic and personalised authority systems that he had known to date – systems for instance where any flaw is denied, as in architectural practice, or where everything is bent to the needs and requirements of the senior male. When growing up, Mike's family had to move around the country in line with the changing location of his father's rep area, as well as adjusting to a shift in family system when Dad came home at the weekend.

At IBM Mike came across an environment in which reason, well-thought-through process and a focus on outcome were dominant. He also came across people who had a 'crunchy' management style; people who didn't shy away from making explicit requests from him for high-quality performance – while all the time not denying that as human beings a gap will nearly always emerge between what was planned and what actually happened. I see shades here again of that crunchy schoolmaster.

Mike had a positive experience at IBM, as at school, of being invited to be his best and of being given the opportunity to step into a range of leadership roles. Mike has a deeply positive relationship with the experience of being challenged; at both IBM and in the schoolroom he met people who clearly and precisely challenged him and on both occasions he found himself flourishing as a result.

The importance of clarity of expression is another of Mike's themes; he frequently described his great skill as being able to articulate clearly the nature of a problem that needs to be addressed. He has felt first hand the power that can be unleashed in someone if they are presented with a clear exposition of a situation and then invited to join in the process of doing something about it.

(c) Counselling

Having a less positive experience of formal management systems and procedures, I found Mike's enthusiasm and appreciation of them sometimes difficult to hear. But there is something about Mike that meant I was able to stay with him and suspend my prejudicial judgement. I think that this may be about my sense that Mike never forgets about the flawed or idiosyncratic nature of human beings. Mike likes reason and structure but knows the human element must be paid attention to if reason and structure are to work.

This provides the context for the third moment in his life I want to dwell on. Even though it was covered quite briefly in our conversation I find myself giving significance to it.

Much as Mike's career has had its ups and downs, so have his marital and non-marital relations. After his divorce from his first wife he saw a counsellor for two years, an experience that made him more aware of how his relationship with his father had clouded aspects of his life. I go to this moment because, at some stage in his life, something softened Mike's approach to leadership.

By the time he had finished at his school as school captain, he described a somewhat dictatorial young man. As part of his prefectorial responsibilities he had to organise rotas so that the prefect body could open up the school at the start of the day and close it down at the end. He recalls having little sympathy for those prefects who did not strictly comply with the demands of the rota. This early disposition may then have been reinforced by the legally mandated superiority of the architect's position on big projects, potentially encouraging a hard and arrogant expectation of authority.

Certainly professional experiences mellowed him and he recalls not getting the best from one contractor in his IBM days when he adopted an intolerant and intransigent approach to their work together. His capacity for self-reflection, applying the disciplines of quality assurance to his own performance, meant that he was able to identify that his behaviours had got in the way of achieving a successful outcome; delivery having a higher priority to him than attachment to a particular style of personal authority.

Yet I am left wondering about those two years of counselling. Two years is a significant period of time to stay in such a process and to stay with it for so long shows a serious commitment. My belief is that this may have helped him develop a softer, more understanding attitude – both towards himself and others. It may also have helped him step out of the charismatic and self-serving shadow of his father and so begin to craft his own unique expression of authority – with its combination of reason, tolerance, participation, challenge and performance.

Mike in (nearly) his own words

Mike is a thoughtful and systematic man. Prior to our conversation I had sent him the questions I intended asking. Set out below are the answers he wrote which I have weaved into a personal statement about how he sees his history and his authority.

> *My work involves close co-operation with professional staff, so much of my day-to-day work is about steering, reviewing and guiding rather than directing. So there is not much 'authority' practised day-to-day. I consult, seek opinion and guide decision making. With other staff I tend to be friendly, open and informative.*

> *These days I am more relaxed and philosophical than previously – mostly because the business has a track record of success over the last six years. I am still keen to gain approval with my bosses – and always hesitant when challenging them.*

> *What I suspect others notice about me is that beneath my friendly exterior I am deadly serious about getting things right! I have heard people say I 'do not suffer fools gladly'.*

> *I first noticed a sense of authority in myself at school. After being expelled from one school at 13 I started at a new one where I was the bottom of the class and the outsider for years. It was not until I was 15 or 16 that I met a teacher who persuaded me to try, effort that resulted in success. This in turn led to positive feedback and a willingness to try at other things. To my surprise I gained places in the class ranking, was made a prefect and ultimately school captain! What gave me a sense of authority, at school, was having a 'role' to play that gave me authority. I found it easy to exercise that control, within the parameters that were given.*

Since then I have had a number of significant experiences of formal roles of authority, in fact most of my work career. As an architect, project manager, line manager, director and CEO. In addition I have had several 'staff' roles where the authority vested in me was project related – working with people to enact transition – as a change manager or facilitator. I think it is in this role that I do my best work; trying to get people to see the problems and challenges and then devise solutions they own themselves.

In terms of how I influence people, my style varies with the situation. With my bosses it is always one of framing the problem, identifying options and then considering consequences and recommendations. With peers, it is much more about problem sharing and guidance provision. With subordinates I try to be clear about what needs to be done when and try to see that ownership exists. I use a lot of energy in meetings and am usually 'taking a lead' in terms of process development and solution brainstorming.

My weakness is in not responding well to challenges in authority – using emotional power to drive things through if logic and reason seem to be failing. I also find it hard to work with strong characters who see things in 'black and white' and are not open to subtlety and compromise.

Reflections on Mike, his history and his sense of authority

When we finished our conversation I made a reference to Lord Browne, the former head of BP. My reason was to contrast my sense of Mike with my sense of what I had read about Lord Browne. With Mike authority exists for a reason, it is about getting things done – that is what Mike enjoys about authority, the ability to shape things. In Lord Browne I see a man who seemed to have fallen in love with the trappings of power – the experience of authority had become an end in itself. I may be doing the man a grave disservice, but the point stands. There is a significant difference between those who wear authority because of the pleasure of authority and those who wear authority in order to influence the world.

In Mike's history I see him revelling in the shift from the architectural practice to IBM, where the purpose of authority shifted from being about supporting the myth of architectural infallibility to supporting the delivery of achievement. At school he experienced the benefits of owning his authority, so that he could achieve better results and in his current job he is using his authority potentially to do himself out of a job – by articulating the need for a single trade association.

I am speculating, but I wonder how much Mike's practice of authority is in reaction to that of his father. I sense that his father's authority was not exercised for the benefit of the family, but solely for the benefit of the father.

The experience of being challenged by the schoolteacher stands out for me as a vivid example of someone using their authority to get others to take responsibility for creating their reality. The schoolboy Mike was shown that he was an active agent in creating his world and there was an alternative reality available to him. He didn't have to stay invisible at the back of the class; he could – if he wanted to – step into the authority of his intelligence and ability. The teacher couldn't do the work for him – he couldn't write that fateful piece of homework, but he could ask Mike to do it. Mike knows that people can be transformed by stepping into this form of responsibility; he knows that people have the ability to respond. This preference for asking over telling may well be the result of being the youngest of four sons – a youngest son doesn't have the formal privileges and status that come with being the eldest. In his professional training, Mike was greatly influenced by attending a facilitators' training course. It seems to have acted as a validation for his preferred form of leadership.

Mike loves clarity, both in terms of setting direction and in terms of establishing how current reality matches that direction. Again I can see the influence of that schoolroom encounter, where the teacher really spelled out the situation as he saw it and by spelling it out brought it to Mike's attention in a way that he could hear. At IBM the systematic and visible process of management chimed with his sense of what authority was for – getting things done, rather than covering backsides. There may be something more to this love of explicitness, but I have no more than a groping sense that it may be to do with an innate disposition or possibly some generalised reaction to a formative experience of the chaotic.

Mike is an optimist; he believes that people have the ability to do things well. If he didn't believe this then his facilitative – asking – style of leadership would make no sense. Again I return to the schoolmaster's challenge and to the benefits that Mike experienced when faced with a 'crunchy' manager at IBM. Colleagues at the time pitied Mike for having to deal with this man, but Mike experienced him as an enabling force. Since Mike has experienced how authority can be used to enable himself, so he seeks to use his authority to enable others.

At times in my conversation with Mike, and afterwards, I have felt more than a touch of steel in him – something almost inhuman. His love of formally documented appraisal procedures, the application of quality assurance principles seemingly to everything he does. The whole world can seem to disappear into a never-ending series of Plan – Do – Measure – Change cycles.

But he does have a vulnerable side and the benefit of knowing what it's like to fail and to scrape along nowhere near the fast stream or the top. His is not a story simply told by a series of onward and inevitable successes – there have been crises and moments of confusion. He has an acceptance of fallibility, although it is tempered by a belief that the consequences of fallibility can be addressed.

Mike's reaction to this story

> While I am surprised by the description I see here of a person I thought I knew – Molly, my counsellor (now deceased) would probably not be. She would recognise most of this and concur with the formative influences from school, to architecture, to practice, to IBM, to BSi and BCA.
>
> Factors not mentioned, like being made redundant from an architectural practice in Hampshire at mid 20s; and finding the end result liberating. Like the divorce that led me to a happy and fulfilling second marriage, reinforce the 'renewable' facts of life.
>
> There is a fear-factor here that still exists 'one day they will find out I have feet of clay' but more and more that is rationalised out.
>
> All the more important therefore to ensure that – because 'authority' is removable – I focus on leadership, facilitating and enabling rather than dictat. But when push comes to shove – a direction is what you will get!!
>
> People do comment that I expect and accept excellence, but praise can be hard to find – the 'gap analysis' always comes first!
>
> If systems and processes reinforce and protect emotional immaturity; what happens when the emotional maturity is achieved? Is the reliance on process reduced? If the authority is wielded with a lighter touch – is it more effective?
>
> I am working now with a very senior, mature and retired guy whom I like. He very rarely gives me an instruction, but asks a lot of questions – he gets the best out of me.

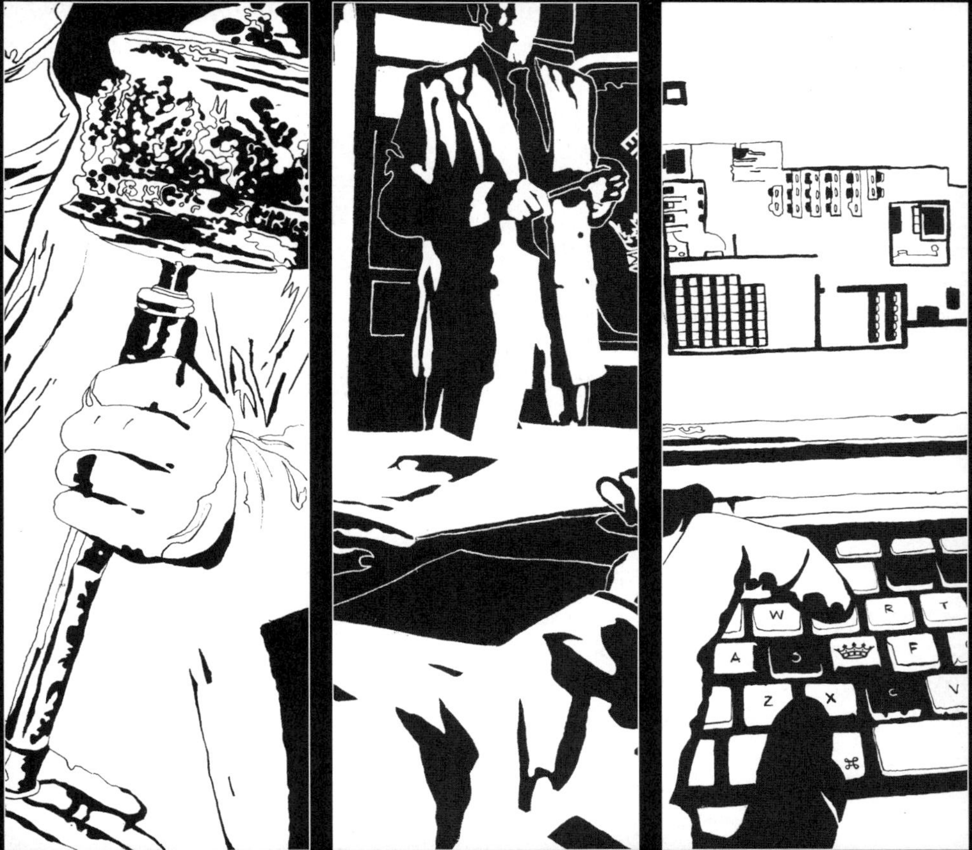

There is a measured quality to these stories; these are lives with miles under the belt, rich histories. For me they speak to what a mature masculine authority can embody, a gentle but rigorous decisiveness – steel being used with good intent. There are two characteristics of this mature masculine that I want to draw attention to:

- The antithesis of heat
- Being imperfect

The antithesis of heat

These are men who do not leap off the deep end; they keep their expressed emotions in check, but not at the cost of being personally inauthentic. With Roy there is the practice of meditation that allows him to clear his inner eye and not be consumed by hot emotions; he is informed but not overwhelmed by his feelings. Bill and Mike are practitioners of reason and fairness; I doubt they often allow their own needs to overwhelm the requirements of the situation in hand. They both know themselves well enough, and are comfortable enough in their own skin, not to derail an activity so that it becomes solely in their own service – there is a hint of altruism to them, but not in a way that makes them invisible.

Heat is not denied, it is simply seen as part of the landscape of what is. Reason, fairness and meditation are ways in which passion can be acknowledged but not seen as the be all and end all. Heat becomes uncontrollable when there is no attempt to ground it in reality or when it is ignored; heat explodes when it is fuelled by fantasy. This cool passion brings with it habits that allow for flames to burn themselves out and for the reality of a central task to be recognised.

Being imperfect

Part of the reality is an acknowledgment of imperfection, particularly by those in authority. Few people in history have achieved enlightenment, so I think we can all safely work from an assumption that we are flawed. To deny flaws or imperfections is to inflame a situation because it cuts us off from reality and encourages fantasies. It is also very irritating for other human beings to be in the presence of those who claim perfection.

What makes imperfection acceptable in authority is the habits of authority being informed by self-awareness, reason and authenticity. This gives authority a coherence and consistency, without tripping over into fantasies that this form of authority is 'the way, the truth, the light'. A genuinely human authority is one that is honest about its intentions and flaws and works with them. Once authority starts being dishonest (which includes denying its imperfections) it creates an environment of fantasy, where grounded action becomes impossible.

endpiece

Chapter 27
What the chorus saw   207

Chapter 28
A singular conclusion   215

Chapter 29
Further exploration   219

ID-chapter

CHAPTER 27

What the chorus saw

To see the stories differently I approached some trusted professional and personal friends and asked them to pick out the stories that spoke to them. This is what they saw.

Clare

If I was envious of anyone it was Martin. There's something really healthy in 'being the king' in the way that he is. [He's] very present… able to take fear out of situations.

Bob broke my heart a bit… responsibility [seemed] so crippling… such a sense of being in control because not being in control is too frightening?

Clare related to Penny and her inability 'to deal with women who were mad'. It evoked for her well-grooved cultural habits where women can behave as if they were 'afraid of themselves'.

She was attracted to Lucy's authority at first because she wanted to see 'how authority can create connection'. Instead she found something else: 'I liked her ruthlessness, her discovery of agency… letting go of having to keep everyone happy.' Bill's story drew her with its theme of 'the burden of authority and how it's no fun'. It left her wondering: 'Where's the joy?'

Lucy, Martin and Penny all spoke to her of living without fear. Penny may have her moments with women of a certain type, but none of them 'lived with much fear'. Along with Bob, these three 'don't get distracted by fantasy'. She also had a sense that 'if I met them they wouldn't boast about how important they were. They haven't built an ego around their authority.'

What burned for her at the end was 'that the purpose of authority is to take the fear out of a situation'.

Michael

They all had to find an individual way to find a way to get things done… [they] found an individual not a generic path… that's what makes them appealing. [They] haven't taken a book off the shelf… that's what makes them individuals… and brings them alive.

Authority has two dimensions. [It] is something personal and it also exists in the context within which it is exercised. A conclusion? Authority doesn't work on the basis of a model.

Janet

What Janet found in the stories changed from day to day – what caught her attention reflected what was playing out in her own life. On the day I spoke to her she started with Bob – 'You poor sod!' – recognising in him her own 'responsibility junkie' habit. Knowing what this habit costs her she 'felt pity for him'.

After Bob came Diana, and Janet 'felt envy. This is the woman who got it together.' There was something 'lovely' in her story and attitude to authority. 'What a sorted lady... not perfect... I envied her sense of contentment.'

'[When] I was reading Stella, I sensed she was... working on herself [which] raised the question of what I wanted to work on.' Authority is a work in personal progress.

When reading Lesley, Janet was having to deal with a specific 'female authority figure'. Lesley's story and the hardness of its first half evoked issues that cut to the quick of '[my] relationship with female authority... [my] relationship with my mother'.

> I liked the more ordinary stories [such as] Bob and Diana. They had humility and ordinariness... a good ordinariness. You don't have to have suffered or be extraordinary to do something special – which is counter-cultural.

Will

Thomas spoke. 'Anyone who goes into authority [is trying to] fix something in themselves... [That] really resonated. I'm trying to fix something.'

Lucy showed 'the glory of naïvety... [of] not being frightened'. Will saw how she changed, how in the beginning she made 'to see the good in everyone' and felt compelled 'to make people better. Now [she] cuts to the chase.'

In Thomas's clients he saw people for whom 'nothing is ever good enough... attention to detail matters'. While finding these traits admirable, Will also saw that 'authority is a two-edged sword', the same attributes in different hands and situations having very different effects.

Luke was about the power and importance of visionary will. 'When leading a team you need a very strong will to maintain the vision when [you're] getting doubt from all over the place... if you give into the doubt you get an inferior product because the powerful vision gets diluted... You need the inner self-confidence that what you're doing is really good.' The challenge is 'when you have someone who believes absolutely... how [do you] bring them down when they're wrong?' As the certainty that Giles' story warns about plays out 'how do you tackle [the] certainty [of others]?'

What stood out in the end was the 'huge range of stories and styles', which were all a reflection of each individual's personality. Credible authority is an authority that comes 'out of you'.

Iain

> Sam's the man who intrigues me. [He had] the best title; the need to metabolise shit. [I] recognised a fellow soul. The story of a slightly isolated adolescent, achievement [being] fuelled by neurotic energy... establishing the feminine qualities of authority. Then in mid/later life 'feeling his bollocks' and saying 'this is alright'. [There is] a sense of him filling out, becoming the hunter and the healer... the leader who has the balls to disrupt things but also the capacity and intent to heal, provide succour and protection. The ability to do this is quite wonderful.

In Sam Iain saw what it took to bring together two fundamental forms of conversation, the 'instrumental and the compassionate'. This is something he 'rarely comes across'.

'It's very easy to talk about masculine and feminine authority traits [in an abstract way]... with Sam [I] saw them burbling up, [felt] the discovery [as he] owned his own manhood, his own energy.' This lived, rather than conceptualised, integration gives Sam a 'vulnerable authority that is a quality any hero/protagonist in any story must possess'. This form of authority is best described for Iain by an insight he was given into why Harrison Ford is such a 'good hero/protagonist in his films. He gets beaten up really well.' As watchers we are 'able to recognise in such a hero our own weakness and vulnerability'.

Penny also struck a chord, particularly as a parent and how 'a lot of your authority [comes from] your own experience of conflict and [conflict] resolution with your own parents'. Penny is also very strong on 'owning your authority'. She talks of pitching to commissioners who need her to be strong, confident, steely... so when they go to argue her case they're 'arming themselves with her confidence.' In her habit of strong direction, and the preference of fascist bastards over those who take no responsibility for speaking with authority, Iain noted 'you don't do anyone any favours by being diffident'. Authority must have its voice and be seen or else people become uneasy.

For Iain the question that runs throughout the book is 'why do you think you want this authority?'

Fiona

Marie's story 'felt real... true'. Her stories of men in male-dominated environments resonated: 'I recognised people who like feeling powerful and having acolytes run around after them.' It left Fiona 'thinking there is a role for a much greater use of psychoanalysis... in business... Executive coaching is a bit fluffy by comparison.' She also recognised in Marie's experience how men behave towards women in masculinised workplaces. While they no longer test Fiona with naughty schoolboy jokes 'I get treated like mother sometimes... [or rather] more like a benevolent schoolteacher.'

When it came to Eve 'I was more interested in how her childhood and view of self' developed. The impact of discovering late on that she had been gifted and how this had led her to change... the flipside of sitting down in her bedroom and crying about injustice... the authority stuff was an overlay on the shifting sense of self... The fact that she's a top-notch regulatory bod [seems] not that important; more important is her philosophy and the way she goes about doing things'.

Jon

'A number of themes stand out, shared by some – but not all – of the stories. There is a theme around balance... the balance between self-interest and the interest of others... [between] exercising authority on behalf of others... and acting on your own behalf.' Jon talked of the balance of ego and non-ego, where 'you have to have some self-respect and belief in yourself to put yourself forward'. In many of the stories he saw 'a servant–leadership type of authority... [with people] acting for and in the service of others. Although no-one [gave it that name].'

Another theme was linked to the servant–leader notion and was particularly strong in Sam's story, where there was 'an integration of authority and nurture'. Although Sam 'talked of it in terms of the male and the female'.

> Then there was something about not always being in the right place to exercise your authority. Sam took a while to find a place where he found he could be himself and from there exercise authority. [This] built on other stories where people had repeated experiences of being good at something... Martin talked to his experience giving him a sense of 'Yes, I'm good at this.' For Sam the emotionality of his [current] work meant he could 'be himself'. This contrasted with his 'experience of being in roles that didn't quite fit'.

'Giles' story was also a realisation of competence over a number of years', although he also 'embodied courage'. The willingness to 'sniff about looking for clues... [his ability to] back himself to make sense of whatever environment he was in. Giles was also very interesting in terms of the balance of self and others. He couldn't be the CEO of a Fortune 500 company because [he wasn't] enough of a bastard. Having [a sense of] balance [between self interest and the interest of others] means you can't do certain jobs.'

'From Adrian I get an ambivalent feel.' Jon wondered about 'what he thinks of his authority and how others experience it. He would vehemently describe himself as not a bully, yet he's very strident and opinionated.' This led Jon to a general observation that 'authority is something that is experienced very differently by people' within the same situation. This 'theme of relational authority', of the experience of authority being something created between people rather than something unilateral, 'came out in Stella's story' as well. Stella talked of 'not thinking of authority as something someone has but being something that is granted to them by others'. Authority is a two-way street and Jon wondered about 'Stella's need to be positive and assertive and what this does to the people who are granting her this authority. Does it infantilise them?... [Does it] let them off the hook from thinking about things?'

Jon saw a tension in Adrian and Stella, the 'wanting the whole team to join in but with a clear idea that it was their [Adrian and Stella's] vision'.

Jon finished with two more observations, one about the stories and one about how he read them. He 'wondered if the role of authority is to keep anxiety in its box and also constrain behaviours... [to] ensure that fears are limited and also that the freedom [of others] to choose is limited'. As to how he read the stories, he was constantly asking: 'What would the story be like [if told from the perspective] of someone who isn't authoritative?'

Eve

'My overall thought – conclusion is that authority is inter-relational. It is not possible to have authority apart from people – therefore the different types of authority are expressions of different types of relationship.' Some of these relationships Eve found attractive, others she didn't. She 'really liked Stella... with her masculine authority in a woman', something she admires but that doesn't work for her. Others come across as people who'd be very difficult to be close to and another seemed to show no interest in understanding others – 'it's up to other people to understand him'. Diana's authority seemed to be the one that was least dependent on others; she radiates 'a quiet assurance in who she is' – which is a strength others value in her.

Authority will play out in terms of the relationships people have with each other; it is not something apart from this. Some of these relationships will be healthy and some will play on particular anxieties and fears; as is the relationship, so is the authority.

Robin

'In conclusion, the stories [that spoke to me] were about truth. In what dimensions of my life do I know the truth? And in what dimensions do I know the truth but ignore it?' In the stories where this came most forcefully to the fore one of the central tensions concerned 'when it is right to wait and see how truth unfolds and when it is time to act. When does authority come from waiting and when does it express itself through action?'

Truth is not a fixed force in these stories, 'we never know truth completely... there is always a gap between text and subtext. The truth shall make you free… and truth is always, in part, elusive.'

Robin saw this struggle and engagement with truth stand out in five stories in particular. In Stella's case he interpreted her story as 'It's been a bumpy road but I'm glad I've got to where I've got to – telling the truth through film, no matter what it costs.' With Adrian it's about 'truth through debate, even though this can be painful'. Lesley was about 'my choice, my life: learning how to tell the truth to myself', while Bob was a more equivocal truth; is he 'struggling and losing. Telling himself the truth but not acting on it'? The last of the truth stories was Bill, 'learning to tell and value truth' above all else.

Without the presence of this ever-elusive and partial personal truth, authority lacks a compelling ethical foundation – and authority without a grounding in ethics is an unguided missile, un-rooted and prone to being buffeted by fashion, easy choices and impersonal justifications.

David

Michaela's was 'an invigorating story that got me thinking'. David's own background includes time as a trade union activist and a belief that 'authority is something that needs to be challenged and confronted'. In Michaela he saw a 'transformation from seeing authority as something you fled from to something enabling'. He was also struck by how 'authority was rediscovered [in post Soviet Czechoslovakia] through the intellectual and artistic discourse. Authority is so often [seen in] reductionist [terms]… it's the tanks rolling in.' With the flourishing of 'the artistic and creative aspects of authority… so it becomes invigorating'.

Authority was 'a moral issue' as well; it had 'something to do about right and wrong – and when it is mediated through a bureaucracy that sense of rightness gets lost'.

CHAPTER 28

A singular conclusion

I am left with one overriding impression – to take on a position of authority (or have one thrust upon you) is akin to standing in a field during an electrical storm with a metal spike sticking out of your head.

With authority comes an exposure to charges of all sorts, some from within and some from the outside world. It has something of the solemnity of the traditional warning given out to those about to wed; authority is not something to be entered into lightly, but soberly. You will be treated differently by people around you. You will all too easily be tricked into all sorts of behaviours. You may even lose yourself.

In order to survive having authority this is what I'd recommend:

- Have somebody who loves you to turn to; who'll keep your feet on the ground and your head out of the mire
- Treat authority as a domestic chore; something that has to exist but isn't any great shakes in and of itself
- Know the fantasies you hold; what vanities are easily stoked, what vulnerabilities readily poked
- Have expertise that is of direct relevance to the situation in which your authority is being exercised
- Know how to get people to tell you how things are rather than how they think you want them to be
- Know how to get people to realise and then take responsibility for the needs, desires and fantasies they're projecting onto you
- Know how to notice and metabolise difficult or consuming emotions that have been evoked in you that may have nothing to do with the actuality of the situation
- Know how much you can put up with and how to recognise when your limits have been reached
- Know how to deal with bastards and bitches
- Have a sense of how much of yourself you're willing to give in the service of others
- Know what 'being healthy' means to you (and what you need to do to keep yourself 'healthy').

If you plan to thrive, it's the same as above – only more so.

The ghosts are out, they're running about

Authority evokes power and responsibility. It evokes the memories of mummy and daddy and their mummies and daddies. It's created in the history of teachers and sages, whiskey priests and ancestral desires for gods, prophets and saviours. Like strong drink it can set you on and set you off. There is no part of your past and present that does not get evoked when you are in the presence of authority – either yours or others.

To see authority as an objective quality that exists according to some fixed framework that belongs outside an individual, their history and the specifics of a situation, is a dangerous falsehood. Authority and how it is experienced and practised lives in the specifics of individuals and their relationships; when its uniqueness and mutability are acknowledged then authority can be consciously worked with and understood. When some external benchmark is overlaid onto it and denies the uniqueness of a particular habit of authority, then authority will be poorly understood – and with poor understanding comes the risk of being consumed by denied or unacknowledged ghosts.

Authority is a particular expression of identity. When that identity is hidden, confused or unexamined, then it is a loose cannon. When it is brought into the light then the opportunity to choose one's relationship to authority becomes possible; you may choose to continue as you always have done, but by choosing to stay the same you have already brought a quality of consciousness to bear that will leave its mark.

In the end, this book has been an exploration into what it takes for authority to be informed by ghosts rather than consumed by them.

CHAPTER 29

Further exploration

This book is a punctuation point in a continuing inquiry into authority. If you would like to do further private reflections into authority I can recommend the following:

(a) Write your own story based around the two questions I used to frame my interviews:

What is the nature of your current authority?
When was your earliest experience of authority?

Once you've answered those questions you can then choose how you go on to explore your relationship to authority in whatever way works for you.

(b) Work with the images within the book, noting which resonate or repel you. Then explore the nature of your relationship to each of the images and how this informs your understanding of authority.

(c) Work through the exploratory framework in Appendix A, in which you will be presented with a specific framing for exploring you and authority.

If you would like to join in a wider public inquiry into authority, working with the same processes as above, you can contact me directly at higginsboot@bulldoghome.com or visit **www.imagesofauthority.co.uk**.

appendices

A: An exploratory framework   222

B: Recommended reading   238

Appendix A: An exploratory framework

This framework was developed intuitively after the writing up of the eighteen stories. In working with it you will be required to work with an imposed language rather than your own. The potential benefit is that this may provoke insights you may not otherwise have had; the downside is that it makes you describe your authority using someone else's terms that do not actually resonate meaningfully with you.

The framework has six sections each of which offers a series of questions and responses. One of the informing principles of its design is that all characteristics of authority identified in it can have either a negative or positive expression.

The purpose of the framework is to provoke a conversation (either internal or with others) using a shared reference point. Its goal is not to establish norms around which people can then be evaluated or ranked.

1. How do you see yourself?
2. How do you see others?
3. How do you see the relationship between yourself and others?
4. How do you see the purpose of your authority?
5. How do you define success?
6. What is the nature of your authority story?

I have identified six criteria with the following headline titles for exploring how someone in authority sees themselves:

- Presence of history
- Touch of steel
- Needs of self
- Sense of potency
- Resilience
- Position

As you read through the associated questions and suggested characteristics make a note of how much – or how little – each characteristic resonates with you. Please note that it is more than possible to hold contradictory positions simultaneously.

1.1 Presence of history

The question here is: *'Do you see authority as historical or ahistorical?'*

- If you see your authority as strongly historical does this mean you are:

- stuck in the past?
  OR
  - able to avoid repeating unhelpful historical patterns (or draw on positive past experience)?

- If you see your authority as strongly ahistorical (i.e. independent of what has gone on in the past) does this mean you are:
  - blind to the past (so likely to be consumed/possessed by it)?
  OR
  - focused on the present?

1.2 Touch of steel

The question here is: *'Do you see your authority as gentle or steeled?'*

- If you see your authority as steeled does this mean you are:
  - likely to invite defensive behaviours from others?
  OR
  - able to hold difficult conversations and make difficult decisions?

- If you see your authority as gentle does this mean you are:
  - keen to avoid confrontation (and likely to store up trouble)?
  OR
  - able to work with the fragility of others?

1.3 Needs of self

The question here is: *'Do you see your authority as addressing or denying your own needs?'*

- If you see your own needs being strongly denied does this mean you are:
  - likely to become a martyr and be personally inauthentic?
  OR
  - seeing the good of the whole as figural?

- If you see your own needs being strongly addressed does this mean you are:
  - narcissistic and self-referencing?
  OR
  - maintaining personal wellbeing and authenticity?

1.4 Sense of potency

The question here is: *'Do you experience your authority as potent or impotent?'*

- If you see your authority as potent does this mean you are:

- overwhelming, autocratic and closed to other voices?
  OR
  - able to set direction and contain anxiety by establishing robust purpose and boundaries?

- If you see your authority as impotent does this mean you are:
  - creating anxiety by not establishing a robust enough set of ground rules?
  OR
  - hoping for self-actualisation in others?

1.5 Resilience

The question here is: *'Do you experience your authority as resilient or ephemeral?'*

- If you see your authority as ephemeral does this mean you are:
  - inconsistent in your purpose?
  OR
  - flexible and adaptable?

- If you see your authority as resilient does this mean you are:
  - pig-headed?
  OR
  - able to keep the course through choppy waters?

1.6 Position

The question here is: *'Do you experience your authority as informed by or independent of formal position?'*

- If you see your authority as independent of position does this mean you are:
  - unable to work with formal procedures or accept the needs of a role?
  OR
  - your authentic self... authority embodied?

- If you see your authority as informed by position does this mean you are:
  - the faceless suit; the trappings not the substance of authority?
  OR
  - the marriage of the formal and the informal; working with a world that is both personal and procedural?

1. How do you see yourself?
2. **How do you see others?**
3. How do you see the relationship between yourself and others?
4. How do you see the purpose of your authority?
5. How do you define success?
6. What is the nature of your authority story?

I have identified six criteria with the following headline titles for exploring how someone in authority sees others:

- Voiced
- Capability
- Presence of history
- Energy
- Flexibility
- Friend or foe

As you read through the associated questions and suggested characteristics make a note of how much – or how little – each characteristic resonates with you. Please note that it is more than possible to hold contradictory positions simultaneously.

2.1 Voiced

The question here is: *'How forcefully do you hear the voices of others?'*

- If heard forcefully does this mean:
  - you allow your own voice to be lost?
  OR
  - you pay attention to the presence of others?

- If heard lightly does this mean:
  - you excessively discount what others say?
  OR
  - you stay well attached to your own perspective?

2.2 Capability

The question here is: *'How perfect do you want others to be?'*

- If you expect the imperfect does this mean:
  - you underestimate what others can do?
  OR
  - you pay attention to the support and development they need?

- If you expect the perfect does this mean:
  - you cannot accept any weakness or imperfection?

  OR
  - you provide a greater sense of what is possible (feed the ambition of others)?

2.3 Presence of history

The question here is: *'How much history do you expect to be present in others?'*

- If you expect people to be without history does this mean:
  - you deny the reality of their projections?

  OR
  - you ground them in the reality of now?

- If you expect people to be full of history does this mean:
  - you live out their fantasies for them?

  OR
  - you bring to their attention what they are asking of you and inquire into its relevance to now?

2.4 Energy

The question here is: *'How active or passive do you want others to be with you?'*

- If you expect people to be passive does this mean:
  - you want them to do as they are told?

  OR
  - you want them to accept what has to be accepted?

- If you expect people to be active does this mean:
  - you want them to be a constant challenge to you?

  OR
  - you want them to take responsibility for their actions?

2.5 Flexibility

The question here is: *'How flexible do you want others to be?'*

- If you want people to be flexible does this mean:
  - you want them to change whenever the wind blows?

  OR
  - you want them to adapt to emerging realities?

- If you want people to be constant does this mean:

- they can only be what they've always been in your eyes?
OR
- you work with the reality of their character?

2.6 Friend or foe

The question here is: *'How much do you see others as friends or foes?'*

- If you see people as foes does this mean:
  - they become scapegoats?
  OR
  - they become a source of challenge and combat (whetstones)?

- If you see people as friends does this mean:
  - your authority becomes subservient to the demands of friendship?
  OR
  - your authority is tempered by affection and tolerance?

1. How do you see yourself?
2. How do you see others?
3. **How do you see the relationship between yourself and others?**
4. How do you see the purpose of your authority?
5. How do you define success?
6. What is the nature of your authority story?

I have identified six criteria with the following headline titles for exploring how someone in authority sees the relationship between themselves and others:

- Nature of interaction
- Boundaries
- Psychological framing
- Positioning of authority figures
- Planned
- Focus

As you read through the associated questions and suggested characteristics make a note of how much – or how little – each characteristic resonates with you. Please note that it is more than possible to hold contradictory positions simultaneously.

3.1 Nature of interaction

The question here is: 'How competitive or collaborative is your relationship with others?'

- If you see your relationship as competitive does this mean:
  - you must win at all costs?
  OR
  - the best course of action wins through?

- If you see your relationship as collaborative does this mean:
  - disagreements must be avoided for the sake of the relationship?
  OR
  - different perspectives are readily expressed and heard?

3.2 Boundaries

The question here is: *'Do boundaries exist in the relationship in order to contain or constrain?'*

- If you see boundaries as containing does this mean:
  - you become responsible for managing boundaries on behalf of others?
  OR
  - anxieties are kept within bounds allowing for robust exchanges?

- If you see boundaries as constraining does this mean:
  - relationships become stuck in a pre-defined pattern?
  OR
  - relationships are focused onto what is relevant to the matter in hand?

3.3 Psychological framing

The question here is: *'Are relationships a matter of projection or are they free of extraneous factors?'*

- If you see relationships as projections does this mean:
  - historic family dramas play out at work?
  OR
  - the opportunity exists to work with nameable patterns?

- If you see relationships as free does this mean:
  - unacknowledged dramas play out and surprise people?
  OR
  - relationships are focused on the here and now?

3.4 Positioning of authority figures

The question here is: *'Are authority figures in a judging or counselling role in authority relationships?'*

- If you see authority figures as judges does this mean:
  - you are continuously appraising and criticising others?
  OR
  - you are encouraging others to do well?

- If you see authority figures as counsels does this mean:
  - you are avoiding challenging the contribution of others?
  OR
  - you are joining others in performing well?

3.5 Planned

The question here is: *'Are relationships planned and clean or emergent and messy?'*

- If you see relationships as planned and clean does this mean:
  - relationships must adapt to fit with the planned order?
  OR
  - relationships can be reviewed in the light of the difference between the planned and the unexpected?

- If you see relationships as emergent and messy does this mean:
  - relationships are haphazard and uncontrollable?
  OR
  - relationships are lively and responsive to what is?

3.6 Focus

The question here is: *'Does the task or the relationship need to be focused on most?'*

- If the task is most focused on does this mean:
  - work is disrupted because of unaddressed relational issues?
  OR
  - work gets done and becomes the focus through which relational issues are addressed?

- If the relationship is most focused on does this mean:
  - work doesn't get done and turns into group therapy?
  OR
  - the quality of all collaborative activity improves as people know how to talk and listen well together?

1. How do you see yourself?
2. How do you see others?
3. How do you see the relationship between yourself and others?
4. **How do you see the purpose of your authority?**
5. How do you define success?
6. What is the nature of your authority story?

I have identified six criteria with the following headline titles for exploring how someone in authority sees the purpose of authority:

- Meeting needs
- Performance
- Provocation
- Anxiety
- Directing
- Purpose

As you read through the associated questions and suggested characteristics make a note of how much – or how little – each characteristic resonates with you. Please note that it is more than possible to hold contradictory positions simultaneously.

4.1 Meeting needs

The question here is: *'Whose needs does your authority meet?'*

- If you see your authority as primarily meeting your own needs does this mean:
  – you see the needs of others as unimportant?
  OR
  – you see your needs as important?

- If you see your authority as primarily meeting the needs of others does this mean:
  – you must sacrifice yourself to the greater good?
  OR
  – you understand the portfolio of needs that have to be met?

4.2 Performance

The question here is: *'What type of performance is your authority in the service of?'*

- If your authority is about demanding delivery come what may does this mean:

- the ends always justify the means?
  OR
  - people surpass what they thought they were capable of?

- If your authority is about accepting what can be achieved does this mean:
  - you sustain mediocrity?
  OR
  - you keep people in touch with reality?

4.3 Provocation

The question here is: *'Is your authority about confronting or protecting people?'*

- If your authority is about confronting people does this mean:
  - people may be damaged but this is a price worth paying?
  OR
  - you invite people to behave as robust adults?

- If your authority is about protecting people does this mean:
  - people become infantilised around you?
  OR
  - you make it safe for people to experiment?

4.4 Anxiety

The question here is: *'Is the purpose of your authority to metabolise or reject the anxiety of others?'*

- If your authority exists to metabolise the anxiety of others does this mean:
  - you internalise whatever fears are in the ether?
  OR
  - you acknowledge and process the anxieties that you wittingly or unwittingly pick up?

- If your authority exists to free you from the anxiety of others does this mean:
  - you leave others crippled by fear?
  OR
  - you insist that people own their own anxieties?

4.5 Directing

The question here is: *'Is the purpose of your authority to maintain or change direction?'*

- If your authority exists to maintain direction does this mean:

- you refuse to adapt in the face of experience?
OR
- you enable others to perform because of your constancy?

- If you authority exists to change direction does this mean:
  - you disable others by shifting with the lightest breeze?
  OR
  - you ensure the collective endeavour stays connected to an evolving environment?

4.6 Purpose

The question here is: *'Is the purpose of your authority to establish or explore purpose?'*

- If your authority exists to establish purpose does this mean:
  - you are dictatorial and deny the value of others' contributions?
  OR
  - you set the boundaries that provide focus and creative limits for others?

- If your authority exists to explore purpose does this mean:
  - you and others exist without purpose or with a purpose neutered by the need not to exclude anyone?
  OR
  - purpose exists in the minds and hearts of everyone?

1. How do you see yourself?
2. How do you see others?
3. How do you see the relationship between yourself and others?
4. How do you see the purpose of your authority?
5. **How do you define success?**
6. What is the nature of your authority story?

I have identified six criteria with the following headline titles for exploring how someone in authority defines success:

- Quality of personal experience
- Growth
- Delivery
- Emotions
- Integrity
- Scope

As you read through the associated questions and suggested characteristics make a note of how much – or how little – each characteristic resonates with you. Please note that it is more than possible to hold contradictory positions simultaneously.

5.1 Quality of personal experience

The question here is: *'Is success about being consumed or being enlivened?'*

- If your authority is about giving yourself to (or being consumed by) others does this mean:
  - you become exhausted?
  OR
  - you have the satisfaction of contributing to the success of others?

- If your authority is about being enlivened does this mean:
  - you become addicted to activity?
  OR
  - you experience a positive energy for life and liveliness?

5.2 Growth

The question here is: *'Is success about learning or material achievement?'*

- If your success is about learning and development does this mean:
  - you never appreciate what has been achieved?
  OR
  - you are becoming wiser?

- If your success is about material achievement does this mean:
  - you don't value intangibles?
  OR
  - you are becoming richer?

5.3 Delivery

The question here is: *'Is success about the outcome or the way the outcome was achieved?'*

- If success is about delivering something in accordance with personal values does this mean:
  - you are dogmatic and intolerant?
  OR
  - doing the right thing always comes first?

- If success is about achieving the outcome does this mean:

- the costs of achievement are ignored?
OR
- the task in hand gets properly appreciated?

5.4 Emotions

The question here is: *'Is success about respect or love?'*

- If success is about love (and being liked) does this mean:
  - you'll do anything to be liked or loved?
  OR
  - you'll seek out what is good in people when you can?

- If success is about respect does this mean:
  - you chase after people whose opinion matters to you?
  OR
  - you seek to be recognised for some personal or professional attribute that matters to you?

5.5 Integrity

The question here is: *'Is success about being true to yourself or true to your role?'*

- If success is about being true to yourself does this mean:
  - you're narcissistic (and solipsistic)?
  OR
  - you hold to principles and values that matter to you?

- If success is about being true to your role does this mean:
  - you are a functionary devoid of personal presence?
  OR
  - you own responsibility for filling a position that needs to be filled?

5.6 Scope

The question here is: *'Does success incorporate the few or the many?'*

- If success is an inclusive experience does this mean:
  - any failure or loss by anyone is denied?
  OR
  - all who have contributed are recognised?

- If success is an exclusive experience does this mean:
  - there are only a few winners and many losers?
  OR
  - those who have contributed most are recognised?

1. How do you see yourself?
2. How do you see others?
3. How do you see the relationship between yourself and others?
4. How do you see the purpose of your authority?
5. How do you define success?
6. **What is the nature of your authority story?**

I have identified six criteria with the following headline titles for exploring the nature of someone's authority story:

- Source of authority
- Attitude to hierarchy
- Moral stance
- Consequences of authority
- Trials and obstacles
- Role of the chorus

As you read through the associated questions and suggested characteristics make a note of how much – or how little – each characteristic resonates with you. Please note that it is more than possible to hold contradictory positions simultaneously.

6.1 Source of authority

The question here is: *'Is authority given or taken?'*

- If authority is something that is given does this mean:
  - you are always beholden to the powers that gave it to you?
  OR
  - you treat it as a valued gift?

- If authority is something you take or create does this mean:
  - your narcissism is fuelled?
  OR
  - it is rooted in a sense of self and situation?

6.2 Attitude to hierarchy

The question here is: *'Do you behave as if hierarchies do or don't exist?'*

- If hierarchies are seen to exist does this mean:
  - people are locked into particular stations and the status quo always prevails?
  OR

– differentials in power, ability and responsibility are transparent and understandable?
- If hierarchies are seen not to exist does this mean:
  – they become hidden and operate only tacitly and informally?
  OR
  – there is a ready opportunity for all to contribute and participate?

6.3 Moral stance

The question here is: *'Is authority seen to be malign or benign?'*

- If authority is seen as malign does this mean:
  – it is feared and avoided wherever possible?
  OR
  – it is treated with healthy scepticism?

- If authority is seen to be benign does this mean:
  – it is turned to too readily?
  OR
  – it is treated as a healthy resource available for all to use or turn to?

6.4 Consequences of authority

The question here is: *'Does authority serve salvation or learning?'*

- If authority is seen as a source of salvation to both self and others does this mean:
  – sacrificial behaviours are encouraged in your self and in others?
  OR
  – authority is seen as contributing to the continued and better existence of self and others?

- If authority is in the service of learning for both self and others does this mean:
  – only approved learning takes place and personal and group prejudices are reinforced?
  OR
  – new or deeper insights emerge?

6.5 Trials and obstacles

The question here is: *'Do trials and obstacles strengthen or weaken authority?'*

- If trials and obstacles are seen to weaken authority does this mean:
  – they should be avoided?

OR
- they provide a healthy reminder of the limits to authority as currently practised?

- If trials and obstacles are seen as a source of strengthening or tempering does this mean:
  - there are no limits to what the current practice of authority can achieve (hubris)?
  OR
  - the practice of authority is kept keen and relevant through continual testing?

6.6 Role of the chorus

The question here is: *'How active or passive are those who observe or experience the consequences of authority?'*

- If the role of the chorus is passive does this mean:
  - they are infantilised?
  OR
  - they don't hinder the hero?

- If the role of the chorus is active does this mean:
  - they get in the way of authority figures (including heroes)?
  OR
  - they take a responsible part in the story and what unfolds?

Appendix B – Recommended reading

1. Complementary texts
I see three books (and a research report) complementing what has been written here:

– As a traditional leadership book, but one which has more of an individual human feel to it, I think that ***Living Leadership: A practical guide for heroes*** by George Binney, Gerhard Wilke and Colin Williams (Pearson Education 2005) comes closest – particularly where it explores how personal demons inform personal choices and behaviours. I did prefer the original research report that had a stronger individual narrative flow and can be found as a 2004 Ashridge research report under the title **'Leaders in transition – the dramas of ordinary heroes'**.
– As an impressive exercise in applying psychoanalytic labels to authority types Manfred Kets de Vries' ***The Leader on the Couch*** (Jossey-Bass 2006) is a good read. It's a little too corporate and work-focused for my taste, but is a good introduction to the language for people who are not used to it.
– As an example of what it takes to break out of established life patterns and find a way that sits more authentically with you I recommend Joseph Jaworski's ***Synchronicity: The inner path of leadership*** (Berrett-Koehler 1996).

2. Research process
This research process did not come about by accident, but is informed by a deeply held philosophy about how reality is created and how human beings connect with each other and with themselves. Three writers have helped me understand the principles and philosophy behind non-reductionist, socially constructed, language mediated research:

– Gregory Bateson and his sometimes impenetrable but worth reading ***Steps to an Ecology of Mind*** (University of Chicago Press 2000). Or, as an introduction, read the essay on Bateson titled 'Framing Bateson' in my own work ***Organisational Consulting – A Relational Perspective*** (MU Press 2007) by Bill Critchley, Kathleen King and John Higgins.
– Richard Rorty is my second touchstone and the following book provides a robust inquiry into the nature of the subjective and for me a fascinating advocacy of the importance of living life as a socially constructed reality – ***Rorty and his critics***, ed. Robert B. Brandon (Blackwell 2000), especially Chapter 1, 'Universality and Truth'.
– John Shotter is my main language influence (he in turn is greatly influenced by the later Wittgenstein, who he referred to as one of his 'textual friends' at

a talk I heard him give around 2000) and the book I find most useful is *Conversational Realities – Constructing Life through Language* (Sage 1993).

3. The woman's voice (the gendered nature of knowing and authority)

In a number of the stories (Eve and Lucy particularly stand out) I sensed the women I spoke to adopting a very different and gendered stance in how they were in the world and their relationship to authority. The writers I have come across that have helped me become more sensitive to the gendered nature of knowing, conversation and authority include:

– Carol Gilligan, *In a different voice – psychological theory and women's development* (Harvard University Press 1993).
– M.F. Belenky, B.M. Clinchy, N.R. Goldberger and J.M. Tarvle, *Women's ways of knowing – the development of self, voice and mind* (BasicBooks Inc. 1997).
– A. Huff, '**Wives – of the organisation**', paper given in 1990 to the Women and Work conference, Arlington TX.
– I have also had recommended to me Janet Holmes' *Gendered talk at work* (Blackwell 2006).

4. Working with not knowing

Martin, Mike and Bill all talk of the importance of not knowing at some stage of their leadership process and this evoked for me the work of C. Otto Scharmer that I know from Bill Isaac's work on dialogue. It also fits with a piece I wrote some years ago on engaging with the uncertainty in organisations.

– William Isaacs, *Dialogue and the art of thinking together* (Random House, NY 1999) p.261.
– Janet Smallwood and John Higgins, '**Finding the flow – learning to let go in organisations**', *The Ashridge Journal*, November 1999.

5. Exploring headwaters

People such as Sam and Roy have become great exponents of understanding why it is they do what they do – they have explored what lies upstream of their thinking. Books that speak to this outside the psychoanalytic literature for me are:

– David Bohm (edited by Lee Nichol), *On Dialogue* (Routledge 1996).
– Robert Dilts, *Changing belief systems with NLP* (Meta Publications 1990).

6. Moving off script

Adrian's company works with the tradition of Augusto Boal and those other radicals who challenge our habits of putting words into other people's mouths. Stella is also attracted to engaging with the reality of others on their own terms, as of course am I (although in a different social milieu). The texts that speak to me of not speaking on behalf of others are:

- Paulo Freire, ***Pedagogy of the oppressed*** (Penguin 1996/1970).
- Augusto Boal, ***Theatre of the oppressed*** (Pluto Press 2000/1979).

7. Living with childhood

Childhood experiences were acknowledged by many as colouring their sense of self and practice of authority. Two texts helped me acknowledge the potency of childhood, one general and one specific to the experiences of boarding schools:

- Alice Miller, ***The Drama of Being a Child*** (Virago Press 1987).
- Nick Duffel, ***The Making of them – the British attitude to children and the boarding school system*** (Lone Arrow Press 2000).

8. Something psychoanalytic

The psychoanalytic literature is vast and its language can be grim – if you are not familiar with it I can recommend the following as a way of dipping your toe in the water:

- ***The Essential Jung: Selected Writings Introduced by Anthony Storr*** (The Fontana Press 1998). I find Jung very strong on notions of personal integration; he is also the father of the idea of Individuation.
- Ian Stewart and Vann Joines, ***TA Today*** (Lifespace Publishing 1987).
- Sigmund Freud, ***Introductory Lectures on Psychoanalysis*** (Penguin 1973).
- To find out more about Bion and his basic assumptions refer to Joan and Neville Symington, ***The Clinical Thinking of Wilfred Bion*** (Routledge 1996); basic assumptions are described in pp.126–30.

9. Something rational/traditional

I am very fond of Roy for his blend of the mystic and the pragmatic. These are two of the books he frequently mentions (the second one also speaks to me of acknowledging Mike's appreciation of good rationality):

- Stephen R. Covey, ***The Seven Habits of Highly Effective People: restoring the character ethic*** (Fireside 1990).
- Jim Collins, ***Good to great*** (HarperBusiness 2001).

10. Power of history

I am always drawn to the power of the trans-generational and influence of archetypes. Two books in particular helped me make sense of this, the first of which is very strong meat indeed, but good for the soul:

- Dina Wardi, **Memorial Candles: Children of the Holocaust** (Routledge 1992).
- Robert Moore and Douglas Gillette, **King, Warrior, Magician, Lover: Rediscovering the archetypes of the mature masculine** (Harper Collins 1990).

11. Good enough parenting

- D.W. Winnicott, **Playing and Reality** (Routledge 1991). This concept is explained more fully here.

12. Authority as personal process

In Stella's story I referred to her programme making as personal process i.e. a way of working through those issues and itches that matter to her. This is an allusion to a paper that has been very influential to my own thinking about research, which describes research as a personal process – where identifying what that personal itch is, is an important part of the process:

- Research as personal process is explored by Peter Reason and Judi Marshall in Chapter 42, 'On Working with Graduate Research Students' (p.413) from **Handbook of Action Research**, edited by Peter Reason and Hilary Bradbury (SAGE 2001).

13. Identity and relationships

Throughout the stories, issues of identity and relationship have been implicitly or explicitly explored. For further reading in this area, particularly the extent to which 'I' and 'We' are the singular and plural expression of the overarching notion of interconnected human beings, refer to:

- Kathleen King's chapter in my book **Organisational Consulting – A Relational Perspective** (op. cit.) pp.31–48: 'Towards Relational Consulting'.
- Norbert Elias, a renowned sociologist who framed the notion of interconnected human beings, whose work is well collected in **On Civilization, Power and Knowledge**, edited by Stephen Mennell and Johan Goudsblom (University of Chicago Press 1998).
- Farhad Dalal, **Taking the Group Seriously** (Jessica Kingsley Publishers Ltd 1998).

14. The film director's experience

Stella referred to the 1973 Francois Truffaut film **Day for Night**.

15. Shakespeare
- 'Uneasy lies the head that wears a crown' comes from **Henry IV Part II**, Act 3, Scene 1.
- 'I have of late, and wherefore I know not, lost all my mirth' comes from **Hamlet**, Act II, Scene 2.

The Shakespearean canon is of course a rich source of meditation on power, authority and its costs and consequences.

16. Modern monsters
The mendacity, the ego, the self-delusion. Tom Bower is a master at exploring the bluster of some of our most notorious 'great men'.

- Tom Bower, **Maxwell: The Outsider** (Mandarin 1991).

He has also written on Conrad Black and Mohammed Al Fayed.

17. Distributed authority
Lesley refers to this concept and it can be found in greater detail in:

- Peter Block, **Stewardship** (Berrett-Koehler 1996).

18. Loss and trivialisation
For a non-trivial examination on the stages of loss and grieving refer to the original work in this area:

- Elisabeth Kubler-Ross, **On Death and Dying** (Simon & Schuster 1997).

19. Habits of censorship
Christina talked to the problems that emerge when people censor themselves in organisations and don't speak to the obvious. She referred to:

- Harlow B. Cohen, **The Dinosaur in the Living Room: Achieving Positive Change by Tackling the Obvious** (AuthorHouse 2005).

20. Other texts referred to
- Fitzroy Maclean, **Eastern Approaches** (Jonathan Cape 1949) and the derivation of Tito's name p.311.
- The book I compared to kissing an electric snake was **Thus Spake Zarathustra** by F. Nietzsche (Wordsworth Editions 1997).
- Milan Kundera, **The Unbearable Lightness of Being** (Faber & Faber 2000).